ST NDARD

)^^

POWER AND CONTROL

Social Structures
and Their Transformation

POWER AND CONTROL
Social Structures and Their Transformation

Edited by
Tom R Burns
and **Walter Buckley**

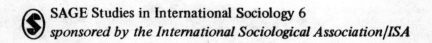

SAGE Studies in International Sociology 6
sponsored by the International Sociological Association/ISA

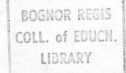

For information address

SAGE Publications Ltd.
44 Hatton Garden
London EC1N 8ER

SAGE Publications Inc.
275 South Beverly Drive
Beverly Hills, California 90212

International Standard Book Number
0 8039 9959 3 Cloth
0 8039 9978 X Paper

Library of Congress Catalog Card Number
76-22900

First Printing

Printed and Bound
in the United States of America

CONTENTS

CONTENTS

1

INTRODUCTION AND OVERVIEW

Hayward Alker Jr.
Massachusetts Institute of Technology

Walter Buckley
University of New Hampshire

Tom R. Burns
University of New Hampshire

In the study of institutions, national societies or even international organizations, the lesson is gradually being learned that they must be treated from a multi-disciplinary, systemic point of view — conventional, economic, political, social, or cultural analysis alone will not do. The papers in this volume move toward such a perspective on power and control, topics that each social science claims as its own. Reflecting various disciplinary affiliations,[1] the contributors to this volume conceptualize power and control as asymmetric relations (or attributes) within social structures, as properties of entire social systems seeking stable control over themselves, and as processes exerting influence over the rise and fall of such structures. Hence, despite differences in language and focus, the reader will find frequent references to structures of power and control, to their interrelationships with other social structures, and to what we refer to as 'morphostatic' and 'morphogenic' processes (respectively, those tending to maintain or to change particular structures).[2]

The first set of papers in the volume concern themselves with concepts and methods for describing social networks and power relationships within social structures. Tools are presented which can be used in empirical research on macro-sociological phenomena, such as complex social networks and control structures. The papers in Parts II and III address themselves to the study of structural stability and change, that is morphostasis and morphogenesis. They transcend the debate of 'structure versus process' or 'static versus dynamic analysis'. Structure and process are in each case integral parts of a systems analysis of structural stability and change.

The issue of 'freedom versus determinism' is yet another topic in the study of social systems and human action, on which several of the papers in this volume shed new light. The Baumgartner et al. and Cohen papers consider societal developments which human actors cannot control or about which they lack awareness as well as stress the fact that 'selective forces' acting to transform social systems often involve some degree of human choice.[3] In a word, social and cultural developments entail both voluntaristic and deterministic components (see also Nagel's and Pattee's papers in this regard).

The study of social power and structure is especially difficult since both of these components are involved. On the one hand, there is the danger of assuming that social systems are regulated by some conscious 'invisible hand' not subject to a considerable degree of explicit direction. Several of the papers in this volume (those of Baumgartner et al., Hardin, and Meier) suggest that in the case of modern societies there may be a greater degree of successful, sophisticated conscious control of societal structures and development than many students of society seem willing to accept. On the other hand, it is also easy to assume an unrealistic degree of unilateral and successful control on the part of power groups, elites, or planning agencies, as they consciously attempt to plan for and manipulate their social and physical environments — with too little attention given to multiple and conflicting decisions and control activities which result in unexpected or undesired outcomes.

Although human choice plays an important role in structural development, control by a society as a whole or by its elite(s) is never complete. Among the reasons for this are the following:

(i) climatic and geographical factors contribute to the structuring of social relationships;

(ii) actors other than a dominant elite within a society, external actors as well as subordinate actors, may exercise some degree of control over social relationships and structures; and

(iii) even the rational actions of apparently consensual elite groups (as well as others) often lead to unintended or unanticipated, structurally significant outcomes.

In the following discussion we present an overview of the papers appearing in this volume, and try to alert the reader to a few of the specific themes and issues raised by the papers.

Anderson and Carlos consider the theoretical origins, development, and present theoretical status of social network analysis. Network analysis emerged principally from the work of social anthropologists engaged in studies of migration, urban areas, and communities in developed societies. Empirical and analytical problems in this research led to emphasis on influential and changing social links which are not necessarily socially prescribed but chosen and developed by individuals and groups. A variety of terminologies have been introduced by anthropologists and sociologists to characterize social networks and to describe exchange and power processes in them. A family of related concepts are: link, sentiment relation, exchange, dependence, power-balance mechanisms, semantic labeling and norms, choice, patron, client, broker, entrepreneur, action set, region and boundary.

Anderson and Carlos conclude that, despite many promising trends and horizons in the literature, the concepts of social network analysis do not form a coherent theory explaining the social and psychological basis of network interrelationships and binding processes, and the sociological and psychological consequences of these processes. The descriptive effectiveness of network analysis is limited because relationships between actors are often insufficiently differentiated (in terms of power, affect, communication, or other dimensions). Other important methodological issues with respect to network analysis which remain to be addressed systematically are: How does one describe the relationship between the influence, exchange, and normative relationships or their interactions with one another? Which relationships in a given temporal and social context should be the focus of attention? To what extent does description of individual or group actors as 'nodes' conceal important structural qualities in their own right as well as their interactions with relationships or network structures? In general, what are the limitations of a description of actors and their relationships in terms of 'nodes' and 'lines'?

Furthermore, network research has remained primarily descriptive rather than attempting to formulate theories of how networks emerge, are altered, maintained, or decay. In short, there has been little attention given to morphogenic and morphostatic processes underlying social networks. This is pointed out, in particular, by the neglect of two interrelated factors underlying social networks: differential resource controls and social structures which can be identified separately. Several related questions which remain to be taken up and investigated are: Does a given social structure tend to generate or shape certain types of network as opposed to others and, if so, in what ways? Do some actors or nodes in a network have greater power than others to create or to maintain or change social networks? To what extent and in what ways is such power dependent on a social structure and the processes tending to maintain and change that social structure? How is morphostasis and morphogenesis of social structure reflected in the distribution of network structuring capabilities and its interaction outcomes or effects? To what extent do the latter 'feedback' to reinforce social structure? More generally, under what conditions are networks reproduced, and in what ways? Anderson and Carlos suggest quite rightly that those interested in the theoretical development of network theory will have to address themselves to these and related questions.

Graph theory has long been associated with network analysis (see Barnes (1972) and Harary et al. (1965)). A graph is a set of points and a set of lines connecting selected pairs of points. Using computer-based graph theoretic techniques, Sonquist and Koenig take on the task of describing and analyzing macro-structural features of a powerful network of interlocking directorates among the 500 largest US corporations. Among the features which they describe and analyze are: center/periphery relationships, cliques (tightly connected boards of corporations with two or more common board members), coteries (cliques plus their satellite companies), and clique diameters. Such a structural investigation is intended as a first step toward enabling researchers to ultimately answer questions about the structure of economic power and control within the US. What is the extent of interlocking in the upper echelon of the American corporate structure? Do some firms or types of firm occupy more 'central' positions? Do financial institutions tend to have a disproportionate number of interlocks? And are they therefore more powerful? If so, is there a regional bias, for example largely confined to the New York-based banks? How do interlock patterns relate to purchaser-supplier relationships including distributional consequences in the wider society? Which of several theoretical orientations characterizing US corporate structure is most valid: e.g. class hegemony, financial control, corporate monopoly, oligopolistic competition, or management domination (over owners)? While the paper by Sonquist and Koenig does not claim to provide anything approaching complete answers to most of these questions, it does point toward research efforts which could lead either to answering the questions or to phrasing more meaningful questions. In addition, although their paper presents a static structural description and analysis,[4] historical research using their techniques can and should be undertaken. Such research would investigate the ways in which network structures develop or change, the relationship between these changes and economic and political developments, such as the growth of government regulation.

Nagel provides a most systematic and consistent methodology for describing and analyzing power within social systems in terms of the methods of causal analysis. His work represents the culmination of a major current in North American behavioral science. In the 1950s and 1960s behavioral scientists in the US were greatly influenced by physical and biological theories, (causally interpretable) mathematical models, and associated experimental or quasi-experimental research methods. The study of social power by scholars such as Lewin, Cartwright, March and Dahl drew inspiration from the natural sciences, combined with a naive but wondrous sense of beginning, de novo, the scientific quest for human nature in its biological, psychological and social aspects.[5]

What could be more naturalistic then Lewin's Newtonian, relational concept (Lewin, 1951: 336):

the power of b over a = the maximum force which b can induce on a −
the maximum resistance which a can offer

A related concept was Dahl's, partly Weberian notion (1969 reprint):

A's power over B = A's ability to get B to do what he otherwise would not do.

Exercised power was to be measured in terms of the probabilities of *B*'s actions in cases when wills were opposed minus a probability when such was not the case, somehow statistically controlling for spurious power attributions.[6]

Another influential work in the same tradition has been that of Simon (1957), who treated power as a type of causation in 'which the behavior of one or more persons alters the behavior of another or others' (see Nagel, this volume).[7]

The elements or components of naturalistic power concepts include personal power and positional power, a priori, and exercised power, and behavioral changes associated with such variables as content and relevancy of subject matter, group identifications and reputational power base (March, 1966: 43). Footnoting much more comprehensive earlier treatments by Lasswell and Kaplan, and March, in his 1957 article, Dahl suggested a list of descriptive power components which have had a considerable influence on later work:

> power *bases* (including resources, a priori socially given positions)
> power *means* (behaviors, actions, employing bases)
> power *scopes* (the sets of *B*'s behaviors affected by *A*)
> power *amounts* (probability changes in specific *B*'s behaviors within the scope of *A*'s power)
> power *extents* (the sets of actions over which *A* exercises some amount of power).

These elements can be incorporated into equilibrium theories when isolated, closed systems of action are assumed.

The conventional formulations based on the naturalistic approach to power analysis have been, as March and Nagel suggest, disappointing in terms of the practicality of applying them in a variety of meaningful empirical settings as well as in terms of their failure to provide many new insights or to raise significant research questions. What Nagel proposes is a new definition of power, nevertheless in the vein of causal modeling, which overcomes several of the weaknesses of similar power definitions: power is the causal relationship between the preference of an actor regarding an outcome and the outcome itself.[8] Nagel's definition can be readily operationalized and applied in complex structural settings, using modern multivariate methods (in particular, path analysis as an extension of the earlier multiple regression approach). The introduction of such methods in line with his conception of power permits the measurement of the power of several actors over the same outcome as well as the inclusion of non-preference causes of particular outcomes.

The methods presented by Anderson and Carlos, Nagel and Sonquist and Koenig are useful tools in describing and analyzing exchange and power relationships within or expressed by social networks under given temporal and social structural conditions. Such methods should be used diagnostically to describe relatively *stable* networks of relationships or causal links representing control relationships in a social system.[9] But ultimately, social scientists need to formulate theories of how social networks or power structures (for example represented by path models) emerge, are maintained, or change. In this quest, attention would have to be given to the relationship between social networks or power relationships and social structure,[10] since they depend on property rights,[11] more or less costly control over material and human resources, as well as on structuring processes (discussed below).[12] Moreover, social networks and social power and its exercise are significant factors in the maintenance and change of social structure.

In general, what is called for are higher order theories of structural stability and change, which could account for the structure and behavior of social systems in different contexts or historical periods, and for changes in their structure and behavior from one context or time period to another. On the basis of such theories, one can not only say that 'X is related to Y in such and such a way', but can state that 'because of the operation of a regulating or structuring process of variable Z, the X/Y relationship would be expected to change significantly in such and such a way' (Baumgartner et al., 1976).

Such a theoretical framework is necessarily multi-level (Alker, 1974, 1975; Baumgartner et al., 1976), entailing a global generative theory which embraces particular or local (descriptive) theories. It would accomplish at least three things:

(i) distinguish or identify different contexts or contextual processes relevant to system structure;

(ii) specify the relationship between context conditions or properties and properties of the system, its structure and dynamics; and

(iii) provide an explanation of (or at least principles or rules specifying) when one or another model of relationships and processes applies, or when the transition from one model to another is likely to occur and how it will take place.

The three papers included in Part II attempt to specify processes and conditions which act to maintain or change social structure and, in particular, to specify those factors which affect the balance between morphostatic and morphogenic processes in a given context. Morphostasis occurs when those committed to the existing structure have sufficient power or resources to overcome or counteract restructuring forces, including efforts on the part of the other actors from inside as well as from outside the social system to restructure it. The existing structure is reproduced. Morphogenesis occurs when those committed to the existing structure lack effective counter-measures against or sufficient control over restructuring processes, including human actions (both intended and unintended), which tend to bring about structural change. The existing structure is transformed (Baumgartner et al., this volume). For instance, morphogenesis is likely to occur either

(i) when a ruling elite is unable to come to grips with an economic crisis, and economic and political disintegration ensues or the way is opened for a rival group to assume power;

(ii) when another group either inside or outside the system gains power capabilities which enable it to effectively challenge the ruling elite (and of course this may occur because of the crisis referred to in (i)); or

(iii) when a social system institutionalizes planned structural change processes.

The elite's relative capacity to deal with a competitive or systemic challenge will depend on several factors:

(1) The material and cultural resources it controls which enable it, for instance, to establish a new level of control or more sophisticated system of regulation to cope with a crisis. In other words, one is interested in the extent the elite has *generative power* within the existing framework to shape new institutions or to change old ones so as either to solve economic problems and/or to gain or keep supporters and to divide opponents (DeVille and Burns, 1976).

(2) The degree of elite unity, enabling it to readily and effectively shape new institutions or to change old ones and to formulate new policies to cope with the crisis or challenge.[13]

(3) The extent to which opposition to the elite is unified and commands substantial resources inside or outside the system.

In their research on system morphostasis and morphogenesis, Hardin emphasizes the factor of expanding resources providing structural generative power to statist regimes, Parkin that of elite unity, and Meier, first, the generative ability of the capitalist state to forge new institutions and policies and, secondly, the fragmentation and political incapacity of the working class.

Specifically, Meier addresses himself to what are two anomalies from a Marxist perspective: on the one hand, capitalism has persisted in the highly developed capitalist countries and, on the other, socialist revolutionary development has occurred in many countries with less developed capitalism, pre-capitalist or semi-capitalist countries in the European south and in the Third World. He attempts to explain the morphostatic character (at least in terms of the basic structure of economic domination) of advanced capitalist societies in the face of 'pervasive contradictions', at the same time that many less developed capitalist societies show or have shown morphogenic potential from a socialist perspective. In the case of advanced capitalist societies, Meier singles out the 'export' of poverty and crisis to under-developed countries, the hierarchization and fragmentation of the working class (both nationally and internationally), the internalization of conflicts and crises into the personality, the development of a variety of ideologies more or less compatible with the existing order, and the development of more sophisticated state controls. Meier devotes the most attention to the morphostatic functions and activities of the state in developed capitalist societies. He argues that the state has come to play an active, generative role – and indeed, has *learned* to play a more effective role – in maintaining the capitalist structure of socio-economic relationships. It does this through state fiscal and monetary policies and infrastructure development; it redistributes wealth to some degree, thereby modifying the existential life conditions and even life chances of individuals and groups within their given socio-economic class position; it also produces public goods and services associated with the welfare state (and in doing so makes up for the inability of the market system to do so effectively) as well as performs directly and indirectly various morphostatic ideological functions. At the same time as the structure maintaining functions of the state have multiplied and developed in their sophistication and effectiveness, the working class and other elements which would be expected to strive for revolutionary change have become or remain fragmented and neutralized – in part due to state action (for example, the welfare activities of the state).[14]

Meier takes for granted the unity of the dominant class and state leadership. On the other hand, elite unity is explicitly treated as a major variable in Parkin's paper on system transformation.[15] Like Meier he argues that highly developed capitalist societies are relatively stable and capable of responding adaptively to new crises. In his view this is precisely because there is elite unity in advanced capitalist societies. In general, Parkin suggests that system contradictions (e.g. between the relations of production and the forces of production) only become significant for the problem of social transformation when a society is characterized by 'disequilibrium' in that the distributions of economic, political and social powers entail considerable incongruence. This gives rise to alternative or competing bases of elite legitimization, the polarization of elites, and less effective responses to crisis or challenge.

Parkin uses the same formulation to conclude that there is instability in Eastern European communist societies. In this case he argues that disunity exists among the ruling elite, in particular antagonisms between the party and state bureaucratic class on the one hand, and the intelligentsia, on the other. The power of the former rests in their control of the political and administrative apparatus, while the power of the latter group inheres in its command of the skills and knowledge which are considered essential for the development of productive and scientific forces in modern industrial society. These opposing groups personify conflicting system elements: at a fundamental level, the contradiction between political censorship of knowledge and information and the need to secure moral support and system legitimacy (which censorship tends to undermine); the contradiction between the legal and political order buttressing the command system (relations of production) and the pressures for further development of productive forces which are subject to constraint by the legal and political order.

Hardin takes issue with Parkin, arguing that either the bureaucratic class and the intelligentsia are not separated into two distinct groups or a distinct 'intelligentsia' is a small group with quite limited powers. The principal argument in Hardin's paper, however, is that communist efforts to expand the economy and welfare functions and to control social distribution contributes to the stability of their regimes. For such expansion and functions rapidly expand administrative bureaucracies, bringing about high rates of recruitment to, and promotion within, the bureaucracies. This tends to 'increase regime support while diluting the significance of recalcitrant holdovers in the bureaucracies'.

In sum, Hardin and Meier see the state in Eastern and Western Europe, respectively, playing an increasingly important structural generative role in the stabilization of the economic order. For Hardin, it is clearly the expanding economy under state control that is the key to the morphostatic process of institutionalization he describes. He argues that a communist regime coming to power in a fully developed society would face great difficulties in institutionalizing itself and achieving stability. Implicitly, Meier also assumes an expanding economy providing the state with resources to engage in more and more control activities.

Social systems based on expansion are likely to face serious crises over the long run, in that quantitative or qualitative changes in the expansion process can be expected. Failure of continued expansion on which morphogenic adaptation is based will mean a relative reduction in resource availability, undermining even an 'institutionalized regime', and fostering the emergence of new forces (see Baumgartner et al., this volume). Problems associated with continued expansion may arise from several sources, among others (DeVille and Burns, 1976):

(i) scarcity of strategic resources on which continued expansion depends;[16]

(ii) the requirements (resulting from continued expansion) for re-organization, the development of new skills, knowledge, and technology; and

(iii) the limited capacity of the environment to absorb pollution from highly developed industrial production, ultimately compelling quantitative and qualitative changes in the expansion process.[17]

Moreover, those persons and groups committed to the existing institutionalized structure associated with an expanding system tend to come into conflict with those associated with an emerging structure or those seeking to establish a new structure based on different principles of purpose and organization. However, such conflicts may remain unfocused or may be regulated or resolved through state action (Meier, this volume: Baumgartner et al., 1975c). The increased efficiency and effectiveness of state action — and its capacity to learn — enable the modern state in capitalist as well as communist societies to better handle crises and to initiate and carry out processes of adaptation.

Many of the points Meier makes about the state in advanced capitalist societies apply equally well to Eastern European communist regimes:

(i) They have developed and will probably continue to develop cultural and material resources for dealing with internal crises (subject to the constraints on expansion referred to earlier).

(ii) In times of crisis, there may be changes in the top leadership as in Poland in the winter of 1970 — corresponding to elections in the Western democracies or coups in Latin America — with the promise of 'solutions' to 'problems'. Such a circulation of elites and promised solutions may, as in the West divert attention from the basic issues and the fundamental reforms which are called for.

(iii) The labor force is more and more differentiated with increasing hierarchization and fragmenting tendencies. This reduces the likelihood of generalized conflict or widespread opposition to the government on particular issues.

(iv) The emphasis on private consumption and consumerism has increased, probably encouraging latent individualistic ideologies.

(v) In general, the increasing social differentiation in communist societies (which is normally associated with 'development') tends to make for conflicts between or among particular groups rooted in particular values in specific settings.[18] Because actors in other settings are not likely to identify with a particular conflict, the likelihood of conflict generalizing into major group struggles cutting across the entire remains minimal (Hardin, this volume).[19/20] Hence, even serious crises may manifest themselves as particularized or localized conflicts (that is, in subsystems), at least in the case of societies which are more or less decentralized and segmented.

But in statist (centralized) societies, in the case of serious political and/or economic crises,[21] multiple conflicts tend to crystalize and become linked to the state (viewed as a unity rather than as a 'differentiated state') in the form of a general conflict. This occurs because the state is the principal actor perceived able through its considerable powers to resolve the crisis and related conflicts. In seeking to realize their objectives or values, particular groups coalesce in an attempt to gain control over, or to significantly influence, the state (or to prevent opposing or potentially opposing groups from doing so).[22] There can be no question of indifference toward struggles going on elsewhere (as might be the case in a highly decentralized system).

What we have tried to suggest here in this brief overview and discussion of the papers in Part II is the complexity of the analysis of morphostatic and morphogenic processes structuring social structures and, at the same time, the possibility that one can engage in meaningful theoretical and empirical research on such a macro-level of analysis.

The papers in Part III are also concerned with morphostasis and morphogenesis, but from a more evolutionary perspective than those in Part II.

Pattee formulates from a biological perspective a general theory of the evolution of power and control hierarchies. He proposes that the complementarity of the 'continuous dynamical mode' of action and the 'discrete syntactical mode' of conception and decision is the essential relationship needed to understand the evolution of control hierarchies at all levels from cells to society. New levels of organization develop from the interplay of dynamical optimization in action and descriptive failure. Failure of description is related to the inadequacy of a syntactical structure, for example a model or a policy, at some essential decision point. Furthermore, Pattee suggests that the syntactical structure cannot describe and enable complete control of the processes to which it relates — in other words there are dynamical processes for which no description exists (see Baumgartner et al., 1975b). On the other hand, the syntactic model of description and regulation imposes constraints controlling or harnessing the processes. That is, descriptive models affect decisions, and therefore, activities and material forces.

This formulation, emerging out of Pattee's work on the origin-of-life problem and related problems of differentiating living and non-living systems, shares some similarity with Marxian analysis based on a systems theory conceptualized in terms of material and ideal factors. But in classical Marxist theory, theoretical primacy is accorded to material elements (this finds expression in the distinction between base and superstructure, in which the latter is viewed for the most part as a product of the former) (Parkin, 1974). Parkin points out, however, that the evolution of Marxist thought is marked by 'a definite trend away from this original position such that the relation between material and ideal factors is progressively reversed'. Meier's paper reflects this trend.

The theoretical framework presented by Baumgartner et al. links material, social-structural and cultural or ideological factors structuring action and interaction systems to structural stability and change and to the development potentialities and tendencies of social structures. The structuring factors operate on the components of social action systems: the complex of action and interaction possibilities, their outcomes or payoffs, and the ideological and cultural orientations of actors in relation to one another. Such structuring may arise from the physical environment. For example, an ecological setting of fertile lands suitable for farming surrounded by infertile, arid, or mountainous areas constrains farmers, at least in early history, from leaving the area. Or the constraints may be social-structural in nature: members of a society are prevented from moving to neighboring areas or alternative territorial systems because of the presence of other ethnic, religious, national, or social groups capable of blocking passage; or there are powerful incentives to stay close to allies or potential allies for protection in case of attack. Or the persons or groups are economically tied to the locale (the area is abundant with resources or highly developed so that the opportunity costs of migrating are especially high). Or religious beliefs tie them to the area.

Ideological, social-structural, as well as geographical and technological conditions, by facilitating or limiting action opportunities, particularly in a differentiating manner with respect to different groups in society, constrain or facilitate the development of particular structures. (Of course, social structures themselves facilitate and constrain in a differentiating manner the resources available to, and the action possibilities of, different actors and classes of actors.)[23] For example, whenever subordinate actors have possibilities of emigrating from domination/dependence relationships (and they are not readily replaceable in them) or of mobilizing to limit such relationships, stratification and hierarchical power structures can develop only to a limited degree. On the other hand, constraints on the emigration possibilities of subordinate individuals or groups typically facilitate the development of hierarchical systems. In general, there is an inverse relationship between opportunities for subordinates to leave or withdraw from a social system and hierarchical development, provided their productive capabilities and resources are not replaceable. Thus, in the case of a dense, growing population practising horticulture in a fertile region which is circumscribed geographically or socially,[24] the emergence and development of hierarchical structures (class systems, state and empire formations) is facilitated by constraints on the possibilities of emigration by those who are subordinated through economic or military means, enabling their labor and the products of their labor to be mobilized and appropriated by those in dominant positions (Caneiro, 1970; Baumgartner et al., this volume).[25]

Elites in a social structure themselves manipulate social interaction conditions in order to structure social relationships and networks and their behavioral outputs. The evolution of higher level social control strategies, techniques, and institutions has occurred through individuals and groups discovering various methods of control themselves as well as adopting methods discovered by others. Of particular interest in this regard has been the development of more sophisticated strategies for meta-management and the manipulation and integration of social structures.

Typically, social groups have multiple structures, actual or potential, or bases of structure, between which they choose collectively, for example selecting a structure appropriate for particular forms of social action in a given context.[26] The choice entails two or more options, specifically conceptions of the alternative structures and related patterns of social action which can be activated or selected. In this regard, Cohen's emphasis on the *prior development* of community-wide leadership structures and institutions which are activated and developed in the face of external threat or other crisis is particularly important.

Cohen describes in the case of the Bura-speaking people of Northeast State, Nigeria, the transformation of an acephalous political system into a system where central leaders obtain increasing power and hierarchical control structures are further developed. Social differentiation and hierarchization arose initially as a result of population pressures or fissionary pressures within local communities, which led to emigration and the joining together of either distantly-related or non-related groups where the newcomers found themselves in a subordinate position. The village leadership and in particular the headman, although not all-powerful, did represent a central political authority cutting across descent groups. Certain rituals, the organization of youth, hunting and to some extent even warfare and defense, were handled on a community-wide basis rather than on the basis of lineage and clan organization.

Such prior social-structural development provided a pattern of social action and structure which, although the power differences may have been initially minimal (and latent), could be activated and developed under suitable conditions such as external threat. In other words, the existing social structure and system of action entailed *structural preparedness* or potentiality-for-development which in the proper context, in this case external threat, could emerge and develop.

The emphasis on and development of community-wide associations and central leadership entailed a corresponding de-emphasis on the structural arrangements of acephalous and local political organization with their tendency for segmentation as population pressures and internal disputes force localized lineages to break off from the wider descant group which produced them. Raiding and other forms of hostility encouraged the development of more defensible, more stable, and densely populated communities.[27] As such communities grew in size and stability, the processes of segmentation which maintained the acephalous form of government were constrained from operating to the same degree. Rather than separation serving as the principal device to settle internal strife, disputes were increasingly handled internally through the leadership mediating, adjudicating, and enforcing decisions, thereby reinforcing the importance and authority of the central leadership.

Cohen also points out that the development of greater hierarchical control and coordination in the face of an external threat coincided in the case of the Pabir among the Bura-speaking people with the emergence of a ruling group in each chieftaincy within which there was intermarriage. Heads of lineages, especially the older ones, formed a council of titled courtiers. This emerging upper class, as its common interests became more apparent and common understandings and organization developed, used its powers to restructure institutions to its own advantage. For example, it disregarded and changed restrictions placed on close marriages so as to strengthen alliances between them, transforming in the process traditional Bura kinship from a highly exogamous system to a more endogamous one, particularly in the higher circles of Bura society. This decreased the corporate nature of Bura patrilineages that produce intra-class feuds and reflects instead an increase in class solidarity across several clans of rulers and nobles allied by common political interests. (Changing the rules of marriage, in this case of political purposes, is an example of the exercise of 'relational' or structural control (Baumgartner et al., this volume, and Baumgartner et al., 1975a).)

In general, conflict with other groups or obvious needs to adapt, whether for purposes of survival or effective competition with other groups, creates a predilection to choose a more centralized type of social structure in which the maximal leadership A has considerable social power. Hence, under conditions of attack or threat of disaster, the value of strong, community-wide leadership and related institutions may become dominant. Community-wide institutions and strong central leadership are perceived as being able to provide more effective coordination for social action and to mobilize more resources than can more local groups or leaders. The membership and local leaders surrender to a greater or lesser extent powers to A or allow A to assume extraordinary powers to deal with internal or external threats or problems for which existing or everyday institutions and patterns of action seem inadequate: war, civil disturbance, disaster or depression.[28] In other words, they encourage or allow the transformation of the system — possibly perceiving it as temporary — in the direction of greater centralized control and hierarchization.

Such social transformations entail the redistribution of power. For instance, local leaders and their membership loose power relative to the central leadership.[29] Those associated with structures or positions suffering a relative loss in power or in control over power resources may resist such developments, at least if these changes are perceived as going beyond that necessary (or as being improperly exploited). Typically, struggles arise over 'decisions' about the structural development of society, in particular, whether power differentiation and hierarchical development will be restricted or amplified further in certain directions (Baumgartner et al., this volume).[30] The outcomes of these struggles will, at least in the short run, depend on the relative power of the contenders — the resources they can mobilize from within as well as from outside the system (Alker et al., 1977).

Both the Baumgartner et al. and Cohen papers examine multi-level structuring processes which lead to the development of social control hierarchies and more systemic forms of power.[31] In these investigations, they focus on positive feedback loops which in certain contexts link initial power differences to differential accumulation of power resources, making the system morphogenetically unstable. As a result, initial differences, even quite small ones, in positional advantage and power accumulation may be amplified into major institutionalized class structures. Such developments, combined with inter-societal exchange, competition and conflict, tend to reinforce internal social stratification as well as stratification among societies. These processes are examined in relation to the emergence and development of the state, empire and other social formations.

NOTES

1. Of the 15 persons contributing to this volume, two are from anthropology (Carlos, Cohen), one from biophysics (Pattee), one from economics (Baumgartner), three from political science (Alker, Hardin, Nagel), and the remainder from sociology. We had one additional contributor to our World Congress session in Toronto, the historian Martin Jay. He prepared a most interesting paper on the concept of totality in Marxist thought, particularly in the works of Lukacs and the Frankfurt school. Unfortunately, because of other commitments, he was unable to orient his paper more to the specific themes of this volume.

2. Cf. the closely related concept of 'sociogenesis' or social learning in the recent work of Dunn (1971); also, the concept of the 'world homeostat system' of Laszlo (1974).

3. However, the factors structuring action and interaction possibilities are of primary importance to social analysis, since they determine what actors can and cannot do, in particular whether they can or cannot engage in mutual exchange or conflict, what types of conflict or exchange are possible, the symmetry or asymmetry of their interaction patterns, and so forth. Within the limits determined by social structural, technological, and ecological constraints, as well as actors' performance capabilities and knowledge – and only within these limits – actors 'choose' and 'decide'.

4. Many of the criticisms of network analysis discussed earlier and in the Anderson and Carlos paper apply equally well to the use of graph theory in social network analysis.

5. Four important reviews that catch much of the flavor and content of this body of research, and parts of the more recent schedule-based approaches are Bell et al. (1969), Cartwright (1959), Dahl (1967) and March (1966). We are particularly indebted to James March on several points concerning naturalistic power analysis approaches.

6. Nothing conveys the idea of the early naturalistic approach better than an ingeniously designed, but structurally superficial, experiment carried out by

March and cited by Dahl (1967). Each of several boys in isolation ranked in loveliness pictures of ten or so girls. Then, although strangers, they interacted with each other in determining a collective ranking of the pictures. A quasi-experimentally controlled, statistical *measure* of *exercised individual* power was the partial correlation of an individual's prior ranking with the final collective result, controlling for the average of the prior rankings. The implicit structural model of influence relations was thus a set of additive multiple regression equations.

7. The similarities of such approaches to prior natural scientific or naturalistic conceptualizations should be noted at the outset. Natural scientists define physical power in terms of work done or energy expended per unit time: one horsepower equals 550 foot-pounds of work per second. Power has the dimensions or component units of

$$\frac{\text{force x distance}}{\text{time}} = \frac{\text{work}}{\text{time}} = \frac{\text{energy}}{\text{time.}}$$

There is a further naturalistic distinction between structure-linked or positional, *potential energy* and *kinetic energy*. In terms of time rates, this distinction is translatable into the notion of potential, exerciseable power and actual, exercised power.

8. An earlier, related treatment based on Harsanyi's addition of opportunity costs to Dahl's 1967 list of power elements is Alker's formulation (1973).

9. There is a long history in the social sciences of focusing on the stability problems of apparently closed or isolated quasi-physical systems, using concepts and methods compatible with equilibrium assumptions (Baumgartner et al., 1976). However, there has been increasing emphasis, as represented by several of the papers in this volume, on open systems and structure creation and change.

10. Naturalistics approaches to the study of social power have been inclined to assume (implicitly) a fixed social structure in the same way that physical laws are supposed to be invariant (see note 9). Thus, the powers or capacities of actors are investigated, as if in a closed or isolated systems.

11. Marxian power analysis, in particular, has viewed political power as grounded in social structure (e.g. Lukes, 1974; Poulantzas, 1973).

12. The power to generate or to structure social structures is a meta-power. As discussed in Baumgartner et al. in this volume, different generative processes or mechanisms have different powers; for example to determine the direction and magnitude of resource flows that sustain or change networks, Nagel-type structures, or social hierarchies.

13. Polarized elites are much less capable of effective response to crisis or threat of crisis, primarily because any adaptation will tend to bring advantages to one group and disadvantages to another (Parkin, this volume; also, see note 30 below). Parkin points out the significance of (many) capitalist societies readily and easily adopting Keynesian economic reforms, thereby counteracting the tendencies toward cyclical crises. This served to convert unemployment from a

possible threat with morphogenic potentiality to a 'social problem'.

14. Human actors are potentially capable of individual and collective goal achievement. In practice, the political and economic institutions within society distort and constrain *differentially* their capabilities to act, including capabilities of conceptualizing, communicating (Habermas, 1970), and transforming themselves.

15. Parkin was not satisfied with the paper he prepared for our session of the World Congress of Sociology and did not wish to see it published at this time. We felt in any case that a sample of his work on system stability and change in industrialized societies should be included. This decision was also called for by Hardin's contrasting analysis of developments in Eastern Europe. We have included therefore an earlier paper by Parkin.

16. The 'export' of poverty and crises to many LDCs may have been a factor not only in socialist revolutionary movements in individual countries, as Meier suggests, but in the increasing class consciousness and organization of LDCs (see Baumgartner et al., 1975d). Such movements are likely to make it increasingly difficult for highly developed capitalist countries (and socialist countries for that matter) to obtain basic resources in exchange for manufactured goods at as favorable terms of exchange as they have enjoyed in the past. This, in turn, will face the leadership in these societies with a more exacting test than they have faced at any time since the 1920s and 1930s (as Chancellor Helmut Schmidt suggested in his talk (September, 1975) before the opening session of the West German Parliament).

17. Some countries, both communist and capitalist, will be better able to make the necessary societal adjustments associated with changes in the expansion process. It will be precisely those societies which lack such capability − or the capacity to develop such capabilities in timely fashion − which will be subject to substantial erosive forces, including those tending to fragment the dominant elites.

18. Ideological differentiation is associated with social differentiation. Differences in objective conditions, life experiences, and opportunities tend to lead to a variety of ideological frameworks defining 'important factors and relationships', values, decision-making algorithms, and perceptions of meaningful 'solutions' to problems (Baumgartner et al., 1975b).

19. Hardin suggests that the particular value conflicts may be internalized within individuals so that the 'organizational dilemma over two conflicting institutionalized values need not define two factions, each supporting its preferred value' (also, see Meier's paper in this regard).

20. The lack of a high degree of social differentiation, especially in the face of an identifiable colonizer or oppressor, may have been a factor underlying one of the anomalies Meier refers to, namely that broad-based socialist movements have emerged in less developed capitalist societies, often as part of their response to, and national struggle against, colonization. One of the major factors making for generalized conflict in Eastern Europe has certainly been Soviet pressure and its army.

21. As occurred in Poland during the winter of 1970-71.

22. 'Intellectuals' often play a role in providing the symbols and concepts which appeal to and bind differentiated groups into a single (although possibly temporary) movement. In any case, the intelligentsia may be an important influence in shaping cultural forces or articulating such forces — with long time lags before the forces usually make themselves felt. Moreover, desertion of a regime by the most capable intellectuals — and this may be accomplished in the most subtle ways — can contribute to undermining the capacity of the regime to maintain or to gain legitimation and to deal effectively with crises or internal and external challenges.

23. A mechanical system where social structure is simply reproduced is obviously not being suggested.

24. Social constraints may derive either from the refusal of hostile neighbors to admit immigrants from neighboring social groups or from *A*'s ability to exercise 'boundary control' through police activities. The costs involved in the two cases are obviously not identical, and may have long-term economic and political implications.

25. On the other hand, there may be a direct relationship between the development and stabilization of centralized hierarchical structures and emigration possibilities under conditions where the resultant loss of population does not undermine significantly the economic base of the society at the same time that it removes those who strongly oppose the established social order (and whose opposition tends to weaken it) (Hardin and Baumgartner et al., this volume).

26. Richardson (1956) in his comparative study of the organization of ships, stresses that during non-emergency activities which account for most of the routine aboard ships, the full measure of vested authority remains latent and a form of authority more suited to non-emergency routine work and living is manifest. But in times of emergency or crisis, the latent structure becomes manifest — there is in effect a meta-choice, selecting a different structure and pattern of action, for example a clearly designated hierarchy of authority to meet the hazards and emergencies which the ship may encounter.' A structure, albeit latent for most of the time, is available to be activated or selected.

27. Of course, this presumes that the groups involved are unable or unwilling to move away, for economic, political, or cultural reasons. Thus, such secondary structural development depends not only on structural preparedness but social ties or constraints that keep the population in place.

28. In general, actors are inclined to support the most powerful or best situated collectivity for protecting their interests, other things being equal. Of course, large or important segments of the society may disagree with *A*'s assumption of power and his policies and have the power to oppose *A* about the direction of system change and development (see note 30).

29. Subordinate actors give up rights and possibilities of action for what they take to be their own or the collective good. But a dilemma arises for them: the hierarchical control structures can be used for collective purposes (mobilization against external attack, internal crisis or disaster, expansion of production, etc.) as well as for controlling or neutralizing opposition and competing elites.

30. Such a social-structural viewpoint suggests that the accepted generaliza-

tion that external threat from, or conflict with, an outside group leads to greater unification and centralization must be re-eexamined. The functional approach to conflict (as exemplified in the work of Simmel and Coser) tends to neglect the fact that societal developments associated with preparations for conflict alter social relationships within the society, with subsequent shifts in power, frequently giving internal advantages to some groups over others. Because of this, there may be opposition and even resistance on the part of individuals or groups that are adversely affected by the processes of change. Hence, the effects of external threat or conflict on a society would depend to a large extent on its internal structure; for example, the degree of unity or cohesiveness in the society, particularly among elite groups. In some instances, integration and centralization may be stimulated by conflict or external threat, in others not.

31. An important feature of structuring processes is the likelihood that they are embedded in multi-level systems. Meta-power or relational control at one level contributes to structuring relatively stable relations at lower levels (see note 12). Structuring processes which are operators or regulators of lower level processes are themselves subject to structuring processes and regulation in a given context. Of particular interest in this respect is the recent emphasis and work on mechanisms controlling the expression of genes in evolutionary theory. For instance, King and Wilson (1975) suggest that changes in gene regulation are the key to anatomical evolution rather than changes in structural genes themselves (the DNA sequences that code for proteins). Adaptation to new environments may come about by means of mutations which alter gene regulation rather than mutations which alter the sequences of structural genes. Thus, the emphasis has shifted from changes in lower level structures to changes in higher level processes of regulation and integration of the lower level structure. Recent research on socio-cultural evolution is based on similar concerns.

REFERENCES

H. Alker Jr. (1973), 'Political capabilities in a schedule sense: Measuring power, integration and development', in: H. Alker Jr, K. W. Deutsch and A. Stoetzel (eds), *Mathematical Approaches to Politics* (Amsterdam: Elsevier).

H. R. Alker, Jr. (1974), 'Are there structural models of voluntaristic social action?', *Quality and Quantity*, 8: 199-246.

H. R. Alker, Jr. (1975), 'Polimetrics: its descriptive foundations', in: F. Greenstein and N. Polsby (eds), *Handbook of Political Science* (Reading, Mass.: Addison-Wesley).

H. R. Alker, Jr., T. Baumgartner and T. R. Burns (1977), 'The Structuring of Dependence', *International Organization*, 31, forthcoming.

J. A. Barnes (1972), *Social Networks* (Reading, Mass.: Addison-Wesley).

T. Baumgartner, T. R. Burns, D. Meeker and B. Wild (1976) 'Methodological implications of multi-level processes for social research', *International Journal of General Systems*, 3.

T. Baumgartner, W. Buckley and T. R. Burns (1975a) 'Meta-power and Relational Control in Social Life', *Social Science Information*, 14: 49-78.

T. Baumgartner, T. R. Burns, P. DeVille and D. Meeker (1975b) 'A systems model of conflict and change in planning systems', *General Systems Yearbook*, 20.

T. Baumgartner, T. R. Burns and W. Buckley (1975c), 'Relational control: the human structuring of cooperation and conflict', *Journal of Conflict Resolution* (Sept.).

T. Baumgartner, T. R. Burns and P. DeVille (1975d), 'Middle East scenarios and international restructuring: conflict and challenge', *Bulletin of Peace Proposals* (in press).

R. Bell, D. Edwards and R. Wadgner (eds) (1969), *Political Power: A Reader in Theory and Research* (New York: Free Press).

R. L. Caneiro (1970), 'A Theory of the Origin of the State', *Science*, 169: 733-38.

D. Cartwright (ed.) (1959), *Studies in Social Power* (Ann Arbor, Michigan: University of Michigan).

R. Dahl (1967), 'The Concept of Power', *Behavioral Science* (1957), reprinted in Bell et al., op. cit.

R. Dahl (1969), 'The power approach to the study of politics', in: D. Sills (ed.), *International Encyclopedia of the Social Sciences* (New York: Macmillan).

P. DeVille and T. R. Burns (1976) 'Institutional Response to Crisis in Capitalist Development', *Proceedings: The Third European Meeting on Cybernetics and Systems Research*, in press.

E. Dunn Jr (1971), *Economic and Social Development: A Process of Social Learning* (Baltimore: John Hopkins).

J. Habermas (1970), 'Toward a Theory of Communicative Competence', in: H. Dreitzel (ed.), *Recent Sociology No. 2* (New York: Macmillan).

F. Harary, R. Norman and D. Cartwright (1965), *Structural Models: An Introduction to the Theory of Directed Graphs* (New York: Wiley).

M. C. King and A. C. Wilson (1975), 'Evolution at two levels in humans and chimpanzees', *Science*, 188: 107-66.

E. Laszlo (1974), *A Strategy for the Future* (New York: Brazillor).

K. Lewin (1951), *Field Theory in Social Science* (New York: Harper & Row).

S. Lukes (1974), *Power: The Radical View* (London: MacMillan).

J. March (1966), 'The power of power', in: D. Easton (ed.), *Varieties of Political Theory* (Englewood Cliffs: Prentice-Hall).

F. Parkin (1974), 'System and superstructure in Marxist theory', Paper prepared for *VIIIth World Congress of Sociology*, Toronto, Canada, August.

N. Poulantzas (1973), *Political Power and Social Classes*. (London: New Left Books).

S. Richardson (1956), 'Organizational contrasts on British and American ships', *Administrative Science Quarterly*, 1: 189-207.

H. A. Simon (1957), *Models of Man* (New York: Wiley).

I

POWER IN SOCIAL STRUCTURES:
DESCRIPTIVE ANALYSIS

2

WHAT IS SOCIAL NETWORK THEORY?

Bo Anderson
Michigan State University

Manuel L. Carlos
University of California, Santa Barbara

I. INTRODUCTION

Social network analysis rests on the premise that a person's social conduct, decision processes, orientations, and attachments should be viewed in the context of his network of relationships. This perspective has dominated the work of many novelists. For example, it is explicitly set forth by Henry James in his classic Preface to *Roderick Hudson*. Indeed, James clearly identified one problem that modern network analysis is striving to deal with adequately. In the Preface he discusses the issue of how one should attempt to isolate, from the very large set of direct and indirect network links in which a person is enmeshed, that

---

For useful comments on various drafts of this paper we want to thank Tom Burns, the late Herbert Karp, Leonard and Donna Kasdan, Michael Loukinen, Marianne Paget, Frank Sim, Carolyn Stell, Susan Taylor, and Werner von der Ohe. Some of the ideas in this paper were originally presented at a working conference on social network analysis at the University of West Virginia, April, 1974.

primary or pivotal subset of relationships which gives us enough information about a person's conduct and attachments to enable us to make
sufficient sense of his behavior and motivations. The pervasiveness of
the network metaphor is also present in the social sciences. In classical
sociology Georg Simmel introduced a form of network analysis by
examining individual behavior in terms of a person's 'webs of affilia-
tion'. More recently, as we shall show, many other sociologists and
anthropologists have employed a network approach in their work.

The purpose of this paper is to discuss and assess the theoretical
origins, continuities, and present status of 'social network analysis'. We
should note from the start that despite many promising trends and
horizons in the literature, there does not exist *a* theory of social
networks which comprehensively explains the social and psychological
bases of network interrelationships and bonding processes. In addition,
we know very little, in a systematic way, about how networks emerge,
are altered, maintained, or atrophy. These limitations notwithstanding,
there are many important insights in the literature into all of these
processes, and some of these we will examine and elaborate on in our
analysis. Our review of the literature will necessarily be selective since it
is voluminous and mostly descriptive in content. Moreover, we do not
wish to cover areas already adequately dealt with by other authors
(Whitten and Wolf, 1973).

The word 'network' merits definition since it is the central concept
in our paper. Viewed in its total dimensions, it refers to sets of direct
and indirect social relations, centered around given persons, which are
instrumental to the achivement of the goals of these persons and to the
communication of their expectations, demands, needs and aspirations.
Networks are thus the conscious products of an individual's attempts to
manage and control his relevant and instrumental transactions. They are
also the product of persons' sentiments and affective orientations, i.e.
their likes, dislikes, loves, enmities, hopes and despairs and other
attachments. Another characteristic of networks is that their individual
links are dynamic. They are constantly being aligned and realigned,
activated or made latent, salvaged or allowed to lapse, as persons and
groups go about the tasks of making their lives.

Our approach in this paper will be as follows. In section II we
explain the theoretical origins of network analysis. We do so by
sketching out the theoretical reasons why sociologists and social anthro-

pologists found it necessary to adopt and use social network analysis and certain integral subconcepts.

In section III we discuss a few micro-theoretical approaches which seem relevant to those concerns which originally led sociologists and anthropologists into network theory. Our discussion in section III focuses on those approaches which seem to us to have the best promise for understanding certain behavioral mechanisms and social-psychological processes involved in the formation, maintenance, and decay of instrumental network links. We do so because we believe that it is precisely these mechanisms and processes which ultimately shape the morphological and bonding characteristics of empirically detectable social networks.

Beginning with section III we begin our assessment of network theory and explore the nature of the obstacles which prevent us from converting network analysis into a rigorous, formal, and empirically-relevant theoretical enterprise. We conclude with some observations on the significance of network analysis and some suggestions about the future directions which network approach might, and in our view should, take.

II. STRUCTURAL FUNCTIONALISM AND THE ORIGINS OF NETWORK ANALYSIS

Much of current thinking and research about social networks emerged from the anthropological study of individuals and groups in complex society and in reaction to the inadequacies of the structural-functional tradition in social anthropology. In the course of their work on urban area problems, in the study of migration, and in work undertaken in European societies, (e.g. in the Mediterranean region or in northern Europe), some anthropologists encountered analytical and empirical issues which could not be easily and meaningfully handled with the conventional theoretical focus and apparatus of structural-functionalism. These problems and issues concern social situations and certain types of societies that call for a good deal of *individual* choice in the formation of a person's instrumental relationships. In light of these problems, a shift toward a model that emphasizes choice behaviors and instrumental bonding patterns became necessary.

In order to explain why this theoretical shift came about and why it was in many ways necessary, let us first spell out the shared characteristics of those social groups for which a structural-functional approach would be natural and plausible. Let S be the social structure of a group of individuals (e.g. a village, a formal organization, or some other community-enclosed collective), and let P be the population that inhabits S. Next, let us assume that a group satisfies the following criteria:

(1) S is an ordered set of social roles;

(2) each role in S contains explicitly formulated and detailed norms and expectations which spell out what behaviors are obligatory, permitted, allowed and forbidden for any incumbent of the role;

(3) each role has as one of its components a set of explicitly defined tasks toward which any incumbent of that role must be oriented.

(4) any task that comes up in S belongs to or is similar to one of the task sets mentioned in (3);

(5) every person in P is an incumbent of a specific, proper subset of S;

(6) each individual in P regards the norms and expectations that define his roles in S as legitimate; and

(7) role membership criteria for all individuals in P are clear, explicit, and non-negotiable.

It should be clear that any society or group of individuals which satisfies these criteria would leave very little room for individual choice behavior. Established norms and expectations, together with the role-tasks, form the constituent parts of all roles in S, telling each person what to do in most if not all social situations. In such a society or group of individuals all networks that would develop in P would be necessarily mapped out by the social structure, S.

This perspective, as many critics have noted, leads to a highly reified conception of social structures, since the latter are conceived of as composed of roles rather than persons. Involved is a by-passing of the ultimate social reality of individual behavior in favor of a certain mode of reality description that ignores the actual conduct of persons in specific situations, whether that conduct be informed or misinformed, rational or whimsical, clear-sighted or prejudiced, self-seeking or caring.

On the whole, then, structural-functionalist perspectives of human and group behavior view social action as being compulsorily normative in character and people as being very strictly limited in their pursuit of social actions and goals. In contemporary network analysis considerably less emphasis is placed on the normative components of social action, though, as we shall note, there is a proper place for normative concepts in a theory of social networks.

Let us now turn to an alternative social structure that we get when we loosen up the structural-functional assumptions and adopt a complex or 'multiplex' society framework (Boissavain, 1974). In the new model, groups have the following characteristics: All roles in S contain general expectations about which behaviors are obligatory, permitted, allowed, and forbidden for the incumbents of the roles. Similarly, the contents of the norms and expectations are to a considerable extent open to negotiation; that is, the notions of what is obligatory, permitted, allowed and forbidden are constructed and accomplished during interactions among the members of the group.

In the modified model of behavior and social structure, new tasks and interrelationships occasionally come up or develop for which there are only rather partial routines and prescribed paths available. Hence, ad hoc solutions and bases for interaction have to be invented. Similarly, the group is not very clearly bounded; that is, new members occasionally drift into the group, and some members are absent for periods of time due to migrations, multiple-group membership, etc. Finally the legitimacy of the norms and expectations that define the roles in S is open to question, in the sense that the norms and expectations have to be continuously validated against experience and in relation to the new tasks faced by individuals and bonds established by the group.

In the above situation, individual choices and non-prescribed social bonds become very important; personal networks are no longer exclusively mapped by prescriptive norms and the formal role structure, including kinship structure, of S, but, rather, emerge largely as consequences of a number of decisions by individuals or groups. Links change a good deal as new tasks are confronted and non-prescribed, multiple bonds are established.

These purposively-constructed networks provide flexible and fluid conditions that help to shape future individual decisions and network relationships in at least two ways: (a) individual decisions and bonding processes will be based on and therefore affected by information and resources that flow through already-established network links, and (b) existing network links will be treated as exchangeable resources; that is, during their negotiations and transactions individuals in S can and do make social contact available to one another at an agreed-upon price.

Such processes and relationships lead to the establishment of indirect links between persons through intermediaries and to the extension of networks. Individual actors in social networks clearly do a lot of the 'work' involved in maintaining, extending, and securing of their linkages. But there also exist certain network 'meta-processes' (Baumgartner et al., 1975) through which some persons come to specialize in affecting the network links of others. Their activities may be only partly visible to those affected. The skillful management of network links becomes the specialized concern for many kinds of brokers (power and influence brokers, resource brokers). A theory of social networks, then placed in the context of our multiplex-society model of behavior and social structure, should therefore have a great deal to say about how individuals extend their activities, make use of brokers, and the limitations that infringe on these processes.

In some contemporary thinking about social networks, the reasoning outlined above has led to some developments that are fruitful for researching and conceptualizing network extension and bonding processes. Fredrik Barth, for instance, has developed what he calls 'generative models' of how social structures emerge as consequences of a large number of individual decisions which are subject to various ecological, normative and interpersonal constraints (Barth, 1966). His analysis sketches, at most, the broad features of the social structures and, by implication, of the networks that evolve, given certain rather vaguely stated assumptions about the constraints and preferences limiting individual choice behavior in network situations. Regretably, however, nowhere in Barth's work do we see in precise detail how a network structure is generated. Moreover, though Barth's thinking is on the right track, it faces formal problems encountered and studied in mathematical theories of decision-making preference orderings.

In line with Barth's approach, there have developed a number of related approaches and concepts which, when more carefully explicated, may provide part of the analytical framework and reasoning that will be required if social network analysis is to grow in the direction of joining individual choice behavior analysis with structural considerations. Such concepts as action-set, comprised of an individual and his instrumental ties, point to the idea that theories of social networks will have to be actor-centered, that actors will have to be seen as consciously and deliberately extending or limiting their networks, and that the analysis must take careful account of the perceptions of individual actors or classes of actors involved in the transactional processes of networks. Hence, it appears that certain components in the psychology of social perception and social information processing are well on their way to becoming an integral part of the explanatory apparatus of network studies. We discuss some of these in the following section.

III. SOME SOCIAL-PSYCHOLOGICAL NETWORK FORMULATIONS

There is some important literature which contains attempts to state the implications of some psychological and social processes which affect individual choice behavior in networks. These phenomena include individual social exchange, dependence, reciprocity, and the formation of indirect network links. Much of the work with these concepts has been done in social psychology rather than anthropology.

Our purpose in this section is to exemplify how a framework which evolved out of social anthropology stands to gain much when combined with approaches used in other fields. We also want to illustrate how the concepts and findings of these social-psychological research programs may help us to understand the dynamics of social network processes that take place in 'real life' groups. We believe that this can provide the starting guidelines for an eventual theoretical bridge between the thinking and research of social anthropologists on social networks, and the thinking and results obtained in the study of small, experimental groups. For us, this is essential if we are to move the theoretical enterprise beyond its current metaphorical and descriptive stage.

In a series of papers published over the last half-dozen years, James A. Davis and his co-workers have outlined and tested several models dealing with the structure of certain sentiment relations in experimental groups (see Davis, 1970). The formulations take their departure from a theory of structural balance and are based on an impressive mass of data.

In the Davis models, sentiment relations and bonding processes resulting from individual choice are interpreted as consisting essentially of affective relations, such as likes and dislikes, between persons in groups. The data and theoretical orientation presented are consistent with a transitivity hypothesis in social relations that can be formulated as follows:

if P_1 likes P_2 and P_2 likes P_3 then P_1 comes to like P_3.

It is clear that this social-psychological process helps to explain why network extensions and bonding processes occur. Starting with certain sets of initial relationships of sentiment and affect, new links can be successively added. Furthermore, if we add the idea that P_1 likes P_2 then P_2 will come to like P_1, we can see how mutual or indirect links may become established in a network.

In order to evaluate the relevance of these ideas for our purposes, the following two arguments must be considered. First, the hypotheses as stated are over-simplified and do not seem very plausible. The process of sentiment and affect transfer does not proceed as automatically as the theory says; we do not develop direct or indirect friendships with all the friends of our friends. The following formulation might make the hypothesis more reasonable:

(a) if P_1 likes P_2 and P_2 likes P_3 then P_1 will come to *expect* to like P_3; *and*

(b) if the outcome of the first encounter between P_1 and P_3 is positive, then P_1 will or may come *to like* P_3; if the outcome is negative, then the likelihood is that P_1 will remain *neutral* in his relations to P_3.

This reformulation tries to capture the idea that we are at best positively disposed toward the friends of our friends. Letters of introduction and reference are based on the potential for this predisposition, although in many cases nothing really comes of such preliminary moves at interaction nor from our attempts to manipulate our friendships. Other factors besides likes and dislikes obviously, at least in our view, intervene.

The problem with Davis's theory is that it neglects the normative aspects of network processes. It also unduly emphasizes the importance of sentiments for the development, maintenance and decay of network links. Obligations in networks frequently develop quite independently of sentiment relations. One frequently recognizes that one has clear and persistent obligations toward people regardless of how one feels toward them, and it is not uncommon that one refuses to take on obligations to others even though one might like them. Political theorists, classical and modern, for good reasons stress the non-sentimental nature of attachments and support in alliances, coalitions, and confrontations (Waldman, 1972).

Processes involving sentiment and obligation are, it seems, quite independent. It does seem reasonable to assume, however, that at least in some instances positive affect may solidify social bonds and obligations and that negative affect may ultimately undermine them. Our purpose here is not to deny the validity of Davis's theory but simply to argue that it is limited as to scope and explanatory range. The growth or extension of sentiment relations in bonding may be a theoretically meaningful process that can be studied in its own right as Davis and his co-workers have done. It seems equally clear, however that the networks which tie people together as members of institutions, neighborhood groups, factions, and other collectivities, contain more than sentiment relations, even though sentiment relations may be present and serve to solidify network links that emerge and are maintained for other reasons.

We suggest that sentiment relations matter most in the earliest phase of the development of network ties. Once a link has become established, its fate depends more on the positively or negatively valued outcomes of transactions between the group members than on sentiment attachments. Hence, Davis's process should be interpreted as pertaining primarily to a pre-transactional phase in social network formation.

Social-psycholgical approaches to network processes can gain much by incorporating the results of Richard Emerson's studies of the concept of dependence (Emerson, 1962). Dependence, in Emerson's view, results from the relative control which individuals have over the resources of other persons. If P possesses many of those resources that O wants, and O possesses few of the resources that P wants, then O is more dependent on P than P is dependent on O. Power in such relationships is defined in terms of relative dependence.

According to Emerson's theory, inequalities of power between persons lead to tension. Under such circumstances, people will attempt to orient their actions so as to reduce this tension. They will not always succeed, but they will generally persist, pursuing their actions in a tension-reduction direction as far as they can.

Emerson specifies four courses of action which serve to reduce tension in a situation of unequal power. Adapted to a network perspective, they are as follows.

(1) The dependent party in a network relationship may decide he needs the resources provided for him by the other party *less* than he originally thought he did.

(2) He learns to live with the tension and accommodates himself to the situation.

(3) The dependent party in a network can try to find alternative sources within other network links of those commodities for which he was originally dependent on the first party. That is, he can try to extend his network to link up with *alternative* suppliers in other networks. As in some patron-client ties, the dependent party can ally himself with other actors who are in a *similar* situation vis-à-vis the same more powerful actor. It is assumed that the more powerful actor in some sense or other needs the dependent actors. Hence, if these can form a coalition, they might be in a position to bargain with him.

(4) Finally, the dependent party in the network relationship can attempt to make the more powerful party more dependent on him than he was before. That is, the dependent party can try to create some commodity that the more powerful person comes to like, want or find desirable. A good example of such a new commodity is social status. The dependent person can give status by flattery, deference and obsequiousness and thus manipulate the more powerful party.

One task for this theory, if it is to contribute and be adapted to network analysis, is to state the conditions that determine how dependent actors choose between the courses of action available to them and how far they can push them. In this respect, Emerson's theory is highly *indeterminate*. He fails to specify or even consider the structural and motivational conditions which determine these choices. More seriously, his formulation does not consider how the more powerful actor in a network might 'catch on' to the strategems for netralization used by dependent actors. A powerful actor will try to prevent coalition formation from occurring among his dependents. He might also try to keep them isolated from other potential 'patrons' so they cannot extend their networks. In turn, of course, the subordinates may see through these strategems of divide and conquer. Were we to apply Emerson's theory to a concrete network situation, it would be important to try to specify the available strategies that can be pursued over time by both the dominant and the dependent actors. A boundary condition that seems to be implicit in Emerson's work is that all the actors are involved in dyadic relationships and are pursuing an exchange strategy of self-maximization. Hence, Emerson's theory is in some ways more important to the analysis of patron-client relations than for our understanding of friendship or kinship networks.

The social-psychological approaches we have briefly reviewed here point to behavioral mechanisms which in various ways contribute to the emergence, maintenance and decay of bonding and exchange processes and an individual's network links. As we have tried to point out, there are serious questions about the scope and applicability of the findings. We have pointed to two scope limitations: (a) the time period involved in bonding and network processes are not clearly identified by the studies examined, and (b) the 'institutional matrix' in which network processes work themselves out are not specified by the studies. To illustrate, sentiment processes play an important role early in the formation of network links; at later phases they at most have supportive functions. Similarly, institutionalized contexts or 'matrices' like friendship, kinship, political and economic action, impose *normative* and *utility-oriented* constraints on the direction, spread, and substance of sentiment relations.

More importantly, events, transactions, and relationships in many networks are *public* events, and hence cannot be treated exclusively as reflecting the personal attachments, dependency relationships, and action preferences of individual actors alone. A *public 'score'* of a person's debits and credits in exchanges is kept by network members-at-large in many social networks. Hence when a person is exchanging with others he makes himself accountable to an *audience* which keeps score of his behavior and transactions. Because of this score-keeping, a person's willingness to help another may depend *less* on the factors that

Emerson or Davis dealt with than on person's anticipated transactions with other actors who will hold him accountable for his treatment of his present partners. Persons, including power brokers, acquire community-wide reputations on the basis of their general transactional performances and their compliance with previously negotiated obligations in network transactions.[1]

Although social network analysis developed as a critique of the normative view of social action (as summarized in section II above), it would be a mistake to focus exclusively on private choice behavior and affective preference in analyzing bonding and other network processes. Normative components remain strong in determining the nature and value of an individual's network ties; that is why social actors distinguish between friends and acquaintances, between close and distant kinsmen or between trustworthy and fairweather allies.

The normative and affiliative or bonding contents of network ties and the significance of each are encoded in the linguistic labels that we give them (see, for example, Bailey, 1971). When a person labels his relationship to others ('my friend', 'mi padrino politico', or political Godfather, 'mi compadre', or fictive co-parent, 'my brother', 'my buddy', and sonon) he signals publicly to an audience the normative bonding and social standard by which his performances in the relationship are to be publicly judged. An important component in social network analysis, therefore, is the identification of semantic domains and social codes that are used to label and determine the significance of network ties in *S*.

Social networks, then, develop, are maintained and decay because of various and different processes, e.g. the spread of sentiment structures, social exchanges and normative-linguistic processes. Given these complexities, it is therefore *not* likely that *a* comprehensive social-psychological theory of networks will be developed in the immediate future. But partial theories, conceptual sets and integrated bodies of propositions can be developed, and have already been stated in part for at least some of the sub-processes involved in networks.

IV. STRUCTURAL DIMENSIONS AND OTHER THEORETICAL COMPONENTS IN THE SOCIAL NETWORK APPROACH

It follows from our modified model of multiplex society (as presented in section II) that a researcher who wants to use social network analysis must view the social structure, S, as generated by a large number of choices made by the actors-in-S. This implies that the research must pay close attention to how actors make their bonding and transactional decisions in light of specific network contexts and consequences. It also means that to understand the relationship of these processes to network structure, the following aspects of networks must remain part of the researcher's considerations: *sentiment relations, power-balance mechanisms,* and *semantic labelings* and *norms* implied by the latter. These factors and processes are critical since they serve to direct attention to critical spheres and dimensions of network interaction; they also suggest ways of organizing the information about relevant social processes being observed.

The literature in mathematical sociology contains other relevant formulations and concepts, besides those we have discussed, that are of great theoretical and parallel interest in studying structural components and dynamics of network ties. We refer here to the work of Harrison White, for example, who has emphasized that close attention should be paid to the issue of the *relative products* of network relations (see Tarski, 1965, p. 92, and White and Lorrain, 1971). He has shown that many persons in networks are often linked *indirectly*. Linkages between relations are called the relative product of the relations. A question of great importance is, therefore, whether a theoretical and empirical meaning can be given to the relative product of two or more relations in a network. If the relation R_1 is 'brother' and R_2 is 'friend', then what is the sociological meaning of 'my brother's friend'? What obligations does one have toward a person just because he is one's brother's friend?

Obligations, affect, and expectations are transferred through *chains* of relations, as White maintains in his 'relative product' hypothesis. Otherwise the custom of sponsorship, letters of introduction and the use of others as references in establishing relations and conducting transactions would lack meaning. That sentiment relations can 'spread' to third parties is indicated by the results of the Davis research program which we discussed earlier. Similarly, it is not difficult to find anecdotal 'evidence' that other relations also transfer through indirect loyalties and ties. For example, in a small Swedish mill town early in this century the managers expected and got a great deal of deference from visiting relatives of workers in the plant. A foreman expected and got compliance on orders issued to workers who were the *direct* subordinates of *other* foremen. To mention another example, if the mother of one's brother-in-law passes through town, one would presumably offer lodging for the night and a meal. There is, however, a colorful American-English term for the *limits* of such obligations which is 'overstaying one's welcome'. Thus, loyalties and the transfer of obligations in direct and indirect network ties have normative constraints as we noted earlier. That some kind of *attenuation* often takes place seems clear, but is this always the case and what factors determine this effect? Social network analysis must begin to specify what kinds of factors and processes are involved in these kinds of spreads of expectation and obligations to which White has called our attention.

If a social network consists of a set of different relations connecting a set of persons, then, relying on White's approach, one can express abstractly and usefully the various indirect relations between these persons by the relative products of the relations. (The same two persons may be indirectly related in various and distinct ways.) Suppose that 'R' stands for status superordination and 'Eq' for status equality. In many cases we may then assert:

$$(P_1 R P_2) \cdot (P_2 Eq P_3) \cdot (P_3 R P_4) = P_1 R P_4 .$$

That is, suppose P_1 is the head of one particular segment of S and P_2 is his direct subordinate, P_3 is an equivalent to P_2 in some other segment, and P_4 is a subordinate of P_3. It is likely that P_1 will expect and receive deference from P_4 (as long as the actors are acting *as* members of S). As far as deference goes, the expression on the left-hand side is *reduced* to use the terminology of White and Lorrain (White and Lorrain, 1971), to the shorter one on the right.

White and Lorrain imply, rightly in our opinion, that it is a major goal of formal structural analysis to accomplish such reductions. They are *not*, however, very helpful in providing guides for how this is to be done in specific cultural contexts. They refer to two 'strategies', a 'cultural' one and a 'sociometric' one. However, they concentrate on sociometric reductions and do very little to develop directives about how to pursue or achieve 'cultural' reductions. The process is very difficult, since one needs to know a *great deal* about the cultural aspects of S in order to write the rules for reduction. And, one might ask, if one knows and can describe that much about S, does one need to write the formal and abstract set of reduction rules about how such interrelationships operate? Most anthropologists would probably respond negatively. However, the response would have to be affirmative for mathematical sociologists who chose to establish the comparability of the formalistic aspects of network dynamics across cultures or types of societies.

White's work raises other issues and has other problems which should be mentioned. In the example used above it is likely that P_1 will expect and receive deference from P_4, but there may be situations in which he may not presume to exercise authority over P_4, although he might do so with regard to P_2. There are empirical and ethnographic case studies reported in the literature that pertain to such issues or what has been termed 'relations between relations'. Although the information is hard to make theoretical sense of, we believe that we would learn a good deal about the reduction of relational chains at least in some situations by attempting to sift through it as we have done below in discussing Bailey's case study of caste, work and authority relations in an Indian village (Bailey, 1960). As it now stands, however, the mathematical formulation of White and Lorrain appears to be curiously void of substantive content and hence also void of useful directives for network studies of non-experimental groups. This, in our view, is due to the disparity in development between the highly developed formalism of some network theories and our application of these theories to substantive or actual cultural processes in field situations.

There are serious problems with non-formalistic approaches which also deserve to be mentioned, because they too make cumulative knowledge about networks difficult. For example, it is easy to find data and pseudo-theoretical explanations about actual cultural process, networks, and the relationships of specific actors in these networks, in the literature. In these works arguments are presented in which the author believes that he has explained something in a phenomenon by describing it and naming it. Most of this non-theoretical literature is composed of anthropological case studies.

Let us briefly look at one case of what we assume is taken to be an explanatory argument dealing with relations between relations. The case is taken from Bailey (Bailey, 1960, ch. VIII), and concerns a dispute that arose and was terminated over a period of two days in an Indian village. The key participants and opponents included the village headman (Ponga) and a minor official (Nrusingh). These two persons were, among other things, commercially related, as buyer and seller of tumeric. Bailey shows that despite the fact that these two persons were on opposite sides of a public caste dispute (Ponga, in fact, heaped abuse on Nrusingh), the conflict did not interfere with their more basic commercial relationship. We quote Bailey (pp. 227-28):

> There is a definite feeling, although it is not put into words, that trading and commerce are in some way outside the ordinary systems of social relations. I had noticed this in Bisipara, at the time of the bitter conflict between the clean castes and the untouchables. In spite of this conflict none of the personal economic links between clean castes and the untouchables – mostly wage-labor – were in the least disturbed. While a case was being fought before the Magistrate and oaths of secrecy were being extracted by their leaders from each side, the normal economic intercourse went on undisturbed. I think that in the Baderi case everyone concerned – Nrusingh, Ponga, and the Konds of Baderi – would have thought it a sign of madness had Ponga attempted to bring pressure on Nrusingh in such a way as to jeopardize their trading relationship.
>
> I have gone to some length to describe the things that Nrusingh and Ponga might have done, but did not in fact do, in order to bring out the element of choice in the situation. There is a temptation to assume that because two persons are connected in several different relationships, then these different relationships must always act upon and modify one another . . . But this is not so: for reasons of conscience, or expediency, or any other reason, it is sometimes possible for the individual to insulate one system from the other, and deliberately to set one relationship to one side and see that it is not brought into play. This is exactly what Ponga and Nrusingh did with their relationship as buyer and seller of tumeric. The different systems of social relations are not inevitably and inextricably connected with one another but are connected only when someone chooses to connect them.

This reasoning is not very satisfactory because commercial relationships do not generally function apart from other social ties. It is asserted time and time again in the literature that social ties, like

kinship and neighborhood relations, do in fact affect commercial transactions. What we need to know is what there is about the commercial
and other ties in Bailey's situation that makes the commercial transaction in his case independent of the dispute. It does not help merely to
say that the actors participate in relations that belong to different
systems; that begs the question altogether. We can always form compound relations (like relative products, relational sums and products);
some of these are sociologically interpretable, some are not. To say that
a commercial tie was not affected by some other social relation because
the two ties formed part of two independent systems is to *relabel* the
phenomenon, not to explain it.

If Bailey were trying to construct a rigorous theory of social networks, it would have been useful for him to point out contradictory
phenomena which his 'theory' does not explain. In the dispute that
Bailey deals with, the chief victim, Manda Kohoro, had three courses of
action open to him in his dealings with the major authority person, the
Sirdar.

> His aim, clearly, was to see that the money which he had handed over should
> find its way to the Government, so that he would not have to pay it again. The
> first course open to him was to insist on his rights at law, ultimately on his
> right to bring a complaint before the Magistrate about the conduct of the
> Sirdar and his subordinate. He could, that is to say, have conducted himself as
> a citizen, and as a person who stood equal with Goneswaro and Nrusingh
> before the law. A second course would have been to remind Goneswaro of his
> obligations as a Sirdar – as Manda's 'king' – and his duty to protect Manda
> from an unscrupulous minor official. Manda would then, in words and by his
> behavior, emphasize his dependence upon Goneswaro, and, by implication, his
> continued faith in the latter's probity. The third weapon in Manda's armoury
> was to invoke the support of his fellow Konds and by their joint pressure to
> cause the Sirdar to straighten the matter out. These three courses are not, of
> course, exclusive of one another and in fact Manda, either willingly or under
> pressure of circumstances, followed all three; but it seems to me that he relied
> mainly on the second course, while his comrades favoured the first, and drew
> Goneswaro's attention to the third factor.

Why Manda chose the particular way of relating to the Sirdar may
not be explainable using any sociological proposition. All we might be
able to say is that Manda acted as he did because of the kind of person
he was and because the Sirdar was the person he was. Another more
aggressive person might have behaved differently. Contrast this with

what Bailey says about the public reaction to Ponga's *not* letting the dispute interfere with the commercial relationship between himself and Nrusingh: 'Everyone would have thought it a sign of madness had Ponga attempted to bring pressure on Nrusingh in such a way as to jeopardize their trading relationship.' This statement suggests that we are dealing with a recognized, regular form of social action for which a theoretical explanation might be constructed (although Bailey does not produce one).

Other anthropological cases of social network analysis with an explanatory ambition make use of strong theoretical assumptions for which no independent tests seem to exist. One example of this is found in a paper by Knapferer (Knapferer, 1969, pp. 181-244) dealing with a dispute in a work situation in an African context. The details of the story need not concern us here. Two men quarrelled and others took sides. Knapferer, in accounting for who sided with him, makes use of a link-summation proposition and a spread-of-obligations proposition, both of which remain implicit and untested. We are not saying that the assumptions are untestable, nor that Knapferer lacks empirical reasons for asserting them in the context he is dealing with. Nor are we saying that it is impermissible in the pragmatics of inquiry to 'feel one's way' toward an explanation, using at times implicit, unexplicated principles. But we are saying that such principles must, when the explanatory enterprise is felt to be successful, be explicated, as clearly as possible, and *this* Knapferer does not do.

The link-summation premise in Knapferer's descriptive data asserts that if two persons are connected by two relations, R_1 and R_2, the resulting bond is stronger than either R_1 or R_2. Hence, the more links P has to a potential ally, O, the more likely it is that P can count on O's support when he *(P)* needs it. In many network contexts link-summation occurs and is recognized by the participants. For instance, persons active in Mexican politics cement their alliances by becoming co-parents or *compadres* (Carlos, 1973). But, assume that P is O's superior in a university department and also his near relative. In that situation O may *not* be able to count on any active support from P when his promotion is being considered. There are social rules about which relations may or may not be part of additive sets. One task facing social network theorists who wish to begin to develop empirical generalizations is to explore the nature of the rules which govern such social relationships.

V. SUMMARY OF THE THEORETICAL COMPONENTS AND PERSPECTIVES IN NETWORK ANALYSIS

To summarize our discussion of the promise and components of network analysis up to this point, we note that social network theory, if it adds up to something, consists of the following elements:

A. A particular conception of social relations and social reality which focuses on the individual social agent and emphasizes individual decisions, interdependence, mutual reliance, and exchange transactions between directly and indirectly linked individuals.

B. A basic or orienting *root metaphor* about the nature and conduct of social relations and bonding processes contained in the term 'network'. The metaphor contains a vision of a web of directly and indirectly interconnected individuals who use their linkages to 'transmit' their expectations, affect, and sentiments and to transact their social affairs. As a metaphor the concept guides the researcher to an aspect of individual behavior and social relations under which a particular type of social structure emerges. *Other,* rival, perspectives use different metaphors (e.g. structural-functionalism uses that of the organic, boundary-maintaining *system*; French structuralism uses that of the *semiotic system*).

C. A family of related *concepts* derived from various fields of study serve to elaborate the root metaphor. Many of those concepts have already been alluded to above: *action set, link, broker, choice, exchange,* and so on.

D. A list of the structural components and *behavioral mechanisms* involved in the conduct of network relations and in the formation of network bonds. We have alluded in several instances to these: sentiment transfer, relations between relations, and power dependence.

E. A loosely structured framework for examining the dynamics and bonding processes involved in the conduct of transactions and interpersonal relations within specific segments of society.

F. A set of empirical and analytical techniques which are useful to the researcher who attempts to use the methodological directives and assumptions of social network analysis in a field situation. Although techniques have not been discussed here, we do refer the reader to

observations we make in the concluding section of this paper and to the
work of Whitten and Wolfe (1973) and of Boissavain (1974).

VI. CONCLUSIONS: FUTURE PROSPECTS
AND DIRECTIVES IN THE USE OF
NETWORK THEORY

Will network analysis continue to have an important place in the work
of sociologists and anthropologists, and, if so, what are the future
theoretical and methodological directions which the research should
take? These are the questions we propose to answer in concluding our
assessment of network theory.

In our view, network analysis will continue, as the growing volume
of literature suggests, to attract considerable and widespread attention
among sociologists and anthropologists for two reasons. First, most
people in complex societies throughout the world spend much of their
lives in networks or in collections of small groups *linked* by overlapping
members; these form and will continue to key structures through which
people conduct their lives and form the social arenas that persons can
comprehend, conceptualize, respond to, manipulate if possible, and feel
secure in. Network analysis makes it possible to focus on and analyze
these processes. Secondly, the activities of persons in social networks,
whether these be in neighborhoods, organizations, or communities, lend
themselves to detailed study by individual researchers. The field worker
is able, to a considerable extent, to keep track of the comings and
goings of individuals in those regions of network activities that center
around other key persons and their interrelationships in neighborhoods,
communities, and organizations. This sort of individual research enterprise fits the style of many anthropologists and sociologists.

Since the network approach lacks a comprehensive set of theoretical
and empirical guidelines, how should future researchers proceed with
network analysis? The following points represent a tentative and preliminary set of directives which in our view might prove helpful for the
further development of social network analysis. The most important of
these is that the analysis should be concerned only with *public* or at

least *partly institutionalized* and *routinized* relationships between *social* actors. A major question then becomes: How do we identify such relationships and distinguish them from private, or more or less idiosyncratic, transitory, and non-instrumental links?

One key to the dilemma would be to recognize that social networks are typically organized *around* more or less enduring structural features of societies. For instance, as we make clear in another paper (Carlos and Anderson, 1974), Mexican political networks are organized around brokers or key actors and organizations like irrigation districts, state and federal bureaucracies, and state or privately owned business enterprises. These individuals and structures form what we might call the *templates* for social networks. They determine the directions and magnitudes of the transaction flows that sustain the networks; although they may also, to some extent, set their policies so as to accommodate, in a partial way, aggregated demands 'assembled' and 'transmitted' by social networks. Similar templates can be identified in a variety of other situations.

Another major problem we must confront in the future regards the need for criteria to determine *how much* of a network needs to be 'laid out' for the analysis of a particular social 'arena'. As we pointed out earlier, network analysis was developed to deal with social structures which do not have definite organizational or corporate boundaries. In such structures one can often expand a person's indirect links indefinitely — we have all had the experience of meeting perfect strangers and eventually discovering how we are linked to them indirectly. It does not usually make sense, however, to include all such indirect links that the members might have when we attempt to specify the network in a group. On the other hand, the operative network of a local group cannot be limited solely to the set of links that exists between the members of that group. Links to outsiders may be very important and therefore require our attention when we analyze processes within a local, bounded group.

Are there then any rules of procedure which in field situations can make it possible for us to search for a middle ground between an indefinite expansion of the networks of individuals and a too-parochial mapping of them? Such procedures have not yet been developed, but some general guidelines derived from what we said earlier can be stated.

Future researchers would do well to keep in mind that all persons have some knowledge about the indirect network links of those persons with whom they have direct links, and this knowledge affects how they adjust and make use of their direct network relationships. At the very minimum these sets of *immediate* indirect links should be mapped out, identified, and analyzed when examining the behavior of individuals in relation to their direct ties. Unfortunately, most of our present know-ledge about people's perceptions of indirect network ties seems to be limited to affective bonds and more specifically to sociometric choices based on linking. Do people have any knowledge about more remote links, i.e. what does *P* know about the relationships between those people that have been selected by the persons selected by *P* but who do not stand in any direct relationship to *P*? In other words, how complex is the network information that the average *P* carries with him, and how much network information can be 'processed' reliably and therefore have an affect on a person's behavior? These are questions that some sociometricians working with experimental groups say can be studied with available procedures for data-gathering. It is unlikely, however, that the individual researcher in a field situation could do the same.

Finally, a social network analysis of a group or a collectivity of interrelated segments and persons should include at least the following steps:

First, one must investigate the extent to which a particular set of persons possesses the characteristics discussed in section II, i.e. are we dealing with a set of relations within or between one or more social networks, or with a structural-functional group (a 'primitive' society) in which individual choice and formation of instrumental relations is limited? A group of the latter type would obviously not be amenable to the application of the network approach as we have defined it.

Secondly, the network resource bases or availability of instrumental ties and the contact links between the actors must be ascertained; these factors will determine the shape of networks and aid in identifying the motivational basis of individual choices and exchanges which are ini-tiated and accepted.

Thirdly, one must identify and state the minimal set of culturally defined relations existing in a network as these are expressed by the *network vocabulary* of the actors in the networks being studied. In this sense the task is similar to conducting a desriptive study of kinship relations (Whitten and Wolfe, 1973).

Fourthly, the normative content or cultural code of exchange of the relation set must be established. This will give information about the value attached to transactions and about which exchanges are seen as mandatory, permitted, and forbidden in *S*. This information will be necessary if we are to develop any hypotheses about the cultural premises for exchange and about what behavioral mechanisms, e.g. network extensions and alliances, are likely to develop in *S* within a particular culture.

Fifthly, one must determine the normative contents or cultural code which applied to the formation and maintenance of indirect links between actors in a given society or social segment thereof, i.e. those normative rules which specify the nature of links which are the relative products of a person's primary, culturally defined, relations. This code would also specify how persons in particular cultures, institutions, or groups achieve or perceive reductions in their network relationships.

In addition to these directives, social network theory contains several allied concepts about the structure of networks and network components which we mentioned above and in the previous section, e.g. action set, dependence, exchange, and such concepts as sentiment relations, patron, and broker. These concepts form a useful checklist enabling the sociologist or anthropologist to further specify what kinds of networks he is dealing with, i.e. they 'sensitize' and orient him to what kinds of interrelationships, transactional events, and persons he should pay attention to in his analysis of the structure of networks.

The above directives, the relevant list of social-psychological and structural concepts we have discussed, and associated analytical-mathematical and sociometric techniques comprise the various fragments of social network theory. Although others may come up with a different inventory of theoretical components (Barnes, 1972), we believe ours to be an accurate and fair assessment of the theoretical core of network analysis. It should now be clear why we insisted from the start that we are not dealing with a refined, tested, and cohesive body of knowledge or with an explanatory theory in the sense that 'explanatory' is used in contemporary methodology.

To conclude and reiterate, in terms of explanatory power and systematized general principles, social network analysis does not add up to much in its present state. At times it appears that network analysis has not moved far beyond being a useful metaphor and a data-gathering and classification technique. Yet, as we have demonstrated, there are many promising theoretical mergers. Similarly, some of the work currently being done in various fields already provides us with what we believe are useful insights and concepts about the dynamics and structure of network relationships, and such relationships, whatever we wish to label them, are central to the dynamics and structure of all complex societies.

NOTE

1. H. White and F. Lorrain (1971, p. 71) state: 'It might even prove necessary in some cases to include data on perception of ties by third parties to obtain more realistic accounts of which secondary ties exist and are effective.' If our argument is right, this is a *common* case in all network relations, whether primary or secondary. Moreover, Emerson's fourth-resolution mechanism dealt with above needs a third party; some collective must validate the signs of deference that *O* tries to give to the more powerful *P*.

REFERENCES

F. G. Bailey (1960), *Tribe, Caste, and Nation* (Manchester: Manchester University Press).

F. G. Bailey (1971), *Gifts and Poisons, the Politics of Reputation* (Oxford: Blackwell).

J. A. Barnes (1972), *Social Networks* (Reading, Mass,: Addison Wesley).

Fredrik Barth (1966), 'Models of social organization', *Royal Anthropological Society, Occasional Papers,* No. 23 (London).

T. Baumgartner, T. Burns, and Peter Schuster, (1975), 'Meta-power and the structuring of social hierarchies', this volume, ch. 10.

Jeremy Boissavain (1974), *Friends of Friends: Networks, Manipulators, and Coalitions* (Oxford: Blackwell).

Manuel L. Carlos (1973), 'Fictive kinship and modernization in Mexico: a comparative analysis', *Anthropological Quarterly*, 46 (2): 75-91.

Manuel L. Carlos and Bo Anderson (1974), 'Political brokerage and network politics in Mexico'. Unpublished manuscript.

James A. Davis (1970), 'Clustering and Hierarchy in Interpersonal Relations'. *American Sociological Review*, 35 (3): 843-51.

Richard Emerson (1962), 'Power-dependence relations', *American Sociological Review*, 27 (3): 31-41.

Bruce Knapferer (1969), 'Norms and the manipulation of relationships in a work context', in: Clyde Mitchell (ed.), *Social Networks in Urban Situations* (Manchester: Manchester University Press).

Alfred Tarski (1965), *Introduction to Logic* (New York: Oxford University Press).

Sidney Waldman (1972), *Foundations of Political Action, an Exchange Theory of Politics* (Boston: Little, Brown & Co.).

Harrison White and Francois Lorrain (1971), "Structural equivalence of individuals in social networks', *Journal of Mathematical Sociology*, 1 (1): 49-80.

Norman Whitten and Alvin W. Wolfe (1973), 'Network analysis', in: John J. Honigman, (ed.), *Handbook of Social and Cultural Anthropology* (Chicago: Rand McNally), pp. 717-47.

3

EXAMINING CORPORATE
INTERCONNECTIONS THROUGH
INTERLOCKING DIRECTORATES

John A. Sonquist
University of California at Santa Barbara

Tom Koenig
University of California at Santa Barbara

INTRODUCTION

According to the laws of nearly all of the states, every corporation must
have a board of directors composed of at least three persons. The board
is selected (generally annually or triannually) by the stockholders and
entrusted with the legal responsibility for running the corporation.
Since the directors are trustees for the owners of the business and have
been delegated the authority to make the key decisions, effective
corporate power is conventionally defined as the ability to choose the
membership of the board (Berle and Means, 1932, p. 66). A majority
vote by the members of the board of directors is theoretically sufficient
to set the policies of the corporation.

Most boards of large corporations are composed primarily of 'outsiders', that is, persons who are neither employees nor retired former
employees of the firm — and the use of outsiders seems to be on the
increase (Conference Board, 1973, pp. 2-4). A great deal of attention has
been focused on these outsiders because they are often officers and

directors of other corporations.[1] The most common full time job of an outside director is chairman of the board or president (who is almost certainly also a board member) of another company (Conference Board, 1973, p. 29). Thus, there is a complex pattern of inter-connections between business firms based on multi-board directors. The prevalence of shared directorships raises the possibility of coordination between interlocked firms or control of one company by another, since control based on financial power can be exercised by acquiring voting positions on the board of a captive corporation. It is important to focus attention on the specific nature of interlocks because an understanding of the relationships between interlocking firms can tell us much about the dynamics of power and control in the US socio-economic system. It is the purpose of this report to provide a comprehensive road-map of the formal interconnections of the entire upper echelon of the US corporate system.

Research into interlocking directorates has been hampered by a lack of common assumptions among researchers. Lawyers (Berle and Means: 1932), economists (Galbraith, 1967; Larner, 1970; O'Connor, 1972), political scientists (Dahl, 1959), sociologists (Mills, 1956; Bell, 1961), psychologists (Domhoff, 1967), business administration experts (Cheit, 1964; Holden, 1945; Dively, 1972), corporation executives (Quinn, 1953), outside directors (Mace, 1971), historians (Kolko, 1962), and Marxist scholars (Perlo, 1957; Menschikov, 1972) have all contributed to the literature on this subject; and each group tends to use different languages, methodologies, emphases, and concepts, and to see different facets as problematic. Thus, past research has tended to cumulate in a confused, rather than in a coherent pattern.

Worse, there is not even agreement, or even much reliable information about the role of a single director, much less about his roles and purposes as an interlocker. Even the business administration efficiency experts are vague on the subject of the director's role in corporate affairs (Dively, 1972, p. 125). Debates about interlocks tend to be polemical because social scientists lack not only information, but even agreement on the most useful questions to ask. The House Judiciary Committee (1965, p. 6) found that despite the obvious significance of interlocks and the amount of time and energy that had been focused on them, there was little empirical evidence as to their actual effects or even their extent. Given the objective presence of the formal social arrangements termed interlocking directorates, most of the questions that have been asked can be reformulated as 'What is the significance of these formal relationships for corporate organizations characterized also by other kinds of interconnections, including stock ownership, trade agreements, purchaser-supplier relationships, competition, and, for many of the persons involved, common memberships in non-business social groups?' Attempts to answer this question in one way or another have, in part, been doomed to failure without an overview of the systemic context in which the interlocking behavior occurs. Because only limited portions of the system have been looked at during a given analysis, instances can always be found to support the contention that another answer is the 'right' one. A more useful stance will be to improve the available descriptive information and to place detailed views of particular interlocking combinations in the context of systemic descriptions. It is the mapping out of one aspect of the upper class as a segmented system of interlocking formal directorate roles that is the objective of this investigation.[2]

WHY INTERLOCKING DIRECTORATES?

A variety of theoretical orientations have been advanced to explain the fact of the network of interlocking directorates that link the US corporate system. They can be grouped together under four rubrics: those deriving from management control theorists; environmental control and reciprocity theorists; financial control theorists; and class hegemony theorists. A review of the four theoretical approaches may be found in Koenig et al. (1974) and Koenig (1974). We summarize the four orientations here.

Management control

The board of directors, for all practical purposes, is appointed by management essentially at will, and is used for advice, criticism, prestige and, to a minor extent, for business contacts. Essential business decisions are made by 'insiders' (directors who are corporate employees), not by 'outside' directors. One version (Galbraith, 1967) emphasizes control through technical expertise rather than by outside directors. Stockholders are viewed as goegraphically disbursed and apathetic. Management uses proxies to control board membership (Smaby, 1974). Outside board members are passive, even ineffectual rubber stamps, though they may add some technological or management expertise and have a perspective which enables them to see things which those too close to the problems might miss (Dahl, 1959; Bell, 1961; Gordon, 1961; Cheit, 1964; Holden, 1945; Dively, 1972; Juran and Louden, 1966; Mace, 1971; Quinn, 1953; and Copeland and Towl, 1968). According to this view, a graph theory-based analysis of the system of interlocking directorates should not yield a network isomorphic with that generated by an analysis based, instead, on economic transactions between corporations.

Environmental control and reciprocity

Interlocks are used by management primarily to facilitate cooperation for mutual benefit. They enable the limitation of potentially disruptive influences or interference from other organizations with whom scarce resources must be shared. They are used when contracts provide insufficient protection and control and when mergers are illegal or otherwise impossible. They are employed especially where both the supply of and demand for a crucial resource are concentrated among a few corporations. Interlocks provide the links through which arrangements for swapping of goods and services and through which quasi-legal coordination of policy can take place. Specific objectives in the establishment of an interlock may include squeezing out competitors, limiting the power of suppliers, and fixing prices. Analysts in this group point out that despite the Clayton Anti-Trust Act, the Federal Trade Commission (1965) found that one out of every eight interlocks was with a potential competitor and that if indirect interlocks (in which representatives of two corporations meet on the board of a third firm) are counted, about 80 percent of all firms are connected with at least one competitor and innumerable potential suppliers and customers (Vance, 1964, p. 73). Often one person or group will control significant blocks of stock in several firms and is in a strong position to encourage those companies to cooperate. Such deals do not necessarily rely on interlocks, but coordination is easiest and most dependable when there is a direct and formal link between the centers of control of the firms involved (HJD, 1965, p. 4; McCreary, 1965; Dooley, 1969; Baran and Sweezy, 1966; Sweezy, 1972; O'Connor, 1972; Thompson and McEwen, 1958; Evan, 1966; and Thompson, 1967). If trade and coordination are the primary motives for interlocks, then patterns of trade and competition should follow interlock patterns.

Financial control

Despite increasing amounts of capital generated from business cash flows in the economic expansion since the Second World War, management still remains heavily dependent on very large amounts of short-term capital. Hence, corporations have remained heavily dependent on large financial institutions such as banks and insurance companies. Capital is essentially the most generalizable of resources, and has a widespread demand. Rapidly changing needs (especially short term) for capital cannot be met through the stock and bond markets, requiring access to bank and insurance company financial reserves. The increasing capital-intensity of many corporations and the seriousness of uncertainty involving access to capital resources makes for an intolerable situation for these corporations. Interlocks with financial organizations help to stabilize this aspect of their environment. Financial institutions take advantage of this to arrange reciprocity agreements between clients and to attempt to maneuver firms into profitable (for the bank) long-term large-scale borrowing and dependence. According to Herman's (1971, p. 52) summary, banks and insurance companies use their financial power to assure themselves of competent company management in their portfolio companies, cut down on 'wasteful' competition, and secure the banking business of the captive company. At times this may generate needed business for the bank at the portfolio company's expense; dependent companies may be forced to act against their own self-interest by powerful controllers of capital. Moreover, the bank can function as an intermediary to negotiate mergers and so gain a piece of the action. This view essentially sees interlocks as devices for control and manipulation of investments by financial institutions (Chevalier, 1970; Fitch, 1972; Menschikov, 1969; Aaronovitch, 1961; Fitch and Oppenheimer, 1970; Perlo, 1957; Lenin, 1970; Vance, 1964; Knowles, 1973; and Perrucci and Pilisuk, 1970). This model predicts that cliques of interlocked firms should tend to have financial power at their core.

Class hegemony

The preceding theoretical orientations have a serious limitation in that they provide 'explanations' for the existence of interlocking director-ates only by explicating the director's or management's public (or perhaps private) rationales. Interlocks are seen entirely as rational means toward an end, rather than also as ends in themselves. They are perceived as basically task-oriented behavior, rather than as having socio-emotional or expressive and symbolic components. Furthermore, they tend to explain interlocking behavior largely in terms of tasks defined with respect to the presumed goals of the firm, or organization, and, except for the management control model, they tend to ignore personal goals of individuals, which may conflict with officially defined corporate goals. The class-hegemony orientation, on the other hand, emphasizes American upper-class participation in business, especially through interlocking directorates as related to a whole series of organ-izational acts which promote upper class cohesion, self-consciousness, and consensus on social issues (Domhoff, 1967; Baltzell, 1958; Mills, 1956; and Hunter, 1959). Being appointed a director is prestigeful and perhaps even expected of a proper sort of upper-class person. Being a member of a network of individuals in the business world outside of one's 'home' company provides common life experiences, common views of reality, definitions of what is right and wrong, and oppor-tunities to validate one's beliefs about social and economic issues and the goals that one ought to pursue with respect to them. These are reinforced by common participation in cohesive upper-class social in-stitutions such as clubs, resorts, and philanthropic enterprises and are passed on to the next generation in select private schools.

Moreover, upper-class persons no longer tend to restrict their hold-ings to large blocks of stock in one or two corporations—portfolio diversification being the norm rather than the exception. Indeed, recent trends in acquisitions, mergers and corporate takeovers suggest that multiple business participation and the exercise of substantial power in each organization constitutes culturally defined 'appropriate' upper class behavior. Thus, active business pursuit, especially including participation in several corporate boards, can be viewed as an end in itself, as expressive as well as instrumental behavior. A consequence of multiple participation is the maintenance of well-oiled communication channels through which business deals of a wide variety can be furthered when need be. Cut-throat competition can be effectively discouraged, and though the intention is not necessarily explicit, the long range position of the small percentage of the population who hold the bulk of the corporate stock can be insured. The model predicts that interlocking directorates should be found to be based in social ties and on class and ethnic background. Thus, cliques should follow ties in elite social clubs and upper-class consensus groups such as the Council on Foreign Relations and the Committee on Economic Development.

As we have noted above, we feel that attempts to decide between these alternative explanations are premature. Better description should come first. Yet, the common view of the latter three models is the assumption that interlocking formal directorate roles imply domination of contemporary economic life by an elite which has well-articulated segments; but we lack a description of the segments. Rather than directing our attention to a deductive strategy of testing hypotheses derived from these orientations (though we have suggested some above) we shall, instead, adopt the strategy of beginning the process of putting together, piece by piece, information that will eventually lead to a model of when each type of link is used in the corporate system and under what circumstances. This first requires a delineation of the segments of the upper echelons of the system, and this is our objective here.

One additional point remains to be made. Interlocks and their meanings are more than just a trivial part of the issue between elitist and pluralist views of power in American society. Pluralists have argued the need to articulate the social mechanisms through which specific issues are initiated, modified, even vetoed, denying that power can be inferred from such data as wealth and income statistics. Elite theorists have taken the opposite point of view, that there is a cohesive ruling class (Domhoff, 1967, 1974; Mills, 1956; and Rose, 1967). These arguments have proceeded largely without the benefit of data on the overall systemic properties of interlocks. Rather, they have been focused on specific segments of the corporate system, i.e. on specific corporate 'interest groups', or on local community groups. The details of the specific set of interlocks are investigated and related to aspects of financial control, reciprocity, management control, and class cohesiveness. There are only a few studies which have attempted to bring to view the systemic properties within which individual interlocking nodes function (Levine, 1972; Warner and Unwalla, 1967; Allen, 1974; and Dooley, 1969).

The main reason for the relative infrequency of systemic studies, those attempting to depict the macro-aspects of the larger system of interlocks, is methodological. Such studies cannot realistically be attempted without both an appropriate set of mathematical techniques and large-scale computing equipment (as well as huge amounts of data from relatively-easy-to-obtain, published sources being put into machine-readable form). Sociologists (and economists, too, for that matter) have been further handicapped by the lack of a vocabulary for discussing structural properties of systems such as the one under consideration here. Figure 1, depicting the relationships between only eight firms, is presented to give the reader a notion of how complex the pattern of interlocks actually is, and the difficulties of working with such relational data even with sophisticated mathematical tools, and computing equipment adequate to handle large arrays. In the remainder of this paper, we attempt to bring together recent advances in computing technology and graph theory to provide the beginnings of a description of the entire upper echelon of the US corporate system, and to enhance the vocabulary we have for discussing its properties.

It is the central premise of this investigation that attempts to depict the more global features of the system of corporate structures will enhance efforts to study its parts in more detail. In addition, structural studies can provide a background at a more systemic level for a useful re-phrasing of the pluralist/elitist controversy. In considering structure itself, one is prompted to turn away from the question, 'Is the system pluralist or elitist?', to one which appears to show more long-range promise, 'In what segments of the structure are elitist (pluralist) tendencies observable, and what factors appear to promote or inhibit the individual behaviors which, when aggregated, lead the observer to

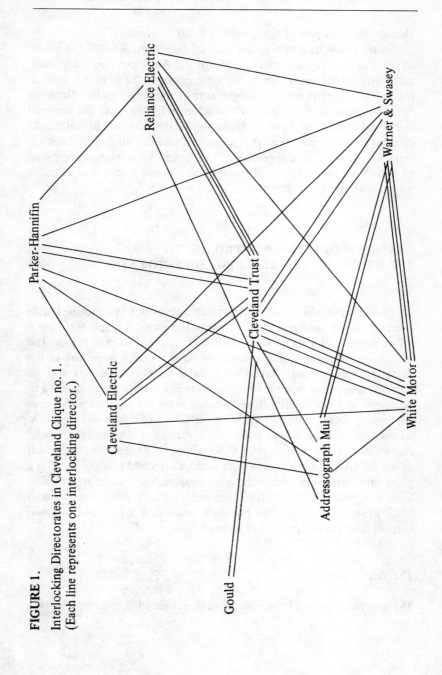

FIGURE 1.

Interlocking Directorates in Cleveland Clique no. 1.
(Each line represents one interlocking director.)

characterize that part of the system as elitist or pluralist?'

We turn now to a very specific set of questions: What is the extent of interlocking in the upper echelon of the American corporate structure? Are connections denser in some parts of the network than in others? If so, what are the components of the dense nodes? Do some firms or types of firms occupy more 'central' positions? Do financial institutions tend to have a disproportionate number of interlocks (Warner and Unwalla, 1967)? If so, is this true for all financial institutions in all identifiable segments of the system, or is it largely confined to New York-based banks? It is our hope that our description will raise more questions than it answers.

GRAPH THEORY AS AN APPROACH TO THE STUDY OF INTERLOCKING DIRECTORATES

Graph theory is that branch of mathematics which is concerned with the analysis of configurations of points and lines. A graph is simply a set of points and a set of lines connecting selected pairs of points. The axioms and theorems of graph theory have received some use in the analysis of sociometric data in the social sciences.[3] Objects such as persons, groups, or other interacting units in a system are considered to be points and the relationships between them are represented as lines connecting these points. In a typical earlier use of this type of analysis, friendships between school children are studied. Each child in a school classroom is asked to nominate those whom he or she 'likes' the most, or would 'like to work on a project with'. Each child is represented as a point and friendship relationships between children are represented as lines in a graph. In the study of interlocking directorates, a person who holds a membership on two boards is treated as a line, and the two corporations are represented as points.[4]

The data

The analysis reported here makes use of published data on interlocking

directorates among 'Fortune's 500', the 500 largest industrial corporations in the US, together with the 50 largest banks, insurance companies, retailers, transportation companies, utilities, and a miscellaneous
group of 47 conglomerates and other corporations whose activities are
typically so diverse they cannct readily be classified as being in one
'industry' or another.[5]

In an economy in which three-quarters of the total corporate manufacturing assets are in the hands of the 500 largest industrial companies
(Federal Trade Commission, 1969, p. 167) it seems reasonable to
assume that the larger firms determine the environment in which the
smaller companies must exist, and thus are the key elements in the
understanding of corporate structures and power (Berle, 1957). Thus,
we do not follow a logic of generalizing from a sample; instead, we
describe all of a dominant population group.[6]

The corporations chosen for inclusion in the data base were those
which appeared in the Fortune 500 listing for the year 1969 (*Fortune*,
May, 1970). The memberships of the boards of directors were obtained
from either the corporation annual reports or from Standard and Poor's
registry of corporation executives for 1969. The original data-base
included 797 corporations, 8623 individuals and 11,290 directorships.
To the original data were added locational information. The corporation's headquarters (also listed in *Fortune*, May, 1970) was used as a
guide, and its location coded using the *1970 Census of Population and
Housing*'s code designations for Standard Metropolitan Statistical
Areas.

The data can best be described as 'hard' in the sense that measurement problems of the type usually discussed under the headings of
'reliability' and 'validity' do not appear. Careful cross-checking procedures were used to resolve directorship discrepancies that appeared to
exist. The validity of the study of interlocks as a device for isolating
'interest groups' and control of corporations by financial institutions is
a more serious problem and will be discussed below.

Analysis of the data

Preliminary investigations of the data suggested that the level of connectedness in the total group of 797 corporations was so high that

defining a link between corporations as one or more overlapping board members would result in the algorithm being used exceeding available computing capabilities by several orders of magnitude. The data would show up as one big clique, a finding which would lend credence to the class hegemony theorists' point of view. Nevertheless, we were committed to the task of isolating the densest parts of the structure whatever its total density level.

As a result, it was necessary to develop a definition of connectedness that was stringent enough to discriminate the very dense from the more sparsely connected regions in the network using a finite amount of computer resources, yet relaxed enough so that at least some connectedness would be found. Two alternatives could be used. One, restricting the number of corporations analyzed, will be reported elsewhere. The procedure reported here was to select that subset of corporations from the original 797 in which every member was connected to at least one other member by two or more common board members. The objectives was to meet the analytic requirement of providing a kind of 'neutral density' filter sufficient to detect contrast in varying degrees of connectedness while screening out more sparsely connected segments. In addition, this criterion had the advantage of being objective, subject to only a small amount of measurement error, and easily interpreted.

Application of the double-interlock criterion as the definition of a link between two corporations yielded a tightly connected central core of 401 corporations. Each was connected to at least one other corporation by a link which consisted of two or more persons who sit on the board of directors of both companies. Among the 797 top corporations studied there were no others having at least one double link to another company in the data-base.

This subset of 401 corporations was then analyzed using Alba's (1972) graph-theoretic techniques as implemented in the computer program devised by Alba and Gutmann (1973). The analysis involved the computation of all maximal complete subgraphs defined in this criterion.[7] Certain of these maximal complete subgraphs were then discarded. These included those which had too few points (two), those which were trees, and others which were not sufficiently complete; that is, they had too few lines connecting the points within them.[8]

A second step in the process involved merging the remaining graphs.

Two subgraphs were merged whenever one differed from the other by only one point (i.e. all of the corporations were the same except one).

In the third step, the resulting subgraphs were again merged. Merging took place during this phase whenever the size of the overlap (the number of corporations the twc subgraphs had in common) was greater than a fixed percentage of the number of points in the smaller of the two groups. The ratio of the count of lines joining points within the proposed new merged subgraph to the count of all such lines possible was then computed (completeness). Subgraphs which had a completeness more probable on a random basis than a predetermined value were left as separate.[9]

Findings (see also Tables 1-5)

Due to space limitations it will only be possible to list a few of our findings regarding the densest nodes in the system of interlocks. Defining two corporations as linked only if there were two direct interlocks between their boards of directors, we located 32 cliques of 3-15 firms.[10] If a company had at least one double link to the central clique, it was labelled a 'satellite' (external connection). Tables 1-5 present selected statistics describing these cliques. We apologize for the chaotic way that these findings must be presented but since our ability to generate statistics has run ahead of theoretical advances in this area, it is difficult to present a coherent picture or to know what information researchers will find useful. It is important to remember that our criteria for a clique are necessarily arbitrary and that firms that are external to the clique by our definition may be internal in another schema.

TABLE 1
Selected Properties of Cliques

(a) Distribution of Clique Sizes:		(b) Distribution of Completeness:	
Number of Organizations in Clique	Percent	Completeness of Clique	Percent
3	31	1.0	31
4	22	0.8 to 0.99	22
5	13	0.6 to 0.79	19
6	16	0.4 to 0.59	22
7	3	0.2 to 0.39	6
8	3	0.19 or less	0
9	6		
10 and over	6	Total	100
			(N = 32)
Total	100		
	(N = 32)		

(c) Distribution of Clique Diameters:		(d) Distribution of Centrifugality:	
Clique Diameter	Percent	Centrifugality	Percent
1	31	0	9
2	44	0.0009 or less	0
3	19	0.0010 to 0.0019	22
4	6	0.0020 to 0.0029	6
		0.0030 to 0.0039	13
Total	100%	0.0040 to 0.0049	13
	(N = 32)	0.0050 to 0.0059	9
		0.0060 to 0.0069	6
		0.0070 to 0.0079	9
		0.0080 and over	13
		Total	100%
			(N = 32)

TABLE 2

Relative Tendencies of Industries to Interlock

Industry	Number of Corporations	Number of Interlocks[1]	Interlock Index
Top 100 Industrials	72	36	1.83
Next 400 Industrials	173	50	0.71
Banks (top 50)	44	35	1.95
Insurance Companies (top 50)	29	14	1.17
Merchandising Companies (top 50)	16	5	0.76
Transportation Companies (top 50)	18	7	0.95
Utilities (top 50)	33	15	1.09
Conglomerates and Miscellaneous (top 47)	16	4	0.61
Total all Companies	401	166	1.00

[1] This column contains only those interlocks within the 32 cliques identified. The remainder of the interlocks were to corporations outside the central cliques.

TABLE 3

Means and Standard Deviations of Properties of Corporate Cliques

Property	Mean	Standard Deviation
Number of Corporations in clique	5.19	2.669
Diameter of clique	2.00	0.880
Completeness	0.74	0.230
Centrifugality	0.0044	0.00314
Number of corporations connected to central clique by one connection	8.91	7.718
Number of corporations connected to central clique by two connections	0.38	1.008
Number of clique memberships held by the top 100 industrials	1.13	1.57
Number of clique memberships held by industrials 101-500	1.56	1.014
Number of clique memberships held by: (top 50)		
Banks	1.09	0.734
Insurance Companies	0.44	0.759
Merchandisers	0.16	0.448
Transportation Companies	0.22	0.491
Utilities	0.47	0.567
Conglomerates & Misc.	0.13	0.336
Number of banks connected to a clique by 1 or 2 connections	1.41	1.434
Number of insurance companies connected to a clique by one or two connections	0.88	1.157
Number of financial institutions in the clique (banks and insurance companies)	1.53	1.191
Number of financial institutions either in the clique or connected to it by 1 or 2 connections	3.81	3.126
Ratio of number of external connections to size of clique	1.69	1.238

TABLE 4

Intercorrelations between Selected Clique Properties

	Size	Diameter	Completeness	Centripetal	External
Size	1	0.83	−0.89	0.22	0.72
Diameter		1	−0.85	0.37	0.68
Completeness (density)			1	−0.28	−0.64
Centripetal tendency				1	0.79
External connections					1

TABLE 5

Corporations Occupying Inter-Clique Liason Roles

Corporation	Rank Within Industry	Clique Memberships	Proportion of Overlap[1]
Industrials:			
US Steel	12	9, 26	0.250
Int. Harvester	31	12, 18	0.167
Banks:			
Bank of America	1	29, 30	0.250
1st Nat. City Bank (N.Y.)	2	13, 26	0.167
Chase Manhatten (N.Y.)	3	13, 27	0.167
J. P. Morgan (N.Y.)	5	9, 14	0.250
1st Chicago City Bank	10	17, 18	0.167
Nat. City Bank (Clev.)	44	10, 22	0.250
Transportation:			
Penn. Central	1	5, 9	0.250
Utilities:			
Am. Tel. & Tel.	1	26, 27	0.111

[1] Number of corporations who have membership in both cliques divided by the total number of corporations in both cliques.

The following definitions may aid the reader in understanding the findings: *Centrifugality* is the ratio of the count of actual lines joining the points within the central clique to those satellites outside the clique to the count of possible lines. *Completeness* is the ratio of the count of actual lines joining the firms within the central clique to the number of possible lines. *Diameter* is the length of the longest chain within a clique that represents the shortest distance between a pair of corporations.

1. The 401 companies have 166 interlocks inside the central cliques and 285 links to satellites.

2. The cliques have coteries containing from zero to 36 satellite corporations. The mean clique has about nine peripheral members. The size of the satellite group is approximately 1.7 times the number of central clique members.

3. All of the cliques had less than a 0.0022 probability of being chance configurations given the overall density of the system.

4. Ten of the cliques had centrifugality measures large enough to occur by chance at least one out of five times suggesting that they are central nucleii of more dispersed, less tightly knit groups.

5. About one-third of the cliques do not overlap any others while one in four had one overlap, and about one-third had between two and seven connections. Our largest (New York-based) clique (which we nicknamed 'grand daddy' of the corporate establishment) overlaps eleven of the other cliques.

6. Of those firms in the center of two cliques (none was central to three or more) more than half are banks and three of these are located in New York (see Table 5). The proportions of overlapping memberships in the cliques range from none up to one-quarter. These overlapping firms may tend to play liaison roles.

7. In almost half of the cliques, a single bank played the financial role in the center. More than four out of five cliques had at least one bank in the clique center, and almost nine out of ten had at least one bank or insurance company. Fewer than one-third had an insurance company as a member. There is a modest positive correlation between the number of banks and the number of insurance companies ($r = 0.27$).

8. Those cliques not centered around a single bank had some other idiosyncratic feature such as multi-regionality of corporate head-

quarters, unusually large size, or (in two cases) a single insurance company in the center.

9. The number of financial institutions is a very good predictor of the size of the clique (0.86).

10. When there are no financial institutions, the clique will invariably be high in cohesiveness and low in size.

11. The top 100 industrials and the banks show almost twice the number of clique memberships as one would expect from the density of the overall system, while conglomerates, smaller industrials, and retailers tended to have less than their share of interlocks. Insurance companies tended to have slightly more than their share (see Table 2).

12. Banks and insurance companies appear to be the most outward-looking members of the central cliques (or, alternatively, they may be the central members to whom satellites look; the distinction is theoretically important).

13. The more financial institutions in the central clique, the greater the centrifugality (0.24) although a great deal of variability is found in cliques with about one-third of their central members financial firms.

14. When clique size is controlled for, the relationship between the number of financial institutions and the completeness of the clique drops substantially (0.79 to 0.32). Thus, the factor related to clique completeness is not domination of the clique by financial versus other types of firms but rather the absolute number of financial firms.

15. The more top-100 industrials or financial institutions, the greater the number of satellites (0.69 and 0.61). This is due in part to the larger boards possessed by these firms, but it should be kept in mind that institutions have the power to regulate the size of their boards and larger boards apparently indicate a desire for the firm to be more widely connected.

16. Clique size and the number of top-100 industrials together account for most of the variation in number of external connections. Number of financial firms has little predictive value when these two other factors are controlled for.

17. The more top-100 industrials in the clique center, the greater the centrifugality (0.47), the greater the clique size (0.59), and the larger the diameter (0.63).

18. Cliques containing one or two banks and a few large industrials may have a wide variety of diameters, but those comprised of other

combinations tend to be very much alike.

19. The larger the number of industrials, the lower the clique completeness (−0.59).

20. There is a trade-off between completeness and centrifugality (−0.28).

21. The larger the clique, the lower its completeness (−0.65), the larger its number of external connections (0.72), and the greater its diameter (0.68).

22. Size and diameter are positively correlated (0.77) and both have modest positive correlations with the number of external connections (0.52 and 0.37).

23. The relationship between centrifugality and clique diameter is mildly positive (0.37), but it is in the cliques with diameters two and three that the maximum variability in centrifugality occurs.

DISCUSSION

Perhaps the most significant fact of the clique-satellite structure of the coteries of top corporations and their interrelations with one another is their regional base. Almost all the cliques were composed solely or predominantly of firms headquartered in a single city or economic region. This lends face validity to a structure adduced entirely on mathematical grounds. It suggests strongly that these are real, cohesive, face-to-face groups that interact with one another outside of the board room. Yet, evidence also suggests strongly that though cliques have regional bases, the level of integration of the total system is high. In other words, face-to-face contacts are by no means limited to regional levels. We have noted overlaps between clique centers at two levels, but we have not even begun to explore the patterns of overlaps involving satellite member with satellite member. Moreover, our mathematical criterion of connectedness between two points was extremely strong, requiring two overlapping board members. In addition, our criterion required that a connection between two corporations be direct; that is the N in our N-clique concept is actually one.[11] We have not elected to extend our definition of connectedness in the system to allow for an intermediary to provide it. This definition doubtless underrates the role that financial institutions play in linking various structural segments.

What remains unclear, however, is what these formal interlocks *mean* in terms of the four theoretical orientations summarized above. Yet, some directions can be discerned. Clique-coterie structures like those depicted here are extremely difficult to account for if only the management control model is operating universally through the system. Moreover, it is difficult to account for the positions of the financial institutions in the cliques using only the management control and reciprocity models. Hence, the financial control logic apparently needs to be invoked, at least to explain some of the patterns.

We suggest that a useful key to the application of the models is contained in the phrase 'explain some of the patterns'. After all, there is no reason why one model should be asked to explain all of them. A typology of interlocks suggests some of the potentially useful applications of models to interlocks:

(1) Bank-bank interlocks: these are supposed to be illegal.

(2) Bank-insurance company interlocks: either financial control or reciprocity may account for these patterns. One conjecture is that when the relative asset magnitudes of the two firms are roughly comparable, reciprocity may explain the interlock; when they are disparate financial control may be operative.

(3) Non-financial interlocks to financial institutions: financial control appears to be the logical choice to explain these except where the assets of the non-financial firm are very large and its capital needs require a consortium of banks and insurance companies to meet them.

(4) Non-financial firms to non-financial firms: reciprocity appears to be adequately able to account for most of these interlocks unless stock ownership by one firm of another's stock is significant.

The management control and class hegemony models, in contrast to the reciprocity and financial control models, depict what the firm may attempt to do in the absence of problems and constraints due to external circumstances. The former accounts for this in terms of the rational behavior of management, the latter in terms of the cultural patterns of which management and being an outside director are a part. In addition, the latter elaborates the circumstances and the mechanisms through which the interlocks are established even when they are for the purposes set forth by the reciprocity or financial control models.

The thrust of this argument is that we may require not one, but several explanatory models, with each explanatory model drawing upon factors from all four of the theoretical orientations. Thus, the problem of 'what do the interlocks mean' receives an answer in terms of a model for describing the circumstances under which they occur.

Besides suggesting theoretical directions, this investigation of the system of interlocks at its upper levels has produced both concepts for dealing with structural properties of interlocking directorates and additions to the methodological tools for dealing with systems. We have noted the regionality of the central groups, developed the concept of the multiple interlock, examined some of the correlates of completeness and centrifugality, explored clique diameter as a concept, and elaborated the positions of the financial firms within the clique structure. We developed an index of propensity to use interlocks that could be applied to other classifications of firms as well as to an arbitrary industry classification. We noted that firms could be isolates, satellites, or central clique members. The clique was seen as a central, tightly connected group surrounded by satellite members and sometimes connected to other cliques through a common member who participates either as a satellite or even as a central member of another clique. The concept of the coterie as the clique plus its satellite members has been suggested. We have noted certain firms which, because of their connections with others appear to be central members of the corporate 'establishment'.

We have demonstrated that graph-theory is a useful tool in the study of the corporate elites. A mathematical model based on these concepts has been used to suggest dense nodes for more detailed study. We computed properties of these nodes and studied their intercorrelations. Some properties were structural, i.e. they were derived from the relations of the node with other nodes in the system; others, like region, are simply attributes of the node itself. Others which could have been used and which, we hope, will be used by other investigators would include properties aggregated from clique members. An example would be total clique or coterie assets. Both the computer capabilities of 'number-crunching' and graphical displays have proven to be indispensable tools.

FURTHER RESEARCH

Ending an investigation with more questions than existed at the start is both satisfying and frustrating. Several lines of exploration are suggested: conceptual, methodological, and substantive.

Many substantive questions remain to be dealt with. To what extent do patterns of trade and competition follow observed interlock networks? Do cliques follow the ties of upper-class members' participation in elite social clubs? What roles do political consensus building groups like the Council on Foreign Relations and the Council on Economic Development play in the structure? To what extent is the structure of purchaser-supplier relations and the structure of stock ownership of one firm by another isomorphic with the structure of interlocking directorates? Where in the structure do political contributions come from?

Two particularly important questions deal with changes in the structure over time and the directionality of the links. A director's 'home' board is that of the corporation in which he is an officer and, presumably, that to which he owes his primary loyalty. Does power flow from home to outside board? If so, financial firms should place their members on other boards, not vice versa. If friendship and personal characteristics are primary there should be no directional pattern. Who are the people with no home boards (or whose home boards are firms too small to make the listings), especially the 'professional directors'? What is the role of outsiders whose 'home' is a university or law firm? Is a connection from a home board to another firm stronger, in some sense, than that provided by an outsider who sits on both boards? Perhaps someone on numerous boards has little impact on them except as a representative from the home board where he spends a lot of time. Maps which are directional may give some clues as to how outside directors are chosen.

Do central cliques reach out to the satellites or vice versa? Answers to this question may tell us something about the power and authority of the central firms. Are double-linked companies cases of reciprocal chief executive officers? If so, this might tend to imply an equality of power as well as a very close link between the two firms.

Do utilities and other capital-intensive firms tend to be 'colonized' by financial centers, or do they reach out to the capital sources and, perhaps, play them off against one another? Are some city groups, for example New York, outreachers while others are colonized by financial centers? Do outsiders tend to come from firms richer or more powerful than the boards they sit on? This would imply a direction of the economy toward increasing centralization. Does directionality change over time? If so, this may imply that influence rather than power flows along network lines.

Other issues related to change over time include the continuity of specific links within a clique, changes in inter-clique linking patterns, replacement of persons occupying a linking role, shifts in position of a firm from the center of a clique to satellite status or vice versa, expansion or other changes in the large east coast networks, increases in cross-regional integration, and the like.

Of great importance is the finding that despite the immensely complex, interlocked set of links between the eastern seaboard cliques centering in New York, there are other nodes. Historical research using the techniques applied in this report could ascertain the way in which the structure has evolved. When did these other nodes appear? What did they look like in embryonic form? What major economic changes can be tied to important shifts in structural patterns? Perhaps if trends can be detected they can be mapped onto existing time series data pertaining to the economic system as a whole. Do changes in patterns (especially links to banks) occur during times of expansion or recession? What are the effects of government regulation efforts, for example the Clayton Anti-trust Act, and trust busting, on changes in interlock patterns as a whole? The possibilities are intriguing.

Other substantive questions include assessing the correlates of clique position. Is centrality associated with asset growth or other financial characteristics? Are there ethnic patterns in the cliques? Are there breaks between old and new money? Why do insurance companies appear to play such a different role than banks as financial centers? What would the structure look like if elite law firms and investment banks were included in the firms studied? How can the system interfaces to government be assessed?

Methodological questions include assessing the implications of using stronger or weaker definitions of what constitutes a link between two groups. What are the most useful criteria for setting parameters in an algorithm like the one used? What additional computer programs are needed to manipulate relational data of this type? What can be learned by studying properties of coteries, properties of satellite groups, and properties of several cliques connected together? When the definition of a connection is extended to include an N-clique of two, what does the structure look like; are the presently isolated cliques the centers of larger groups? In what ways are isolated firms different from satellites or central clique members?

With these questions we return to the starting point of this investigation. We sought to provide a road-map of the entire upper echelon of the US corporate system, to describe its segments, to develop the vocabulary and the methodology for dealing with investigations into system properties, and to couch our description in terms germane to existing theoretical orientations. Our road-map is still sketchy, but if the net increase in the number of questions to be asked is any indication, we have had some modest success.

NOTES

1. See, for example, House Report No. 11593:1913; National Resource Committee, 1939; Federal Trade Commission, 1951; House Judiciary Committee, 1965; Committee on Banking and Currency, 1968.

2. The advice and guidance provided by Prof. G. William Domhoff is gratefully acknowledged. Statistical advice came from Prof. Robert H. McGuckin, computer programming support from David Trumbo, Pennie Greene, Steven Abraham, Anthony Shih, Robert Poolman, Anthony Pepitone, Bradford Smith and Hugh Kawabata, and the computer programs were obtained with the help and support of Prof. Richard Alba. Students in several seminars helped explore the data and crystallize the ideas. Not the least of these was Robert Gogel.

3. For a review of the literature, see Roistacher (1972).

4. In an alternative conceptualization in which the objective is to study upper-class cohesiveness, the person is represented as a point and common membership in a club, on a board of directors, or in some other social organization is a line connecting two persons. The resulting graph has many more points than that under consideration here and presents considerable computational problems. We shall return to this conceptualization at the end of our discussion.

5. The authors are deeply indebted to Prof. Michael Schwartz of SUNY, Stony Brook, N.Y. for permission to use the data put into machine-readable form by him and by his students.

6. The dominance is evidenced by the fact that the assets of the top 100 industrials are approximately twice those of the next 400! (Federal Trade Commission, Economic Report on Corporate Mergers (1969), p. 706).

7. A graph is *connected* if every pair of points in it is connected by a path. (In this case a path is two different persons, both sitting on both boards of the connected firms.) The *distance* between two points is the length of the shortest path between them (this is also termed the *geodesic*). If there is no path between two points, the distance between them is infinite. The *diameter* of a connected graph is the length of its longest geodesic. A *complete* graph has every pair of its points adjacent. A *subgraph* is a set of points and the lines connecting them (but *not* the lines connecting them to points not in the subset). A subset is *maximal* with respect to some property (say, connectedness), when it loses that property upon addition of another point to the subset. Put another way, a subgraph is maximal whenever the entire subset of points has a particular property, or every pair of points has that property − and when you add another point, either the subgraph loses the property or some pair of its points now does not have the property. For example, in Figure 2, *A* and *B* are adjacent; but *A* and *C* are not adjacent in 'G'. The sequence (*A, B, C, E, B, C, D*) is a walk, but not a path. The sequence (*A, B, C, D*) is a path with length three. The sequence (*B, C, E, B*) is a closed walk and a cycle. Graph 'G' and subgraph (B, C, E) are connected. The distance from A to C is two. The diameter of (*B, C, E*) is one. Graph 'G' is not complete, but subgraph (*B, C, E*) is complete. Subset (*B, C, E*) is a maximal complete subgraph, since every pair of points is adjacent, but if you add any other point not every pair will have this property.

FIGURE 2.

An example: graphs 'G' and 'S'.

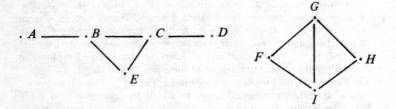

8. The program parameter settings used were: $N = 401$; choices = 16; power = 1; overlap = 0.33; trivial group size = 2; adjacency matrix distance length = 1. Density and significance levels were defaulted to be computed from the data.

9. The requirement for minimal completeness used was 0.33.

10. A listing of the members of the groups and more explanation of their mathematical derivations and statistical properties will be found in *Insurgent Sociologist*, Spring (1975): 204-29.

11. Notice that our definition was so strict that in the typical clique illustrated in Figure 1, the elimination of a single interlock between Cleveland Trust and Warner and Swasey would result in the configuration lacking a maximally complete subgraph and consequently not being identified as a clique.

REFERENCES

Samuel Aaronovitch (1961), *A Study of British Finance Capital* (London: Laurence and Wishart).

Richard D. Alba (1972), 'A graph-theoretic definition of a sociometric clique', *The Journal of Mathematical Sociology*.

Richard Alba and Myron Gutmann (1973), SOCK: A Sociometric Analysis System (Columbia University Thesis, unpublished).

Michael P. Allen (1974), 'The structure of interorganizational elite cooptation: interlocking corporate directorates', *American Sociological Review*, June.

Jack G. Augustson and Jack Minker (1970), 'An analysis of some graph-theoretical cluster techniques', *Journal of the Association for Computing Machinery:* 571-88.

Paul Baran and Paul Sweezy (1966), *Monopoly Capital* (New York: Modern Reader Paperbacks).

A. Bavelas (1948), 'A mathematical model for group structure', *Applied Anthropology:* 16-30.

A. Bavelas (1950), 'Communication patterns in task-oriented groups', *Journal of the Acoustical Society of America,* 57: 271-82.

Daniel Bell (1961), *The End of Ideology* (New York: Free Press).

C. Berge (1962), *The Theory of Graphs and Its Applications* (Transl. Alison Doig) (New York: Wiley).

Adolf A. Berle and Gardiner C. Means (1932), *The Modern Corporation and Private Property* (New York: Macmillan).

Adolf A. Berle (1957), *Economic Power and the Free Society* (New York: Fund for the Republic).

Philip Bonocich (1972), 'Technique for analyzing overlapping memberships', in: Herbert L. Costner (ed.), *Sociological Methodology* (San Francisco: Jossey-Bass Inc.).

Philip Bonocich (1976), 'Factoring and weighting approaches to status scores and clique identification', *Journal of Mathematical Sociology* (in press).

R. E. Bonner (1964), 'On some clustering techniques', *IBM Journal of Research and Development,* 8: 22-32.

R. G. Busacker and T. L. Saaty (1965), *Finite Graphs and Networks: An Introduction with Applications* (New York: McGraw-Hill).

D. Cartwright and F. Harary (1956), 'Structural balance: A generalization of Heider's theory', *Psychological Review,* 63: 277-92.

D. Cartwright and F. Harary (1968), 'On the coloring of signed graphs', *Elemente der Mathematik,* 23: 85-89.

Earl F. Cheit (ed) (1964), *The Business Establishment* (New York: John Wiley).

Jean-Marie Chevalier (1970), *La Structure Financiere de l'Industrie Americaine,* (Paris: Edition Cujas).

J. Coleman and D. MacRae Jr (1960), 'Electronic processing of sociometric data for groups up to a thousand in size', *American Sociological Review,* 25: 722-26.

Conference Board (1973), *Corporate Directorship Practices* (New York: New York Stock Exchange).

Melvin T. Copeland and Andrew R. Towl (1968), *The Board of Directors and Business Management* (New York: Greenwood Press).

Robert A. Dahl, Mason Haire and Paul Lazarsfeld (1959), *Social Science Research on Business* (New York: Columbia University Press).

J. A. Davis (1968), 'Structural balance, mechanical solidarity, and interpersonal relations', *American Journal of Sociology,* 68: 444-62.

J. A. Davis (1970), 'Clustering and hierarchy in interpersonal relations: testing two graph theoretical models on 742 sociomatrices', *American Sociological Review,* 35: 843-51.

J. A. Davis and S. Leinhart (1971), 'The structure of positive interpersonal relations', in: J. Berger (ed.), *Sociological Theories in Progress,* vol. 2. (Boston: Houghton Mifflin).

George Dively (1972), *The Power of Professional Management* (American Management Association Inc.).

G. William Domhoff (1967), *Who Rules America?* (Englewood Cliffs, N.J.: Prentice-Hall).

G. William Domhoff (1974), *The Bohemian Grove and Other Delights* (New York: Harper & Row).

Peter Dooley (1969), 'The interlocking directorate', *American Economic Review,* June.

William M. Evan (1966), 'The organization set: toward a theory of interorganizational relations', in: James D. Thompson (ed.), *Approaches to Organizational Design* (Pittsburg: University of Pittsburg Press), pp. 173-91.

R. Fitch and M. Oppenheimer (1970), 'Who rules the corporations', *Socialist Revolution,* 1 (4-6).

R. Fitch (1972), 'Sweezy and corporate fetishism', *Socialist Revolution,* 2 (36).

C. Flament (1963), *Applications of Graph Theory to Group Structure* (Englewood Cliffs, N.J.: Prentice-Hall).

L. R. Ford and D. R. Fulkerson (1962), *Flows in Networks* (Princeton: N.J.: Princeton University Press).

Fortune (1970), 'The Fortune directory of the 500 largest industrials', *Fortune,* 15 May.

John Kenneth Galbraith (1967), *The New Industrial State* (Boston: Houghton-Mifflin).

T. C. Gleason (1969), *Multidimensional Scaling of Sociometric Data* (Ann Arbor: Institute for Social Research).

Robert Gordon (1961), *Business Leadership in the Large Corporation* (Berkeley: University of California Press).

F. Harary (1955-56), 'On the notion of balance of a signed graph', *Michigan Mathematical Journal* 2: 143-46.

F. Harary (1969), *Graph Theory* (Reading, Mass.: Addison-Wesley).

F. Harary, R. Z. Norman and D. Cartwright (1965), *Structural Models: An Introduction to the Theory of Directed Graphs* (New York: Wiley).

Edward Herman (1971), 'Review article', Unpublished, Wharton School of Business, Philadelphia).

Edward Herman (1973), 'Do bankers control corporations?', *Monthly Review,* June.

Paul Holden, Lounsbury Fish and Hubert Smith (1945), *Top-Management Organization and Control* (Palo Alto: Stanford University Press).

C. H. Hubbell (1965), 'An input-output approach to clique identification', *Sociometry,* 28: 377-99.

Floyd Hunter (1959), Top Leadership, USA (Chapel Hill: University of North Carolina).

J. M. Juran and J. Keith Louden (1966), *The Corporate Director* (New York: American Management Association, Inc.).

James C. Knowles (1973), 'The Rockefeller financial group', *Warner Modular Publications,* Module 343.

Thomas Koenig (1974), 'An investigation into the significance of corporate interlocks in the American economy', Unpublished Master's thesis, department of sociology, University of California, Santa Barbara.

Thomas Koenig, Robert Gogel and John Sonquist (1974), 'Corporate interlocks and social class', Unpublished, University of California, Santa Barbara.

Gabriel Kolko (1962), *Wealth and Power in America* (New York: Praeger).

Robert Larner (1970), *Management Control and the Large Corporation* (New York: Dinellen Publishing Co.).

V. I. Lenin (1970), *Collected Works,* vol. 22 (Moscow: Foreign Languages Publishing House).

Joel H. Levine (1972), 'The sphere of influence', *American Sociological Review,* 37: 14-27.

R. D. Luce (1950), 'Connectivity and generalized cliques in sociometric group structure', *Psychometrika,* 15: 169-90.

R. D. Luce and A. D. Perry (1949), 'A method of matrix analysis of group structure', *Psychometrika,* 14: 95-116.

Myles L. Mace (1971), *Directors: Myth and Reality* (Boston: Graduate School of Business Administration, Harvard University).

D. MacRae Jr. (1960), 'Direct factor analysis of sociometric data', *Sociometry,* **23**: 360-71.

Edward McCreary, Jr. and Walter Guzzardi (1965), 'Reciprocity: A customer is a company's best friend', *Fortune,* June.

S. Menschikov (1972), *Millionaires and Managers* (Moscow: Progress Publishers).

C. Wright Mills (1956), *The Power Elite* (New York: Oxford University Press).

James O'Connor (1972), 'Question: Who rules the corporation? Answer: The ruling class', *Socialist Revolution,* Jan./Feb.

O. Ore (1962), 'Theory of graphs', *American Mathematical Society Collected Publications,* **38.**

O. Ore (1963), *Graphs and Their Uses* (New York: Random House).

E. R. Peay, Jr. (1970), 'Extensions of clusterability to quantitative data with an application to the cognition of political attitudes', Unpublished doctoral thesis, University of Michigan.

Victor Perlo (1957), *The Empire of High Finance* (New York: International Publishers Co. Inc.).

Robert Perrucci and Marc Pilisuk (1970), 'Leaders and ruling elites: The interorganizational bases of community power', *American Sociological Review,* **35**: 1040-57.

Theodore Quinn (1953), *Giant Business: Threat to Democracy* (New York: Exposition Press).

R. C. Roistacher (1971), 'Peer nominations of exploratory behavior', in: M. J. Feldman (ed.), *Studies in Psychotherapy and Behavioral Change, No. 1, Theory and Research in Mental Health* (New York: State University of New York at Buffalo, Buffalo), pp. 113-24.

R. C. Roistacher (1972), 'Peer nominations, clique structures and exploratory behavior in boys at four junior high schools', Unpublished doctoral dissertation, University of Michigan.

Arnold M. Rose (1967), *The Power Structure* (New York: Oxford University Press).

G. Sabidussi (1966), 'The centrality index of a graph', *Psychometrica,* **31**: 581-603.

Alpha Smaby (1974), 'Coping with corporate power: The CAPUR crusade', *Progressive,* July: 19-23.

S. Spilerman (1966), 'Structural analysis and the generation of sociograms', *Behavioral Science,* **11**: 312-18.

Standard and Poor's (1969-74) *Poor's Register of Corporations, Directors, and Executives, United States and Canada* (New York: Standard and Poor's Corporation).

Paul Sweezy (1972), 'The resurgence of financial control: Fact or fancy?', *Socialist Revolution,* March/April.

James D. Thompson (1967), *Organizations in Action* (New York: McGraw-Hill).

James D. Thompson and William J. McEwen (1958), 'Organizational goals and environment: Goal-setting as an interaction process', *American Sociological Review,* **23**: 23-31.

United States Congress, House Subcommittee on Domestic Finance of the House Banking and Currency Committee: *Chain Banking: Stockholder and Loan Links of 200 Largest Member Banks* (Washington, 1963). *Twenty Largest Stockholders of Record in Member Banks of the Federal Reserve System* (Washington, 1964). *Bank Stock Ownership and Control* (Washington (1966). *Control of Commercial Banks and Interlocks Among Financial Institutions* (Washington, 1967). *Commercial Banks and Their Trust Activities* (Washington, 1968). *Growth of Unregistered Bank Holding Companies* (Washington, 1969).

United States Congress, House Committee on the Judiciary, Anti-trust subcommittee (1965), *Interlocks in Corporate Management* (Washington, D.C.).

United States Federal Trade Commission (1951), *Report on Interlocking Directorates* (Washington, D.C.).

United States Federal Trade Commission, Subcommittee on Anti-trust and Monopoly (1969), *Economic Report on Corporate Mergers* (Washington, D.C.).

United States National Resources Committee (1939), *The Structure of the American Economy: Basic Characteristics* (Washington, D.C.: US Government Printing Office).

Stanley C. Vance (1964), *Boards of Directors: Structure and Performance* (Eugene: University of Oregon Press).

W. Lloyd Warner and Durab Unwalla (1967), 'The System of Interlocking Directorates,' in W. Lloyd Warner, Durab Unwalla and John H. Trimm (eds.), *The Emergent American Society: Large Scale Organizations* (New Haven: Yale University Press).

4

DESCRIPTION AND EXPLANATION
IN POWER ANALYSIS

Jack H. Nagel
University of Pennsylvania

As many others have observed, conceptual confusion seriously impedes social scientists' attempts to understand power phenomena.[1] Proliferation of apparently incompatible frameworks and definitions stems in part from extra-scientific sources: ambiguity and varied connotations are inevitable when analysts borrow popular terms from ordinary language. Ideology also hinders agreement, as scholars fight political struggles on the conceptual battleground.

At least part of the confusion, however, results from an intellectual failure: insufficient recognition of the varied questions we ask using power concepts, of the different levels of theory needed to answer them, and of the relations among these levels.

In particular, too many theorists neglect to distinguish between descriptive and explanatory uses of power terms. Instead, many believe that power should serve as a 'major explanatory concept' in social theories (March, 1966). This belief, pursued too narrowly, can impede research in at least three ways: Some of its adherents try to build explanatory or motivational properties directly into their definitions of power — for example, by treating it as the ability to coerce or, more broadly, as the ability to manipulate others' utilities or well-being. Petitioners soon arrive, however, seeking recognition for the power of non-violence, expertise, or some other neglected capacity. Ensuing disputes about human motivation or practical tactics are joined in the definitional arena, where no rules for recognizing a victor exist.

Others, realizing that concepts alone do not really explain anyway (at least not in the prevailing deductive sense of explanation) contend that theories of power must come first, leaving the success or failure of models to determine the survival of whatever concepts they include. Unfortunately, attempts to explain events adequately in power terms quickly lead to theories of formidable complexity. Consequently, proponents of this position tend to be pessimistic about the usefulness of power in social theory.

Finally, the explanatory focus induces some observers to reject certain rigorous definitions and measures because they appear suited only to ex post facto assessment and lack the predictive quality implied by the conception of power as potential or capacity.

This emphasis on explanation in formulating and evaluating power concepts seems to me premature and incomplete. Without a more general notion of power, how do we decide what kind of explanation is a power explanation? When capability concepts of power conflict, on what grounds are we to choose among them? And do we not retain a strong, legitimate interest in knowing the distribution of power in social systems in order to evaluate even when we cannot adequately explain?

DESCRIPTIVE POWER ANALYSIS

Answers to these questions require a satisfactory descriptive analysis of power. Essential elements in this analysis are a definition of power, measures of power, and principles of power inference.

Power as Causation by Preferences

The orthodox tendency in modern political science, at least since the influential work of Simon (1957), has been to treat power as a type of causation 'in which the behavior of one or more persons alters the behavior of another or others' (Frey, 1974). Some authors further stipulate that the controller must intend the effect his behavior causes.

While there are persuasive reasons for accepting a causal conception of power, the conventional formulations have been disappointingly unproductive of new insight and are subject to serious substantive criticism, especially when applied in field research. In particular, their emphasis on activity leads to neglect of 'non-decisions', patterns of outcomes maintained without overt conflict, and to ignoring rule through anticipated reactions, in which one actor adjusts to another's wishes in the absence of any recognizable influence attempt.

Influence through anticipated reactions is a crucial anomaly. Theorists cannot ignore it, because in real systems it is ubiquitous and often vitally important — for example, as a chief means of voter influence in electoral democracies (Cell, 1974). Yet behavioral definitions of power, with or without intentions, cannot admit the phenomenon without strenuous and questionable complications. This obvious weakness, if solved, might point the way to additional improvements in our conceptual and methodological tools for analyzing power.

The solution I propose is a redefinition of power as causation by preferences, combined with a new analysis of preference as a dispositional concept. More precisely, *a power relation, actual or potential, is an actual or potential causal relation between the preferences of an actor regarding an outcome and the outcome itself.*

Social power has always implied the ability to realize wants or desires. For reasons that remain obscure, but may have had to do with conceptions of causality, those who viewed power as causation by behavior eliminated reference to the want-regarding aspect of the concept (though in practice they smuggled it back in). Definitions of power as intended causation were designed to remedy this defect; but the idea of intention, with its connotations of consciousness, excludes rule by anticipated reactions (as well as other modes of influence, such as the shaping of behavior by reinforcement that, although not consciously intended, does produce preferred outcomes).

Preference, a more general notion, avoids these difficulties when interpreted properly. As a disposition, preference can be characterized by multiple conditional definitions, each relevant only under specified circumstances. One conditional definition applies when an actor knows that an outcome is contingent, at low cost to herself, on her own actions. We then infer her preference from her choice behavior, such as an influence attempt. This is the situation to which the behavioral and intentional definitions of power are suited.

The preference definition subsumes them, because the influence attempt can be viewed as caused by the preference. We can also define preference by referring to behavioral reactions *after* an outcome has occured. These reactions — e.g. of pleasure and gratitude or rage and retaliation — are precisely the kind, anticipation of what might induce another actor to do as the reactor wishes. The proximate cause of the compliant response is, of course, the respondent's own anticipation, but the notion of preference as a temporally extended disposition enables us to treat the anticipation, if it does correctly correspond to the preference, as the effect of the preference. Thus, in both cases the controller's preference causes the respondent's behavior.

Preferences need not be inferred only from behavior during power interactions. Because of the 'openness' of conditional definition, or the possibility of specifying new responses to characterize the attribute under other test conditions, preferences may be assessed by additional observations. Possibilities include survey research, interviewing, content analysis, projective tests, inferences from social roles, and deduction from theories of motivation. The problems here are formidable, but achievements in attitude scaling and (less practically) utility theory give preference a definite and sometimes even quantifiable character altogether lacking from the far too general notion of behavior and from the too specific and subjective idea of intention.

Thus, the preference definition of power includes causation by intended behavior and influence attempts, captures power phenomena missed by the conventional definitions, and offers hope for easier operationalization and measurement of power.

Despite these advantages, resorting to preference in defining power may seem an epistemological retreat to those who share B. F. Skinner's rejection of internal states in explaining behavior.[2] Actually, the key conditional definitions of preference can be stated in such a way that all reference to mental or emotional states is avoided. Furthermore, in proper Skinnerian fashion, the causal explanation can be extended back to behavioral or environmental antecedents of preferences. Nevertheless, we start from the disposition in power analysis precisely because our interest in power stems largely from its relation to the achievement of desires (or if one prefers, attainment of reinforcing consequences and escape from aversive ones).

The use of 'outcome' as the effect variable also deserves comment. This term is intended to make the definition an extremely general paradigm, applicable to most objects of power identified in the literature: the behavior of individuals; systemic outcomes such as tax rates; psychological variables, including beliefs and attitudes; and power structures themselves, as in the delegation of authority or the construction of constitutions.[3] The generality of this pattern makes it imperative to specify the outcome variable by stating the domain (actor or set of actors influenced), scope (behavior or attribute influenced), and time period for which the hypothesized power relation is thought to be valid.

Use of Causal Models

The major payoff promised by causal definitions of power has always been the possibility of transferring to power analysis standard social science techniques for inferring and measuring causality. The actual flow of benefits, however, has been in the reverse direction, as it was his interest in power that induced Simon (1957) to undertake his pioneering analyses of causal ordering and causal inference. This work has had enormous impact in the social sciences, but ironically it has not been extensively or systematically applied to the problem that motivated it.

This failure can be explained partly by reliance on behavior or intentions as the causal variable in orthodox power definitions. Defining power as causation by preferences removes this hindrance. A second barrier to transfer was a disjuncture in the interests of causal modellers and power analysts. The former became, for a time, preoccupied with causal inference rather than coefficient estimation, while the latter sought power measures more than principles to justify power attributions.

The second obstacle has disappeared during the past decade with the increasing vogue of path analysis. Among other virtues, its utility for both estimation and inference and focus on indirect causation give it great advantages in the study of power — certainly as a heuristic and possibly, though under limited circumstances, as an operational technique as well.

We can gain a better perspective on these advantages if we first consider some more general implications of the proposed power definition when combined with Simon's explication of causality.

According to Simon (1957, p. 11), 'causal orderings are simply properties of the scientist's model' — relations between variables in a theory, not between real objects or events. Power relations, as a special type of causal ordering, are therefore also properly understood as orderings of theoretical variables. Consequently, any power attribution presupposes a theory of the outcome over which power is thought to be exercised.

Specifically, a theoretical structure involves power if variables denoting preferences concerning an outcome have causal precedence over variables denoting the outcome itself. Recursive systems of static equations, of the type assumed in conventional social science causal modelling, provide the best-known example of a causally ordered structure. Such structures are power models if preferences are exogenous in the equation that determines the outcome. It is important to note, however, that more sophisticated models can also represent power relations. Block recursive structures depict power relations if preferences appear in lower-ordered blocks than the outcome variable. Dynamic models represent power if preferences of one time period determine outcomes in the next.[4] Even non-recursive static models, in which preferences and outcomes simultaneously determine each other, may be interpreted as representing asymmetric power relations, if equilibrium observations and an underlying recursive dynamic process can be assumed.[5]

Let us now proceed to summarize briefly the benefits that result when we combine the preference definition of power, the perspective on causality just presented, and statistical path analysis. Parenthetical page references indicate passages in Nagel (1975) to which the reader can refer for greater detail.

Justifying Power Attributions: Recognition that power attributions are hypotheses subject to normal methodological strictures and rules of inference imposes discipline and offers opportunities. Because more than one theory may be compatible with a given set of data, it is important to consider every reasonable alternative model that might explain an outcome. Simply finding evidence compatible with a favored theory is not sufficient to sustain it. Each power hypothesis must be shown superior to its competitors — an injunction seldom heeded in power research. Treating each power attribution as a causal inference puts at our disposal three modes of justification:

(a) principles of specification extraneous to the statistical model, such as observed temporal ordering of preference and outcome, experimental intervention, or demonstration that known mechanisms intervene between the cause and effect;

(b) use of theory-trimming to eliminate supposed power relations that are not supported by a significant statistical correspondence between preference and outcome; and

(c) use of test equations to evaluate complex theories of power, provided that over-identified structures can be specified. These last two methods offer new possibilities for choice among theories when qualitative observations, as is often the case, fail to select convincingly from among competing power hypotheses (45-53, 74-79, 118-19, 125-40).

Advances in Measurement: Existing power measures have had limited influence. Most apply only to simple dyadic relations (e.g. Dahl, 1957) or to highly restricted forms of power (e.g. the voting power indices[6]). As a set they appear confusingly varied and even mutually incompatible (Riker, 1964). Application of path analysis largely eliminates these problems. Use of multivariate methods permits measurement of the power of several actors over the same outcome, as well as inclusion of non-preference causes. Moreover, it can be demonstrated that Dahl's amount of power and Banzhaf's voting power index are special cases of path measures, while March's measurement concept and the Shapley-Shubik index are closely related and eminently compatible (40-45, 54-74, 91-100).

Assessing Indirect Influence: In large systems, power typically operates indirectly — as through elected representatives, authorized subordinates, or foreign puppets. Particularly troublesome and the subject of much ideological dispute is the influence exercised indirectly by controlling an intermediary's preferences, as in manipulation, indoctrination, and inculcation of false consciousness. Power as the

causation of outcomes by preferences readily permits us to conceptualize such forms of control, for there is no reason why another
actor's preference should not be the outcome controlled. Path analysis,
of course, was devised to measure causal effect exercised through one
or more indirect chains of influence. The intervening variables may be
either preferences or non-preference factors, such as perceptions. The
effect on preferences of non-preference variables can also be depicted.
When an actor's preference functions as intervening variable, the causal
effect exerted through that path can be partitioned between the actor
himself and the more ultimate causes by treating the unexplained
residual of the preference as the actor's own 'autonomous' preference.[7]
Thus, just as with power generally, it is unnecessary to think of indirect
influence in all-or-nothing terms (42-45, 89-90, 101-13, 125-40).

Actor Selection: The basis for designating collective actors has per-
sistently evoked controversy among group theorists in American
political science (Greenstone, 1975). The present approach to power
analysis tends to remove restrictions on actor designation, rather than
impose them. Actor selection should be evaluated fundamentally by the
causal explanatory power of the ensuing theory, though for reasons of
substantive interest one may well want to estimate the power of actors
who turn out to be ineffective.

Contrary to the Bentleyan tradition in political science, activity,
organized or otherwise, is not necessary to exercise influence, though
direct participation may certainly augment the power of an individual
or group.[8] Nor, to consider another test used in group theory, is it
necessary that a social category exhibit a strong consensus before one
can treat it as a single actor. Internal dissension is certainly likely to
weaken a group's influence; but, as the Downs (1957) model of electoral democracy demonstrates, it is possible to conceive of power
exercised by a broad category (all voters) that exhibits high variance in
preferences.[9]

The opposite situation can also obtain. Two or more sociologically
distinct groups may consistently exhibit nearly identical preferences. If
so, the problem of multi-collinearity can make it statistically impossible
to distinguish their influence. The researcher may then be forced to
treat them as a single actor, as indeed they may be in practice. On the
other hand, if causal ordering between the two actors' preferences can
be demonstrated, they can be separated again in an indirect influence
structure (119-20, 124-25, 154-56).

Nondecisions: The first step in constructing outcome and preference scales is to determine the possible states of each event in the outcome category. Only one of these states will have occurred in reality. When overt struggle settles a recognized political issue, then political actors will have actively promoted one or more of the non-occurring possible states. When the outcome results from non-decision-making, then the investigator must imaginatively reconstruct the alternative possible states and gauge preferences across them by criteria other than political activity. If these tasks can be accomplished and if, using criteria discussed above, a causal ordering between preferences and outcome can be sustained, then it is perfectly meaningful to speak of and assess power over non-issues.[10] (115-17, 120-23).

Anticipated Reactions: Conundrums associated with the closely related problem of rule through anticipated reactions are, not surprisingly, resolvable using our framework. For example, should we attribute power to A if B alters his behavior to conform to a mistaken idea of A's preference? The answer is no, because to demonstrate a causal link between A's preference and B's behavior, one must observe A's preference independently. If B responds not to that preference, but to his own imagination, then the causal link with the preference is severed. Similarly, independent observations of preferences may enable us to assess power when two parties correctly anticipate each other's reactions and adjust their behavior accordingly, without overt struggle, negotiation, or communication. Using behaviorist definitions of power, it is impossible even to conceputalize influence in such equilibrium situations (31-33, 142-46).

The Zero-Sum Issue: Ever since Parsons first posed the question, considerable attention has been given the problem of whether power in a system is a fixed or variable-sum quantity. The former implies that any gain in power by one actor must be at another's expense, while the latter suggests the less conflictful possibility of an actor or actors gaining power while no one else loses. Our perspective permits a definite answer to this question. If power is causation by preferences, then the total variance explained by preferences is an appropriate measure of the sum of all actors' power. This amount can expand if the causal effect of preferences increases at the expense of unexplained variance and/or non-preference causes. Such increases can occur for a variety of reasons — improved skill in exercising power, better communication, better mobilization and coordination of human energies, reduction of the impact of irrational impulses, and avoidance of unnecessary struggles. Once all variance in an outcome is due to preferences, however, power over that outcome becomes a fixed-sum quantity (158-68).

Limits of Power: Finally, our analysis should produce some sensitivity to situations where power is not a useful variable in explaining social outcomes. Among conditions that limit its usefulness are the following: failure of preferences to explain causally a significant portion of outcome variance; inability to specify an identifiable model; instability of preferences relative to the time period of observation, as when there is strong reciprocal interaction among preferences or quick feedback from outcomes to preferences; and lack of differences among preferences of actors, unless they can be shown to be causally ordered or one wishes only to assess their cooperative power. The point of these strictures and others that might be listed is to stress that not every situation should or can be interpreted in power terms. Nevertheless, these new developments in descriptive power analysis should, I hope, expand our ability to think about and to assess power and influence in large-scale social systems (178).

POWER AS EXPLANATION AND POTENTIAL

These benefits of descriptive power analysis may still leave unsatisfied those who conceive of power as a potentiality or who want power to be an explanatory concept.

Explanation, of course, is relative — both to what one wants to explain and to know how far one wants to follow the regress of causes. One could, for example, take the results of a descriptive power analysis as given and use them to account for other variables, such as when we attribute rage to powerlessness.

Descriptive analysis itself does depend on an explanation of the outcome in question, a theory in which it is explained, partially or entirely, by causally prior preferences — and by the distribution of power across actors. But the latter addition is merely tautological, since we infer the power distribution from the relation between preferences and outcomes. One could use the estimated power coefficients to explain or predict future outcomes, but this is blind projection, and we have no guarantee that the coefficients will be stable.

Satisfying explanation and insightful prediction depend upon the construction of theories of power — models in which power coefficients themselves are endogenous.[11] An ideal theory of power would generate numerical power coefficients, given the values of parameters and exogenous variables. Power coefficients could then be derived in two ways — deductively from the theory of power, and inductively from outcome and preference observations and the theory of the outcome. It would then be possible to test and improve theories of power by comparing theoretical coefficients with empirical estimates.

From this point of view, statements about power potentials are, or should be, equivalent to predictions about power coefficients. Any use of power or influence to indicate a potential or capacity is therefore an empirical hypothesis, derived from an implicit or explicit theory of power, one that may be strongly or weakly supported by past experience. Formerly, writers employing a concept of potential power have generally left their theories implicit and untested, though often the actor in question possesses a widely effective power resource, such as weapons, wealth, or legitimacy.

Reasonable grounds for attributing potential power or even a set of deduced power coefficients are not sufficient to predict an outcome nor even to predict that an actor will influence an outcome. In path models of power, outcome variables are depicted as additive functions of terms representing the product of each actor's power with her preference. If an actor has no preference concerning an outcome, or if her preference is weak compared with others, then her effect on the outcomes will be nil or insignificant. This construction formalizes the common-sense assumption that personal causality depends on both ability and motivation. It considerably complicates power theories of events, particularly in the predictive mode; statements about potential power require only a theory of power coefficients, while statements about predicted or probable power require both a theory of power and a theory of preferences, or at least knowledge about preferences.[1][2]

Still more satisfying explanations would be provided by a dynamic theory of power coefficients, one that would predict shift points in statically estimated models or, perhaps, more continuous changes in power distributions.[1][3]

Thus, ascending levels of theoretical complexity are implied by different types of power attribution. A simple model of the outcome suffices to estimate exercised power from known preferences and outcomes. To explain exercised power or to attribute potential power, a static theory of power coefficients is needed, one that must include new variables. To predict exercised power in the near future, one must add hypotheses about preferences. To attribute possible future power or to explain changes in power, one needs a dynamic model of power coefficients; and to make extended predictions of exercised power (should one wish to be so rash), the dynamic theory of power must be supplemented by extended predictions about preferences.

Explanations traversing all these levels have thus far been grand verbal theories of history, of which Marx's is the prototype and the most influential. Formal explanatory power theory in behavioral science is at a fledgling stage. Existing models are difficult to operationalize, limited to simple systems, and incorporate few types of power. We are a long way from being able to make confident deductive statements about power in complex systems. Therefore, relatively atheoretical, inductive, descriptive power analysis may play an important role — testing explanatory theories as they develop, giving some idea of the results of patterns too complex to deduce, and providing information of intrinsic evaluational interest. In using these static models, however, we must avoid ascribing permanence or inevitability to the results they yield. Power distributions in complex societies are subject to dynamic processes that we do not yet fully understand and that we may hope some day to make more responsive to human preferences.

NOTES

Many of the ideas in this chapter are developed more completely in my recent book (Nagel, 1975). I am grateful to Yale University Press for permission to present them here and to Way Shen for valued help.

1. Throughout this essay, I use 'power' in the generic sense. Some authors devote strenuous efforts to distinguishing among various power terms, such as influence, authority, control, force, violence, persuasion, manipulation, and so on. There *are* distinctions in the modal use of these terms in everyday language. (For a good analysis of three of them, see Bell, 1975.) Moreover, some of these distinctions have both explanatory and normative importance. Nevertheless, like several precursors, I believe that priority should be given to determining the generic meaning common to all these terms. I suspect that distinctions, when we are ready to make them, will be more numerous and more precise than our ordinary vocabulary equips us to handle.

2. Russell Hardin called this problem to my attention. As Herbert Simon (1975) has pointed out, the 'behavioral' movement in political science, unlike the behaviorist school in psychology did not in principle reject explanation by psychological mechanisms. Nevertheless in power analysis their choice of vocabulary had unfortunate effects.

3. On power over power, or relational control, see Baumgartner et al., ch. 10, this volume.

4. Ambiguities arise, however, if outcomes feed back to affect preferences, or if feedback relations exist among the preferences of two or more actors. See Nagel (1975, ch. 9).

5. One might also switch to a symmetric definition of causality, instead of insisting on asymmetry between cause and effect. I have not followed this course, but its implications for power analysis might be worth exploring.

6. For a thorough, clear account of the Shapley-Shubik and Banzhaf voting power indices, see Brams (1975).

7. Although developed independently, this is exactly the view of autonomy taken by Skinner (1971, pp. 41, 55, 189), except that Skinner is confident that science can reduce the residuals to zero.

8. To be rejected even more emphatically is the egregious pluralist fallacy of equating political activity and interest or preference. As Greenstone notes, the possibility of repression and the problem of collective action decisively refute this complacent view.

9. It is sometimes supposed that in such models power accrues to the median voter (whose preference is approximately adopted by vote-maximizing parties). This is not so. If that voter were to change her preference to a position at one end of the ideological spectrum, the parties would not follow her. The median voter *benefits* most from party policies, but *influences* them little more than any other voter. In Downsian models, power is more properly attributed to the entire distribution or, concretely, to the electorate or constituency as a collective actor.

(On power and benefit, see Nagel, 1975, pp. 157-58).

10. Because preferences cannot be inferred from activity in non-decision-making, it may be tempting, in the absence of other indicators such as surveys, to resort to an objective interest approach to power analysis. I have rejected this course, principally because it seems too vulnerable to normative dispute. (Contrast Greenstone, 1975.) Nevertheless, when one feels confident in assessing an actor's objective interests, it may be worthwhile to include them in the causal analysis, especially to see under what conditions they determine 'subjective' preferences (108-13).

11. The ideas developed in this and subsequent paragraphs are quite comparable to those presented independently by Alker (1973), though he does not use the causation by preferences definition and depends heavily on a single power theory, that of Harsanyi (1962).

12. In the confusing Harsanyi-Alker vocabulary, 'power in a mere schedule sense' corresponds to measures or predictions of potential power, while 'power in a schedule sense' incorporates knowledge of utilities and so corresponds to predicted or probable power.

13. This level of power theory corresponds roughly to Alker's 'power in a contingent schedule sense'. If a dynamic theory shows that change or stability in power distributions depend on human preferences, then it explains what Buckley et al. call 'relational control'. (See Baumgartner et al., ch. 10, this volume.)

REFERENCES

Hayward R. Alker (1973), 'On political capabilities in a schedule sense: measuring power, integration and development', in: Hayward R. Alker, Karl W. Deutsch, and Antoine H. Stoetzel (eds), *Mathematical Approaches to Politics* (Washington: Jossey-Bass).

David V. J. Bell (1975), *Power, Influence and Authority: An Essay in Political Linguistics* (New York: Oxford University Press).

Steven J. Brams (1975), *Game Theory and Politics* (New York: The Free Press).

Donald C. Cell (1974), 'Policy influence without policy choice', *Journal of Political Economy* 82: 1017-26.

Robert A. Dahl (1957), 'The concept of power', *Behavioral Science* 2: 201-15.

Anthony Downs (1957), *An Economic Theory of Democracy* (New York: Harper & Row).

Frederick W. Frey (1974), 'Political power', *Encyclopedia Britannica*, 15th edn, **14**: 697-702.

J. David Greenstone (1975), 'Group theories', in: Fred I. Greenstein and Nelson W. Polsby (eds), *Micropolitical Theory,* vol. 2 of *The Handbook of Political Science* (Reading, Mass.: Addison-Wesley).

John C. Harsanyi (1962), 'Measurement of social power, opportunity costs, and the theory of two-person bargaining games', *Behavioral Science* 7: 67-80.

James G. March (1966), 'The power of power', in: David Easton (ed.), *Varieties of Political Theory* (Englewood Cliffs, N.J.: Prentice-Hall).

Jack H. Nagel (1975), *The Descriptive Analysis of Power* (New Haven: Yale University Press).

William H. Riker (1964), 'Some ambiguities in the notion of power' *American Political Science Review* 58: 341-49.

Herbert A. Simon (1957), *Models of Man* (New York: Wiley).

Herbert A. Simon (1975), Personal communication to the author.

B. F. Skinner (1971), *Beyond Freedom and Dignity* (New York: Bantam).

II

THE CONTROL OF SOCIAL STRUCTURES: MORPHOSTASIS AND MORPHOGENESIS

5

IDEOLOGY AND THE CONTROL OF CRISIS IN HIGHLY DEVELOPED CAPITALIST COUNTRIES

HANS-PETER MEIER
University of Zurich

INTRODUCTION

There are two interesting anomalies in the empirical course of crisis and the development of revolutionary consciousness and movements according to the Marxian predictive model. On the one hand, stagnation is found in the highly developed capitalist countries, that is those fulfilling in three ways the socio-economic criteria of maturity for internal revolutionary situations: extensive penetration by capital within the nation, monopolization, and capital monopolized by the state. On the other hand, countries with less developed capitalism, precapitalist or semicapitalist countries in the European south and in the Third World, are by-passing the socio-economic criterion of maturity for internal revolutionary conditions.[1]

These cases found in two segments of the international capitalist system reflect the same cause: they result from the international penetration by capital in its newest neo-colonial forms. Today it seems even less valid to regard courses of crises as limited to national and

endogenously conditioned events than previously in times of direct
imperialism and colonalism. Rather conditions, triggers, and courses of
crises are exported, imported, or reimported, that is we have to understand them always as *international phenomena* conditioned by exogenous as well as by endogenous factors. Thus, in Portugal the endogenous class antagonism mediated by the exogenous course of crises,
such as the international strengthening of anti-imperialist liberation
movements, resulted in the open crisis of a dominant, fascist regime.
This example serves to point out the direct types of international
connectedness of national crises of class domination. The majority of
such interdependencies are more indirect ones. Clearly, the strengthening of revolutionary liberation movements is conditioned by their
alliances with the socialist state system.

The two deviant cases are probably complementary phenomena of
the same cause, as suggested, on the one hand, by the objective relative
under-determination of revolutionary consciousness of the working
class in the highly developed capitalist countries, and on the other
hand, by the objective relative *over-determination* of revolutionary
consciousness of working class and pauperized masses in the Third
World. Relative under-determination of revolutionary consciousness in
the highly developed capitalist states results from utilizing the export of
pauperism and the import of prosperity, two strategies for controlling
internal crises through the neo-colonial forms of international labour
division. Both effects produce the syndrome of a working class aristocracy in the richer nations in comparison to the pauperized masses of
the poorer ones. Although a unified class according to objective relations to the means of production, they remain radically divided with
respect to their degree of development and to concrete life situations,
especially at the level of consumption. The relative under-determination
of consciousness increases the likelihood of susceptibility to ideologies
containing forms of false consciousness.

The relative under-determination in the rich nations corresponds to
the relative over-determination of revolutionary consciousness of the
working, unemployed and pauperized masses in the poor nations. Here
the consciousness of being exploited by the international monopolies
(anti-imperialist consciousness) *coincides* with the consciousness of the
bridge-head function performed by their own feudal bourgeois or
bureaucratic-militaristic dominant elites in the system of international

exploitation (an element of socialist consciousness).

How is it possible on the other hand that — in contrast to the cumulation of crises in Portugal — in the US the structure of domination could 'overcome' its endogenous crises (inflation, unemployment, Watergate, etc.) as well as its exogenous crisis resulting from its actions as an aggressive imperialist power in the Vietnam War?

In the 'Eighteenth Brumaire of Louis Bonaparte' Marx suggests that the bureaucratic-militaristic state machine, instrumental for the exploitation of classes by minorities, has not become linearly and progressively decayed over time. On the contrary, Marx concluded, 'that all revolutions perfected more this machine rather than broke it' (Marx and Engels, 1973). Thus, through crisis and conflicts this machine was not only reproduced but *simultaneously improved*. The highly developed Western countries which are, at the same time, parliamentary and democratic states are characterized by the longest historical experience of maintaining and developing the capitalist domination-function and the corresponding domination-structure. Both the premature revolution in the Third World and the delayed revolution in the highly developed capitalist countries[2] relate to the theoretical problem of base and superstructure, their interrelation and the function of the political system in these relationships.

THE POLITICAL SYSTEM AND THE RELATION OF BASE AND SUPERSTRUCTURE[3]

The political system functions as the principal regulator of crisis. These crises are based on contradictions or antagonisms within and between the relations of base and superstructure of the corresponding society.

The base is defined as the ordered totality of the following relation sets. First, the relations between actors and physical environment conditioned by the technological level of productive exploitation of nature (means of production); secondly, the relations between actors themselves conditioned by their relations to the means of production, to the production process and to the products (mode of production).

The latter, in sum, constitute the socio-economic class and stratification structure of a society.

The political system as the principal control actor of crisis is conceptualized as a superstructural phenomenon. The superstructure is defined as the ordered totality of the following relation sets.

(1) The relations among actors (political class relations) mediated by their relations to the legal state (parliament, government, bureaucracy, military, etc.), as the main subsystem of the political system, and by their relations to legal or illegal, formal or informal but more or less direct political associations (parties, unions, interest groups, etc.) as the complementary subsystem of the political system.[4]

(2) Abstracting from other non-direct political relation sets of superstructure, we have to consider also the relations among actors mediated by their conscious-mental (re-)production of the physical and social environment, and therefore of the universe of present and of transmitted historical relation sets in a society. The communicative relations producing and mediating the corresponding codes, such as institutions of primary and secondary socialization, media, etc. are the main material aspect of this conscious-mental production. Later we shall consider three of their forms: the relations among actors mediated by culture, ideology, and class consciousness.

Each regularity postulated relative to these relation sets of base and superstructure is founded on the premise that at a definite point in time certain configurations within and between these relation sets are invariant (morphostatic aspect) or that they in a definite span of time change invariantly (morphogenic aspect).

Superstructure is defined, in analogy to base, as the ordered totality of relation sets. Regarded as entities they are also characterized by a relative functional autonomy or self-dynamics in social processes. We can define a societal formation as the ordered totality of relations between the base — conceived as an ordered totality of its own relation sets — and the superstructure, conceived as an ordered totality of its own relation sets. The second basic sociological law[5] postulates again a causal-functional invariance[6] in the development of this ordered totality of relations between base and superstructure relation sets. This invariance should be conceived, on the one hand, as hypotaxis of superstructure with respect to the base (property of reflection), and, on the other, as hypertaxis implying the controlling of the base by superstructural parameters. Depending on the range and quality, by which the base's contradictions are reflected as such in the superstructural relation sets, they appear also as antagonisms in the superstructure. The latter motivate eufunctional or dysfunctional forces reproducing equilibriums of previous societal formations or readapting to equilibriums in newer ones.

The properties of reflection and control in base-superstructure relations imply an antinomy. This antinomy can be demonstrated by the relative degree of freedom, from constraints by reflection, of superstructural control which is able to more or less transcend the reflection process[7] or the self-dynamics of the base processes themselves.[8] Conversely, the more pervasively the main contradictions of base *is reflected* in superstructural contradictions, the less the degree of freedom in control function. As a result, development of superstructural relation sets would not only be subordinated to those of the base but even subsumed. In this case political processes would seem as pure derivatives of socio-economic relations, i.e. processes of capital movement. Such a result is disproved by most historically-known revolutions and counter-revolutions. The reflection of socio-economic class relations as political ones has never been characterized concretely by one-to-one relationships. The flexibility of Lenin's praxis in analyzing class relations remains a significant example in this respect. In order to discuss for the purposes of this paper transformations from contradictions into crises as well as the function of the state in them, we emphasize the following attributes of relations between base and superstructure:

(1) The base's contradictions become more or less *pervasively*[9] crystallized as contradictions within and between superstructural relation sets. However, certain relation sets in the superstructure such as aesthetic codes, language as such (abstracted from the socio-linguistic functions in mediating social relations), can be relatively immunized against contradictions in other relation sets of base or superstructure. Marx (1974), for instance, emphasizes the fact of transhistorical validity of some aesthetic items and codes created by ancient culture.

(2) Social change as a transformation of relation sets must be conceived in a non-mechanistic manner; that is we wish to emphasize the fact that relation sets in reality are transformed by dynamic *behaviour patterns*.[10] The latter, while in sum determined by the relation sets, can operate relatively autonomously in relation to these –

a fact of which we must take account in explaining such transformations. Finally, abstracting from these behaviour patterns means
also to abstract from their actors as special relation sets (personality
systems) mediating basic and superstructural processes. The personality
system represents another relation set distinguished in regard to the
basic and superstructural ones.[11] The personality system, which is
neither subsumable under the base nor under the superstructure, functions as real 'infrastructure' in social and political processes. Modifying
subjectively the behaviour patterns in regard to the context of relation
sets objectively conditions personality systems. Actors are enabled to
behave not only reactively but also *creatively* in this context.

CONTRADICTIONS, CRISIS AND STATE

The terms 'contradiction' and 'crisis' should be clearly distinguished.
Crisis means the manifestation of objective contradictions located
within and between the relation sets implied by the three aspects of
social being — base, superstructure and personality — outlined above.
The term 'contradiction' relates to these structural properties of a
society which define the objective conditions necessary but not sufficient for the outbreak of a crisis or the particular patterns of its
course. By analogy with linguistics, the set of contradictions in a
society relates to its manifestation as crisis, in a similar way as the 'deep
structure' of language items relates to their 'surface structure'.
Methodologically, it is non-optimal to explain crises simply in terms
either of their 'surface structure' or, alternatively, simply in terms of
'deep structure'. Rather, crises should be understood by optimally
combining the inductive and deductive methods, i.e. viewing 'crisis' and
'contradiction' as mutually dependent — the crises deriving from the
contradictions while simultaneously shaping them.
    The transformations of contradictions into crises does not entail
linear-causal or mechanistic processes. On the contrary, such transformations are the results of complex interactions between contradictions producing the crises and feedbacks from these crises, which
again modify their 'deep structure', i.e. the objective contradictions in a

society. The degree of freedom, in transformations from social contradictions into crises, determines simultaneously the scope for the intervention of the self-dynamics of other factors in such transformations. Historical, cultural and situational contexts and specific objective or subjective attributes of the actors[12] — e.g. classes, strata, groups or individuals, and in particular institutions — take an active part in mediating such transformations. Thus, the state not only influences but tries to control such transformations, i.e. processes of crisis-crystallization.

In reconsidering the two cases which depart from the linear pattern of crisis development contained in the Marxian model — i.e. the relative under-determination of the revolutionary situation in the highly developed capitalist countries, and its relative over-determination in the less developed ones — we must draw analytical distinctions concerning the *pervasiveness* of contradictions as well as the *quality of crisis development* in a society.

As shown, contradictions 'pervade' the relation sets, constituting the structure of a society, in different ways. The degree of pervasion of contradictions is, in a historical sense, a function of the type of societal formation to which a society belongs — but also a function of the further specific attributes mentioned above, which make in some respects each society a unique case. For our purposes we conceive the degree of pervasion of contradictions as a simple dichotomous variable, specifying the under-developed capitalist countries as societies with *less pervasive* contradictions than the highly developed ones which have *more pervasive* contradictions. Less pervasive contradictions mean that contradictions, induced by a capitalist development pattern, have still not fully penetrated the domain of superstructural relation sets, of which the political structure constitutes a part. That is, although these countries are characterized by features of a capitalist socio-economic class structure, the latter is not or only partially reflected in political structure. Converseley, the highly developed capitalist countries are specified as societies with a 'ripe' structure, i.e. with a set of more pervasive contradictions. In this case the latter transcend the base relation sets and penetrate the superstructural ones, implying that the socio-economic class structure is more or less completely reflected in that of the political.[13]

The quality of crises is conceived also as a dichotomous variable

which specifies them as having disruptive as opposed to non-disruptive
consequences with regard to the stability of certain relation sets in a
society – in particular its socio-economic or political class-domination
structures. A crisis, then, may result in disruptive consequences when
its course is of a *cumulative* nature. In this case, those actors seeking to
prevent a crisis from taking a disruptive course are not able to isolate it
within, fragment it between, or divert it away from, the crucial relation
sets. Conversely, the capability to isolate, fragment or divert the course
of the crisis gives it a *non-cumulative* character, not disruptive of those
relation sets, the stability of which is essential for the maintenance of
the status quo – but probably disrupting other 'non-essential' relation
sets or behaviour patterns, for instance, of the personality.

In particular the state's activities in playing an active part in transforming contradictions into crises can cause the crisis to take a course,
the pattern of which *diverges* considerable from the linear model –
designated above as Marxian, although never explicitly stated by Marx
with reference to the imperialist phase of modern history. This postulates that the most intensive and disruptive crises should occur in
societies with the most pervasive contradictions, i.e. in the most highly
developed capitalist countries. However, in modern history, we observe
a systematic shift to a non-linear model of disruptive crisis development
and revolutionary crisis solution.

On the one hand, in the semicapitalist or capitalist countries of the
Third World or southern Europe with less pervasive contradictions we
find a trend towards crises taking a cumulative course, which is simultaneously of a disruptive character with respect to socio-economic class
domination. This acceleration of crisis development in the less developed countries results from the relative over-determination of the
internal revolutionary situation. The acceleration is caused by mechanisms such as the import of potentials and triggers off crises from the
highly developed capitalist countries. Evidently, in the nations of the
Third World additional factors operate in practice to reinforce objectively and subjectively the over-determination of the revolutionary
situation for instance, the coincidence of anti-imperialist and nationalist mobilization with elements of socialist consciousness promoted by
the specific situation of building a new nation.

On the other hand, in the highly developed capitalist nations with
the most pervasive contradictions we find a trend towards crises taking

a non-cumulative course, i.e. not threatening the socio-economic class domination. Here a trend towards the relative under-determination of the revolutionary situation dominates, which contrasts with anticipated potential of crisis implied by the relatively pervasive objective contradictions of these societies.

This fact results from the mechanisms *which displace the crises of a disruptive quality beyond the domain of those political relation sets, the adequate functioning of which is a functional prerequisite for the maintenance of the socio-economic class domination.* One of the mechanisms relies upon the export of crises into other countries, in particular to those of the Third World. Other mechanisms are the displacement of crises into parts of superstructural relation sets, which do not belong to the functional prerequisites for maintaining socio-economic class domination. The internalization of crises into the personality may be considered as a further form of crisis displacement. Measures by which crises are temporarily moderated, for instance through reformist intervention by the state, may be distinguished from strategies of crisis displacements. As the principal agent or central coordinator of such strategies, the modern capitalist state functions in a multitude of ways — in particular by utilizing specific ideological strategies. These facts call for a careful consideration of the functioning of the state in controlling crises in the highly developed capitalist countries.

Functions of the Modern Capitalist Interventionist State

The modern capitalist interventionist state has to be conceived as a complex organized system performing different functions in regard to the relation sets of base and superstructure. These functions are hierarchically ordered as primary and secondary ones. The systemic character of the state's functions implies that only synthetic methods of inquiry as opposed to analytic ones are adequate; that is, we cannot generalize from single functions to the whole function of state, but conversely, in determining specific single functions we must refer to their relations to the overall function of the state. In departing from this methodological principle, one may mistakingly define ideologically secondary functions, in reference to the hierarchy *means* functions, as *goal* functions.

The maintenance of the socio-economic domination structures within and outside the country is the primary function of the capitalist state. It includes *protective* and *promotive* forms. Passing from protective to promotive forms in carrying out the primary function increases the degree of direct or indirect mediation of exploitation by the state; state investments, infrastructure development, direct participation in economic domains, etc. This transition is historically reflected in the change from the 'watchman state' to the imperialist and, finally, to the monopolistic state. In previous forms the capitalist state's control function was restricted to the repressive protection of exploitation, other forms mediating the capitalist exploitation having still been scarcely developed. In this phase the crisis of private production mode culminated in direct confrontation of the impoverished masses with the capitalists themselves or the corresponding state protectors. The legitimation gaps of the capitalist state objectively and subjectively − in experience and in consciousness − coincided directly with the crisis of private production mode and its visible protection by state. The resulting legitimation crisis of the state stimulated the Keynesian revolution of developing capitalist domination instruments mainly as a consequence of the crises in the 1920s and 1930s. It was one of the main preconditions for developing the secondary functions, especially the welfare function (Banaszkiewicz, 1972).

Secondary functions include the political, ideological (Wesolowski, 1967, p. 65) and psychic forms of domination or their readaptation to changing conditions in maintaining economic domination. The diverse secondary functions of the state are again ordered by different weights. These different weights are functions of the time variable i.e. historical categories. In some periods the welfare activities are dominant, in others ideological ones. The latter for instance, frequently occur in times of transition to forms of 'exceptional states'.

However, the essential common property of these secondary functions of the state is that they define more or less well adapted means functions in reference to its primary function, i.e. goal function.

One of the secondary functions concerns the reproduction or readaptation of political relations, including the form of the state,[14] to the conditions to be presupposed as necessary and sufficient for performing efficiently the primary and secondary functions. It is evident, that since the bourgeois revolution and mainly as a consequence of the transition from the protective to the promotive form in maintaining the primary functions, this capacity for self-adaptation has increased extraordinarily. The relative competitive relation between private and increasing public accumulation forced the state not only to maintain the primary function but also to perform it in an optimal and cost-favourable manner. The result of this on the one hand, efficiency in bureaucracy, planning, etc. and, on the other hand, the tendency to substitute the more cost-intensive activities of state by less cost intensive ones. In this way repression is replaced by the welfare function or, as both are still relatively cost intensive means,[15] by the even less cost-intensive ones, the ideological or psychic ones.

A second complex of secondary functions of state refers directly to the domain of socio-economic relations: first, the redistributions as modifying the existential life conditions of individuals within the given socio-economic class position (redistributive function), secondly, the production of a public infrastructure (infrastructural function); and thirdly, the correction of certain costs externalized by the private production mode (external cost-reducing function).[16] The ideological function, as the third of the secondary state functions, influences the conscious-mental production of a society determining specific relations among the actors. Culture, ideology and class consciousness are mediated by the communicative relations directly produced or influenced by the state's educational or informational policies.

Finally, as the fourth type of secondary state functions we have to consider its direct or indirect influence on the personality, its psychic and mental competence. The majority of the other functions can in different degrees mediate eufunctional or dysfunctional effects on development or conditions of personality.

The set of differentiated functions of capitalist state corresponds to a structure differentiated in parts performing one or more of these functions or functioning for coordination of the diverse state activities. The centralization of information and administration in regard to the differentiated parts reflect again this functional and structural differentiation of state.

Learning Capacity of State. The elaborate repertoire of the modern capitalist state for the domination and control of crises results from functional and structural differentiation, reflecting the history of learning processes to maintain the class domination by the capitalist state and by its elites against the threat from the proletariat – a history extraordinarily rich and nationally diverse. Nevertheless, today and in the future some common specific properties characterize the control processes of crisis by highly developed capitalist states.

(1) The functional and structural differentiation of the capitalist state is improving its capacity to control crisis in a multi-stable manner, that is political crises no longer appear as those of the *whole* state but rather – as crises or conflicts in one or more of its parts – in parliamentary democracies for instance as a crisis of a government's coalition, or as a crisis of a party split by divergent fractions, etc. The military and bureaucratic subsystems, the essential structural parts for performing the primary function, remain intact. Regarded in a cybernetic sense, the state system becomes more and more capable of maintaining the stability of the whole system by enlarging the tolerance levels for instabilities induced by disturbances from the environment in specific subsystems. Historically, this capacity of the state is based on achievements by the bourgeois revolutions such as formal democracy, division of power, etc. Marx, in the 'Eighteenth Brumaire', describes the interesting configuration in crisis management, by which the socio-economic class relations in France could be maintained by the 'division of labour' between the executive power of Bonaparte and the parliamentary power of the bourgeoisie. The crisis of parliament became a functional prerequisite for strengthening the executive power and for preparing the coup d'état by Bonaparte. That is, the crisis in specific parts of the state system – in times of extreme emergencies or of maximal entropy of crisis[17] even of the state as a whole – becomes eufunctional for the protection of the overall socio-economic interest of the dominant bourgeois class (Marx and Engels, 1973).

(2) A further property characterizing these learning processes and development of state capabilities is based on the change from passive to more active ways of performing its functions by using elements of the scientific-technological revolution for the consolidation of power relations and domination. As a consequence the goal functions and means functions of the state in defining the goals and means of attaining them are performed not only in a compensative mode by negative feedback but also by feed-forward mechanisms which facilitate the taking of preventive measures against anticipated or coming crises.

The types of learning capacity[18] refer, in different degrees, to all categories of domination, i.e. also to the state's control of the crisis consciousness of the population in capitalist countries, the form of domination considered in the following discussion.

The Politics of False Consciousness – the Ideological State Function

The strategic relevance of the ideological state function results from the power of forms and contents of consciousness, by which behaviour patterns can be controlled, given the power of the context of relation sets, by which they are determined objectively.

The conscious-mental production defined as an integral part of superstructure implies primarily the three categories of consciousness: culture, ideology and class consciousness. These categories functionally mediate specific relations and behaviour patterns both among the actors themselves and in relation to their artificial or natural environment. On the one hand, the universe of relation sets and behaviour patterns, directly or indirectly realized or experienced, are in a passive and active way *reproduced* by these consciousness factors constituting the main dimension of collective and individual memories in a given society. On the other hand, the relation sets and the behaviour patterns are again *modified* by the specific forms and contents of these consciousness factors.

Culture is regarded as the socio-historical consciousness space of a specific society, belonging to *all of its members* and given by corresponding social-historical level of praxis. Simultaneously this consciousness space constitutes the space of possible ideologies which mediate different reference systems for the interpretation of environment for *specific collectives* of society. Finally, ideologies themselves – within the given cultural consciousness space – again determine characteristic spaces specifying the chances for certain forms of class consciousness which specific socio-economic or political classes adopt and which mediate their different objective interests as consciously contrasted, subjective interests.

Essential to a theory of state and politics is the fact that consciousness factors, by influencing each other, control also their truth values reciprocally. Ideologies as forms of false consciousness, for instance, mediate forms of false or distorted class consciousness too. Through the performance of ideological functions, the production and diffusion of ideological items, the state intervenes in the formation processes of class consciousness — the development of the class-for-itself.

Within a given cultural consciousness space we can discriminate different types of false consciousness. First, ideologies produce non-consciousness with respect to specific domains of reality — for instance religious myths and ideologies following the establishment of the modern cultural consciousness space by the scientific-technological revolution. Secondly, ideologies can imply the *inversion* of originals and copies in cognitive acts of reality — for instance the effects of *camera obscura* implied by idealistic conceptions, criticized by Marx and Engels. It is evident that within this inverted sphere of consciousness many relatively true cognitions are possible, still excluded by the first form of false consciousness. Thirdly, ideologies can mediate relations between *false originals and copies* in cognitive acts of reality. Ideologies can finally evoke *nivellation-* or *precision-errors* in the cognitive adoption of reality, that is prejudice in the sense of cognitive 'over-generalizing' as opposed to 'over-differentiating', which are caused by deviation from the optimal point in combining holistic with partial perspectives in cognitive acts of reality. In the course of history by transcending these (and other) stages of false consciousness, science coincides progressively with ideology — making possible the consideration of ideologies as factors mediating right consciousness.

The capitalist state needs to mask its particularism as universal interest forms of false consciousness or non-consciousness itself. But the politics of false consciousness and its connection to the context of other state functions have qualitively changed. The conditions of this change are based on objective factors, in sum defining and reinforcing the objective phenomenon of the relative under-determination of class consciousness among the Western working classes. On these objective conditions the readaption process of the state's ideological function is also founded, on the one hand by modifying historical ideological strategies, and on the other by learning newer ideological strategies for the control of potential or actual crises in society.

International Aristocracy of Western Working Class and State Strategies of Ideological 'Superation'. The first form of relative, objective under-

determination of consciousness of the working class in the highly
developed capitalist countries is based on the established — primarily
consumptive — aristocracy of the Western working classes relative to
the pauperized masses of the Third World. Historically, this aristocracy
emerges, both as a result and as a condition, of the course of the
transition from the protective to the promotive ways in performing the
primary function by the state. Thus, the aristocracy resulting from the
imperialist or neo-colonialist phase of capitalism is at the same time
reinforcing it primarily by the use of the corresponding *ideological
potential.* This change of the primary function of the capitalist state
creates the structural opportunity to penetrate the consciousness of the
aristocratic strata of working class with social-chauvinist elements and
ideologies. Lenin (1970) identified these strata of the working class as
'... imperialist privilege-corrupted upper strata of working class in
America and Europe'. Working-class aristocratic structures and ideologies claiming *the unity of national interest,* which are utilized by the
state, mutually reinforce each other. This ideological strategy creates
false consciousness by nivellation of domestic class antagonism, while
simultaneously contrasting the international differences of the working
class.[19] The imperialist phase of the capitalist state still remains in
symbiotic connection with latent or manifest elements of this unity-
ideology which, in borderline cases reinforced by racist items, culminates in the populist or fascist idea of fatherland.

This ideological strategy is referred to as 'superation', that is, the
cognitive perception of objective contradictions or antagonisms between economic or political classes are superated by ideological items
negating them. Ideological superation transfers the diversion outside of
the internal crisis potentials based on contradictory class relations, that
is, *exteriorization* of aggression. Superation is the ideological prerequisite for the imperialist war, but in some sense for the defensive
antifascist war too. The last is the paradoxical fact of internal fascism
evoked by the struggle against fascism: all Western nations engaged in
the Second World War, in the defensive antifascist front, are still
characterized by memory traces of this historical phase of ideological
superation of the domestic class antagonisms. In the Western nations'
alliance the Second World War meant a phase of ideological and
material *stasis,* interrupting the prewar class struggles, and transcending
them by ideologies of national unity. Since the Second World War,

reactivation strategies of nationalistic-superative ideologies are still
founded on this memory strata. Primarily during the time of the Cold
War, they were used in intimate connection with anticommunist
themes.

Domestic Aristocracies of Strata within the Western Working Class and
State Strategy of Ideological 'Contamination'. The second form of
relative under-determination of consciousness among the Western working classes is based on aristocracies of strata within them. The first and
the second form of objective under-determination favour the susceptibility of the Western working class, or of parts of it, to forms of false
consciousness in a *cumulative* manner. Ties to actual forms of coincidence of working class interests with national interests exist primarily in those countries which import cheap labour. Therefore, the
international division of prosperity among the working class becomes
more visible in the nation itself and therefore the international and
domestic aristocracy effect culminates. According to this, we find in
the highly developed capitalist countries with high proportions and
concentrations of immigrant labour aggravated conflicts between
domestic and foreign workers as ideological inverted enemies: these
collisions are intensified and exploited in an agitating way by neo-
nationalist populist or neo-fascist movements. Examples of this are the
populist-fascist movements in Great Britain, in an earlier stage ideologically headed by Powell, later taken over by the National Front; in
France the Ordre Nouveau; and in Switzerland mainly the Schwarzen-
bach movement launching several referenda against the 'Ueberfremdung
von Volk und Heimat', supported primarily by strata of the working
class.

Seen historically, the *domestic* aristocracies are connected with the
conjunctural prosperity and the development of other state functions,
primarily the infrastructural and redistributive activities by state before
and after the Second World War. In particular, the phenomenon of
limited mobility for certain substrata within the working class is promoted. For instance, the limited mobility operates as differential distribution of education between generations, at the same time mediating
differentially professional mobility, consumption, and prestige.

But, also relative to other aspects of life situation, the phenomenon
of relative deprivation evokes or reinforces already existing differences

among the traditional working class. The distribution of goods categories, favouring differentially limited mobility within the classes, promotes at the same time, objectively, the strategy of ideological diversion. In this way the character of *state multi-regulation* of potential crises becomes obvious. The intended effects of selective distribution of goods are – qua selectivity – simultaneously adapted to the prerequisite of ideological state function which intends to blockade or to render more difficult the formation, for itself, of a class totality. This process relies upon as well as contributes to the division of a homogeneous trade-unionized working class as class totality and splits it in particular interest groups. Consequently income struggles degenerate often into struggles about income- or consumption-privileges of only substrata within the class, favouring the splitting of political class totality.[20]

Class consciousness contains ideally the synthesis of the universal interest of the class vis-à-vis society (consciousness of its historical mission) with the particular interests and needs vis-à-vis the concrete existential conditions of members. Both processes – the international and the domestic aristocratic effects – and the connected cumulative under-determination of consciousness favour the ideological splitting of universal and particular interest components.

This is a further form of false or distorted consciousness among Western working classes. The susceptibility of parts of the Western working class to reformist-pragmatic ideologies – and to the neo-liberal substitutional ideology since the Cold War, the ideology of convergence – primarily results from this ideological deficit.

The domestic aristocracy – or relativity of deprivation – forms the objective opportunity structure for the strategy of ideological contamination. Contamination has to be differentiated from the strategy of ideological superation. It is based on the contamination of left-liberal elements with right revisionisms of the socialist high ideology in order to build up a reform ideology of the middle which neutralizes or moderates crises. Contamination tries to replace the high-ideological form of conflict between the contradictory high ideologies, that is, liberalism vis-à-vis socialism.

High-ideological, superative and contaminative ideological strategies form therefore the main patterns of the ideological repertoire of capitalist states vis-à-vis crises. These types of ideological state activities can occur successively according to a step-by-step function of substitution. During the phases the crises become more intensive or cumulative; the strategy of ideological superation can be *preventively* utilized. It serves as a strategy in borderline cases when high-ideological or contaminative strategies lose their efficiency. Ideological superation dominates within the ideological repertoires of crisis management, emerging when legitimacy deficits of the state — caused by the breakdown of the other ideological strategies — are to be covered up or the 'exceptional state' or the reduction of welfare functions have to be ideologically justified.

Changes of the Relation between Society and State as Sources of False Consciousness on the State. The change of state functions becomes itself a source for a third form of relative under-determination of consciousness facilitating false forms in the sense of distorted or inverted perceptions of the real state functions: illusions about the welfare function on the one hand and illusions about state socialism on the other. Both produce not only an ideological effect of masking the private mode of production but also of its protection and promotion by the primary functions of state.

By the quantitative and qualitative increase of secondary functions, especially of welfare activities, the state seems to be not only protecting the interests of the dominant socio-economic class, but also the protector of certain material or non-material life conditions of the working class. In other terms, the capitalist state is ideologically identified also as protector of some of its own interests, and not just as a *corrector* of costs externalized by the mode of private production. The temporary or periodic contradiction between the primary function and the secondary redistributive function, in addition, operates so that the capitalist state is forced to search for more mediated forms for combining optimally the primary state function with the redistributive and other secondary activities. Thus, *it works less as a direct agent of one specific class, than as a regulator of the class relations as a whole.* These changes of state functions facilitate — in comparison to the direct class-agency functions of state in previous history — that the welfare function becomes ideologically hypostasized as a goal function itself, while in fact remaining a means function more or less optimally adjusted to the primary goal function of the capitalist state. The susceptibility of the Western working class to welfare-state illusions is strongly reinforced by these objective changes of state functions and its utilization in ideological strategies. The welfare-state illusion itself exists again as a consistent element of the convergence ideology.

Likewise the increasing mediation of private production and appropriation or distribution of products by state implies an objective loss of visibility of the conditions and effects of private production and appropriation — facilitating the susceptibility to illusions about state socialism. For instance, the conjunctural crises — or generally the spontaneity factors of private production — seem to be crises within *parts* of the state or of the state itself, as contradictions crystallized within and between specific state activities between policies of anti-inflation and of full employment, policies of expenditure and of accumulation by taxes, policies of social welfare and of conjunctural prosperity, etc.

While the welfare-state illusions evoke an increase in the state's legitimacy and of loyalty vis-à-vis the state among working-class supporters, the state-socialism illusions cause the reverse.[21] The experiences of alienation objectively conditioned by private exploitation appear — refracted in the prism of this ideology — purely mediated by the state and its bureaucracy. Therein is also rooted the aversion against the state — a strong ideological element of populism. But the quintessence remains, that both forms of false consciousness about the state among its supporters are creating a *cumulative* ideological effect of masking the dominating socio-economic class and power relations.[22]

Psychic-Mental Competence of Personality. Finally we have to outline a fourth form of under-determination of consciousness among the Western working class, qualitatively different from the forms of under-determination discussed above: the deformation of personality, of its psychic-mental competence, protected or promoted by the state.[23] Psychic-mental competence is understood as the total internal physic, psychic and mental capacity of the personality to engage in a conscious and rational way with the conditions — primarily the alienating conditions — of natural, artificial, social, political and cultural environment. Diverting potential crises based on class contradictions to crises and dysfunctional conflicts within personality is the latest stage of crisis regulation in the highly developed capitalist countries, qualitatively different but intimatively connected to the outlined ideological strategies. The state can play a decisive part in mediating shifts of crisis interiorization to personality. Examples for such mediations are namely the protection or promotion by state of:

(a) individualistic ideologies, for instance of types of the 'American dream ideology', which blocks collective forms of articulation and reinforces internalization processes of conflicts;

(b) the distorted or false needs primarily evoked and reinforced by passive forms of consumption implying dysfunctional effects on personality;

(c) the exposition to mass communicative stimulus overflow which transcends the personality's capacity to interpret and integrate them;

(d) the stress symptoms implied by the spontaneity of the capitalist labour market or conjunctural cycles or by critical life periods; and

(e) the unequal exposure of individuals to physical and social stresses in residential and work environments.

As a consequence of these and other processes reducing the psychic-mental competence of individuals to meet the objective conditions of alienation actively and in a conscious, rational way, they become 'alienated' from consciousness or displaced from it. That is, conflicts become internalized, instead of being solved by actively coping with the objective environmental conditions of alienation.

The stability or lack of conflict on the political level, the stagnation of revolutionary labour movements in some Western countries is in inverse proportion not only to the degree of the ideological class-domination outlined above (Wesolowski, 1967, p. 76), but also the degree of state protected deformation of personality. The latter evokes or reinforces behaviour patterns such as internal reactions, i.e. disturbances of mental health,[24] forms of abusus, suicide, etc. on the one hand, and external reactions of a particular character, i.e. conflicts between minorities, generations, groups or criminality, on the other. The aggravating property of this domination form is primarily due to the fact that disturbances of psychic-mental competence remain more irreversible than, for instance, memory traces created by ideological domination. Through the reduction of psychic-mental competence the necessary condition for reversibility, the competence for conscious action itself, becomes affected or even destroyed.

NOTES

1. The premature revolution in these countries only partially penetrated by capital is defined as a direct transition from the feudal or precapitalist phase to the phase of revolutionary change implying not only anti-colonial but also socialist contents and intentions. In most of these countries penetrated by multinational monopolies – frequently allied directly with the domestic domination-structure – capital penetration occurs less extensively (in a geographical sense) but more intensively.

2. It is evident, that this group of capitalist countries is non-homogeneous in respect not only to historical, social and cultural but also economic conditions. In particular, the US significantly deviates in its political culture and technology of domination from the other Western highly industrialized nations. The latin countries of the European south can be distinguished from the middle and northern European part of this group – not to speak of Japan as a further deviant case. The abstraction from these differences does not allow us to specify the behaviour of individual countries.

3. The following remarks are intended more to challenge than to elaborate a general frame of reference for conceptualizing the relations between state and society. That is, it serves more as a framework for systematization of possible fields of state intervention in the universe of social relations, than as a model for explaining concrete intervention processes, which we intend to discuss later.

4. We understand political system as a more general concept than 'state'. Parts of it, which remain eufunctional for the whole political system by reproducing the disequilibrated totality of the base's relation sets, represent the legal aspect including again the corresponding parties, associations, actors, etc. We have to distinguish it from the parts of the political system which are dysfunctional for the reproduction of the disequilibrated conditions and eufunctional for the readaptation to the equilibrium of a new structure of society. Intended and realized results of functions can diverge, that is intended eufunctions can in fact reinforce dysfunctions (and vice versa).

5. Hochfeld formulates it as '... functional subordination of the ideological-institutional superstructure....' to the economic base (Wesolowski, 1967).

6. By the term 'causal-functional invariance' we refer to the following three-step procedure of approaching the complex problem of relationships between base and superstructure:

(1) The statement of a correlation between the development of the base's relation sets and the development of the superstructural ones. Most work in the social and human sciences still refers to such invariances observed in history and in the development of societies or societal formations.

(2) Through further steps of analysis the simple statements of correlational interdependencies should be replaced by hypotheses about causal dependencies.

(3) Finally, through proceeding to find the functional interdependencies of such relation sets as a function of time, the dependencies as linear-causal ones are

again negated, that is we have to conceive the invariances between relation sets of base and superstructure not as simple correlations or as linear-causal dependencies, but as dialectical categories.

7. The modern history of Japan exemplifies the relative autonomy of the traditional-feudal relations in superstructure immunized and resisting the pervasion of the contradictions of the base induced by capitalist development.

8. This is pointed out by the fact that in capitalist society the technological component, that is the means of production, is losing its relative self-dynamics, still characteristic of classic capitalist societies, because of intensified central planning by the state of scientific and technological production and educational training.

9. One should distinguish between the pervasiveness of contradictions and the antagonistic or non-antagonistic quality of contradictions. The degree of pervasion means the range of basic contradictions simultaneously reflected as superstructural ones. The latter attributes relate to the type of disequilibria of a specific society; thus, in the following, implying antagonistic contradictions within semicapitalist or capitalist societies characterized by modes of private property.

10. In German the word 'behaviour' (Verhalten) derives from the same root as the word implying the static aspect, i.e. the relation sets (Verhältnisse), reflecting linguistically the link between the two aspects (Hahn, 1966).

11. This is not to re-establish a dualism between personality and society such as is found in the models of man in classic liberalism, anarchism or in more scientific form of anthropologistic or psychologistic reductionism. A comprehensive discussion of the personality issue in Marxism is given by Sève (1969).

12. Actors involved in transforming contradictions into crises are not only those objectively involved in the contradictory relations but also those subjectively involved as well in the corresponding behavior patterns. The involvement of an actor in an objective contradictory relation defines only a necessary but not sufficient condition for the actor to be a participant in such a transformation. For instance, although a member of the 'class-in-itself' objectively involved in an antagonistic class relation, an individual is not necessarily engaged in crisis-related behaviour of a quality of the 'class-for-itself'.

13. 'High pervasiveness' of the socio-economic contradiction, between labour or production by the majority and control or adoption of production by a minority, as political contradictions implies the emergence of corresponding infrastructures and/or contending forces which also politically articulate the socio-economic antagonism. Later we shall show how those mechanisms explaining why it is that the crystallization of the socio-economic contradiction as a political one has decreased since the Second World War in many of the highly developed Western countries – in spite of the fact that these nations, principally in recent times, have been confronted with many crises. The history of differentiated adaptations of the 'division of labour' in translating the socio-economic class domination into political, ideological or psychic class-domination, actively mediated or coordinated by the state is considered to be the principal cause of this fact. 'Less pervasiveness' refers to the fact that the socio-economic

contradictions have still not or have only diffusely shaped political infrastructures and/or those contending forces which articulate *this* socio-economic antagonism as a political one.

14. That the formal property of the capitalist state as a political democracy remains a secondary attribute non-operating independently for more social equalization is empirically supported by a cross national analysis of 60 Western and Third World countries (Jackman, 1974). Jackman concludes that 'political democracy exerts no significant effects (additive or non-additive) on social equality'.

15. The costs necessary for the state decrease according to the degree as its control activities refer to motivational categories of more informational than energetical character (Kossecki, 1974).

16. The three types of state activities produce categories of 'public' goods which, according to their degree of instrumentality for the promotive maintenance of primary functions by the state, become quasi-public goods. Social class position and stratification determines the objective demand of actors for categories of public goods. But, as shown empirically, political attitudes and the ideological orientation of individuals exert a relatively autonomous effect, constituting a subjective demand for such goods (Meier and Müller, 1974).

17. At such stages the development of a crisis the equilibrium of contending forces — involved objectively and subjectively in a transformation from contradictions into crisis — is labil, i.e. the possible outcomes of the crisis course are less redundant. The more redundant the latter the more stable is the equilibrium of contending forces. High lability of an equilibrium implies opportunities to transform it into a disequilibrium of contending forces, i.e. one of a coalition of actors dominates the others. Such a disequilibrium can define a new equilibrium of forces relying upon modified, more or less contradictory, social relations.

18. Formally this learning capacity perfecting the state repertoire of control strategies of crises is based on the 'principle of requisite variety' (Ashby); the greater the variety of contradictions or of latent or manifest crises in the environment of the state, the more the variety of its structural and functional elements provided for its control (primarily for maintaining optimally the primary function) has to be increased.

19. In this case, the class identity (in a conscious or psychic-emotional sense) is absorbed by the national identity. However, neither this nor, conversely, nihilism against national individuality of class identity, but only the synthesis of both class and national identity, defines the optimal linkage between the two crucial identity principles.

20. This makes rather difficult the interpretation of political contents and intentions of the recent strike movements in the highly developed Western countries.

21. This dualism reflects itself clearly in the oscillating movements of majorities in Western parliaments and governments: on a phase of emphasized state monopolist tendency follows usually a phase of increased welfare activities trying to correct the legitimation gap resulting from the former, that is, the state monopolism can only coexist with pragmatic social democratism.

22. This masking effect implies that, for instance, the environmental or

energy crises are not blamed on the real actors primarily causing it and gaining the
profits from it, but becomes ideologically related to the state – in fact trying to
correct some consequences of it. The increasing transnational crossing of large
concerns, which implies an increased autonomy vis-à-vis the particular home state
but in the same time strengthens their connection to the capitalist states as whole
system, reinforce strongly this masking effect.

23. Primarily in this domain the state intervenes frequently by non-inter-
vention. Through this form of 'activity by passivity' the modern capitalist state
violates traditional conceptions of the state function – challenging also the state
promotion of self-realization of its members – that is, postulates which have
already been articulated by the early social democratic and some of the liberal
humanistic traditions.

24. Epidemiological research concludes that the mental health among the
members of the Western lower strata is significantly lower than among members
of the higher strata – so just that class is most affected, which needs the highest
psychic-mental competence necessary for reactivating class struggle.

REFERENCES

J. Banaszkiewicz (1972), *Państwo i partia w systemie kapitalistycznym*
(Warszawa), 113.
E. Hahn (1966), 'Theoretische Aspekte der soziologischen Erkenntnis', *Deutsche
Zeitschrift für Philosophie*, 1: 27.
R. W. Jackman (1974), 'Political democracy and social equality: A comparative
analysis', *American Sociological Review*, 39: 29.
J. Kossecki (1974), Cybernetyka kultury (Warszawa), 139.
W. I. Lenin (1970), *Ausgewählte Werke*, Vol. 3 (Berlin), 707 (translated by us).
K. Marx (1974), *Grundrisse der Kritik der politischen Oekonomie* (Berlin), 31.
K. Marx and F. Engels (1973), *Werke*, Vol. 8 (Berlin), 197 (translated by us).
H. P. Meier and R. Müller (1974), 'Determinanten der Nachfrage nach öffent-
lichen Gütern', Soziologisches Institut, Universität Zürich (unpublished
paper).
L. Sève (1969), *Marxisme et Théorie de la Personalité* (Paris).
W. Wesolowski (1967), 'Marx's theory of class domination: An attempt at
systematization', in: K. Lobkowicz (ed.), *Marx and the Western World*
(London), 62.

6

SYSTEM CONTRADICTION AND POLITICAL TRANSFORMATION

Frank Parkin
Magdalen College, Oxford

1

David Lockwood has drawn attention to two related but analytically distinct types of integration in society: social integration, referring to the relationship between groups — more especially classes or strata; and system integration, referring to the degree of connectedness between institutional parts of the social order.[1] The former type of integration concerns the social relations between actors, so that the problem of order in society is posed in terms of moral or normative categories. The second type of integration directs attention to the somewhat more technical or non-normative aspects of order, concerning as it does the degree of 'fit' or compatibility between various functionally connected institutions. Both types of integration are of course central to Marx's theory of social change. For Marx, the antagonisms stemming from weaknesses in social integration (exemplified in the extreme case by class polarization) plus the weaknesses in system integration (the contradiction between the forces of production and the relations of production) are understood to be the twin mechanisms responsible for social transformation. As many critics have pointed out, the exact nature of the link between these two different processes was never

This paper first appeared in the *European Journal of Sociology* (1972), 13: 45-62. Copyright © 1972 by Frank Parkin. Reprinted by arrangement with the author.

clearly specified by Marx. But it does seem apparent that system contradiction is regarded as causally prior to the cleavage, and ultimate conflict, between classes, since it's not until these contradictions in the system become irresolvable that the stage is set for the final showdown between contending classes.

Given the importance that this notion of system contradiction occupies in Marx's whole theoretical scheme it is, as Lockwood points out, rather surprising that it should have been largely disregarded by sociologists — even by those specifically concerned with conflict models. Instead, the main preoccupation has been with class antagonism, which can in some respects be regarded as a derivative phenomenon. This is, perhaps, partly because of the difficulty in establishing clearly the "breakdown mechanisms" in different societies, including capitalism. Moreover, given the apparent ability of this particular system to survive the almost countless prophecies of imminent collapse, through crises of overproduction, the falling rate of profit, or whatever, it is understandable that sociologists should have come to regard the notion of system contradiction with some suspicion.

In this paper I try to show that the concept can be usefully employed in analysing certain aspects of the problem of order in industrial society. And there is a certain pleasing irony in the fact that it seems particularly appropriate to the understanding of state socialist societies, notwithstanding the official Marxist view that the overthrow of capitalism heralds the end of internal contradictions. The view advanced here is that the notion of system contradiction is only useful when considered in relation to certain aspects of the stratification order, and more particularly, with what could be referred to as "power equilibrium" and "elite differentiation". By power equilibrium is meant simply a high degree of congruence between the various dimensions of stratification, such that economic, social and political power follow roughly the same pattern of distribution. Power disequilibrium is said to occur where these three elements of the stratification order do not exhibit the same general profile. It may be suggested that under this condition there will typically be alternative or competing bases of elite legitimation, so giving rise to a differentiation or polarization of elites. In a nutshell my argument is that only when a society is characterized by elite differentiation do system contradictions become significant for the problem of social transformation. Where, on the other hand, the stratification order is in equilibrium, the elite structure will typically be one of uniformity, not differentiation. Under these conditions, weaknesses in system integration will not generally entail a threat to the social order.

In a sense, the whole of the scheme adopted here could be said to rest on some kind of equilibrium model; but not so much the equilibrium model derived from structural-functionalism, as that implicit in Marx's own formula. The difference is of course that the structural-functionalist approach is to treat the social system as a self-regulating mechanism operating in a timeless void. Whereas for Marx, the states of equilibrium and disequilibrium are understood as alternating processes by which societies are moved along in a sequence of historical change. One could say that, for Marx, a society becomes ripe for social transformation when the stratification order is in disequilibrium; that is, when the class which is (say) economically dominant through its control of the productive process is not the class which is politically dominant. The tensions which this imbalance generates can only be resolved by one and the same class winning mastery over all the elements of power – social, economic and political. The paradigm case is of course that of an ascendant bourgeoisie being politically subordinate to a declining aristocracy. The ideal-type bourgeois revolution can thus be seen as the mechanism which restores the stratification order to a state of equilibrium by concentrating all the dimensions of power in the hands of one social class. The next stage in the developmental sequence is then scheduled for that point in time when capitalism itself would give rise to new forms of disequilibrium which would be resolved in the same conclusive manner.

Crucial to the understanding of this whole conceptual scheme is the role of the ascendant class. For Marx, a social class only assumes dominance in society when it is the social embodiment of those institutional and material forces which define the essential character of the social system – or its "core institutional order". Thus the historical progression of societies through different stages is closely linked to the ascendance of that particular class whose members possess the qualities and attributes best fitted to cope with the newly emergent material forces and new institutional tasks.[2] In true Darwinian fashion a class dominant in one epoch is earmarked for liquidation as soon as the social forces on which its dominance rests have given way to new conditions, so preparing the ground for the ascendancy of a different class better able to respond to the new challenge. Not until a social class has reached this state of ascendancy within the framework of the old order is it able to bring about system change by assuming political mastery.

Now it is clear from all this that the successful transition from capitalism to socialism must, in terms of Marx's theory, presuppose the emergence of a class which embodies a distinctive set of social and productive relationships of a non-bourgeois kind which contain the promise of resolving the contradictions within capitalism. To use Marx's gynaecological metaphor, the embryo of the new socio-economic system must always mature in the womb of the old order. It was therefore necessary for Marx to show that embryonic forms of socialism were developing within the body of capitalism, just as bourgeois social relations and a market economy had been slowly nurtured within the old feudal order. And Marx did in fact detect two different tendencies within capitalism which he took to be early forms of the emergent productive forces which would come to replace private property relations, and so prepare the ground for the demise of the bourgeoisie. The first of these developments was the rise of the joint stock company. He saw the separation of ownership from control, and the expansion of the shareholding system, as a corrosive force at work on capitalist property relations; and although this in itself was not to be understood as social ownership in its pure form, it was a transitionary stage to this ideal.

> In stock companies the function is divorced from capital ownership, hence also labour is entirely divorced from ownership of means of production and surplus labour. This result of the ultimate development of capitalist production is a necessary transitional phase towards the reconversion of capital into the property of producers, although no longer as the private property of the individual producers, but rather as the property of associated producers, as outright social property [...].[3]

As Marx saw it, this development heralded 'the abolition of the capitalist mode of production within the capitalist mode of production itself' and could thus be understood as 'a mere phase of transition to a new form of production'.[4]

A second and parallel development was the growth of the workers' co-operative movement. For Marx, this movement brought into being a new kind of property in which 'the antithesis between labour and capital is overcome'.[5] The co-operative factory system demonstrated 'how a new mode of production naturally grows out of an old one, when the development of the material forces of production, and of the corresponding forms of social production have reached a particular stage. Without the factory system arising out of the capitalist mode of production there could have been no co-operative factories'.[6]

Here then is evidence for the kind of development that Marx was intent on discovering — a new social form arising within the shell of the old — which for him is always a precondition for the ascendancy of a new class (in this case the proletariat), the class which is the social embodiment of the emergent productive forces. It is no part of Marx's scheme to suggest that a class which has *not* reached such a position of ascendancy could effectively become the new dominant class. As Avineri has recently pointed out, the notion that the proletariat could assume power while it was still the totally subordinate class is a purely Leninist one.[7] For Lenin, the proletariat could make the revolution first and then set about creating the social and economic foundations upon which its political supremacy would rest. This is a complete reversion of Marx's priorities. For Marx, political power can only *actualize* the potential already *existing* within the society; it cannot fashion social and material realities according to some abstract formula or design. It could be argued then, that the revolution failed to bring about socialism in the Soviet Union not simply because it occurred in an economically backward society (which is the standard explanation) but because the proletariat was not the ascendant class.[8] For even if a society was economically advanced, the transition could still not properly be made while the proletariat was the totally subordinate class. Indeed given the fact that proletarian ascendancy does not appear to coincide with advanced industrialism, and that the cooperative movement and joint stock ownership no longer seem to be transitionary or embryonic forms of a new social order, then the very possibility of the successful transformation from capitalism to socialism becomes highly problematic. Expressed somewhat differently, in so far as the bourgeoisie remain the socially, economically and politically dominant class, then the stratification order is in equilibrium. And under this condition there is no internal tension that has to be resolved through radical social transformation. This point is touched upon again later when the elite structure of modern capitalism is under discussion.

II

As far as state socialist societies are concerned, the same equilibrium condition does not prevail. One could say in fact that the seizure of power created disequilibrium in the stratification order where previously there was none. Moreover, it is precisely as a result of this that weaknesses in system integration are a more distinctive feature of socialist society than of modern capitalism. Now weaknesses at the system level tend to find expression at the social level in the form of conflict between groups or collectivities; indeed these opposing groups may be even thought of as personifying conflicting system elements — that is, as social typifications of diffuse structural processes. In socialist society the key antagonisms occurring at the social level are those between the party and state bureaucracy on the one hand and the intelligentsia on the other. The power of the former rests upon their control of the political and administrative apparatus of the state, giving them effective legal guardianship of socialized property. The social power of the latter group inheres in its command of the skills, knowledge and general attributes which are held to be of central importance for the development of productive and scientific forces in modern industrial society. Examples of weaknesses in system integration, of which these conflicts are the social symptom, have received ample documentation. Probably the most familiar are those problems associated with the attempt to maximise industrial efficiency within the framework of a highly centralized political economy. The command system appears to operate quite effectively during the early stages of development, when the primary emphasis is on capital accumulation; but at more advanced stages of growth, and with the emphasis shifting to light industry and consumer goods production, the dirigist system becomes increasingly dysfunctional. It is when the crucial phase of the 'second industrial revolution' is reached that the command mechanism becomes unable to cope satisfactorily with the volume of information and detailed decisions necessary to the smooth working of the economy. The leading east German economist, Fritz Behrens, was only one among many who pointed to a 'contradiction [. . .] between the form of state direction of the economy and the content of the quickly developing economic substructure'.[9] Attempts to resolve this contradiction have raised the delicate problem of how to curtail the economic powers of the central apparatus without eroding the party's monopoly of political authority. Resistance to economic reforms has been strongest among members of the party apparatus and state administration, whose personal authority would be seriously undermined by a radical switch from plan criteria to market criteria. Seen in ideal-typical terms, the controversy over the economy is most sharply expressed in the form of conflict between the apparatchiki and the intelligentsia, respectively the main opponents and advocates of reform.[10] Czechoslovakia was an exceptional case only in the extent to which the latent but ever-present tensions between these two groups erupted into open political conflict — a showdown precipitated by the inability of the existing system to cope with economic crisis.[11]

It is not in the least fanciful to suggest that the crisis came about as a result of the forces of production coming into direct conflict with the social relations of production; in other words, that the legal and political order buttressing the command system had become a 'fetter' on the further development of productive forces. The events leading up to and culminating in the 'Prague spring' might thus be seen as a paradigm case of system contradiction leading to pressures for internal transformation in line with the classic Marxist formula. Furthermore, a latter-day Marx seeking to locate within socialist society an ascendant class closely identified with the transformation, and capable of pushing it through, would doubtless find the intelligentsia the obvious candidate for the post. It seems clear that in all socialist states the intelligentsia occupies a position of high social and material standing in the stratification hierarchy by virtue of its command over socially valued knowledge and expertise. In empirical studies of status ranking, moreover, they are invariably shown to be higher in the scale of social honour than the party bureaucrats. In a sense, then, this group is popularly regarded, and seems to regard itself, as the social embodiment of those scientific, economic and creative forces which are felt to be indispensable to the quest for modernity and social progress.[12]

However, as in some previous epochs, the ascendant class in socialist society is not the class which wields political power. Indeed, it is because political authority is concentrated elsewhere — in the hands of the party apparatus — that the stratification order can be characterized as one of disequilibrium. And this is a social condition which generates internal tensions that can only be fully resolved through a reconstitution of the different elements of power in the hands of the same social group. Seen from this angle, equilibrium could be restored by the accession to political power of the intelligentsia and the displacement of the apparatchiki. Once this was achieved (and again the events in Czechoslovakia give some indication of possible lines of development) the new men of power would be in a position to de-politicize the economy by introducing strategic shifts from plan to market.[13]

It must be emphasized here that contradictions in the productive system should be understood as a particular case of a more general condition. Dysfunctions in the economy are largely attributable to the informational blocks which a highly centralized political structure tends to set up. But the central control of economic and technical information is merely part of a more generalized political surveillance over the dissemination of knowledge in all its forms. The embargo on the free circulation of ideas and information is a strategy designed to enhance system stability through the suppression of all social knowledge which detracts from official versions of reality. The existing socialist order would in fact be seriously undermined by any relaxation of the controls on knowledge, since the party's criteria of what counts as social fact cannot often be squared with common-sense criteria. However, the party's claim to the monopoly of truth is in effect self-defeating in that it negates the regime's attempts to secure moral support and system legitimacy. Direct political censorship of knowledge and information results not in the desired conformity of outlook but in widespread scepticism or disbelief in the validity of officially blessed facts. The sanctification of revolutionary truth is especially difficult to achieve in east European societies because of the state's inability to seal off competing versions of reality which emanate from neighbouring western sources. The credibility, and hence the legitimacy, of the socialist regime is naturally most suspect in the eyes of those with greatest access to external information — the intelligentsia — although clearly the broad mass of the population does not lack opportunities to compare official claims against personal experience. Thus although the present system would be unlikely to survive under conditions of free enquiry and open debate, the regime's very attempt to suppress politically unacceptable knowledge destroys those claims to moral authority by which it seeks to rule. This contradiction seems irresolvable within the existing order and is probably of greater import for system stability than are the contradictions associated with the productive sphere. Indeed, it may be quite possible for socialist states eventually to overcome many of the dysfunctions of a command economy without dismantling the apparatus of political control, as in the case of east Germany. But this would not eradicate the basic contradiction between the political censorship of knowledge and the quest for legitimacy, as again the east German case illustrates all too vividly.

III

As previously suggested, one important reason why disequilibrium in the stratification order leads to pressures for internal change is that this is the social condition most amenable to the differentiation of elites. And part of the argument advanced here is that only when elites exhibit a high degree of differentiation are weaknesses in system integration likely to result in pressures making for system change. The reason that social disequilibrium and elite differentiation go hand in hand is that a non-crystallized stratification order provides multiple bases for elite recruitment and legitimacy. Medieval society provides the archetypal illustration of this, though a similar situation prevails in many kinds of pre-industrial society. In the standard case, the society will contain groups like the clergy, whose claims to authority rest upon sacramental knowledge; a military caste basing itself on the possession of arms and warrior skills; a merchant class deriving wealth and influence from the monopoly of trade; and so forth. Each group seeks to legitimize its power and privileges by reference to different criteria, and there are no commonly accepted criteria which could provide the basis for a uniform status order. Thus, where there are multiple bases of social legitimacy within the same society, the scene is set for the diversification of elites, all basing their claims to power on the possession of different status attributes.

In industrial society, this situation does not usually occur to the same extent. The long run tendency is for the reward structure to become closely tied to the division of labour, so that occupational and educational criteria come to provide the cornerstone of the whole edifice of stratification. Now, both socialist and capitalist versions of industrial society each contain an alternative source of elite recruitment and legitimacy to that primary one associated with the division of labour. In capitalist society, property ownership is the one obvious alternative; while in socialist society it is party office. Party elites and propertied elites might thus be said to be in a roughly similar structural situation in so far as the values which underwrite their privileged position are different from the values which guarantee the position of most other groups in society. To the extent, then, that we can detect quite distinct bases of legitimacy, the way seems clear for elite differentiation or cleavage in both types of society.

However, it would seem to be the case that this particular development is much more characteristic of socialist society than of modern capitalism. At any rate, there is no obvious counterpart in western society to the kind of elite polarization which manifested itself in Czechoslovakia, and which typically exists in a rather less dramatic form in most east European states. The question is, then, why should elite structure be more unitary under capitalism than under socialism? Two reasons may be suggested. The first is to do with purely social aspects of elite recruitment. In socialist states the cleavage between the political bureaucracy and the intelligentsia is partly a matter of social background and education. The typical member of the party apparatus, especially in the important middle levels of the hierarchy, will be of peasant stock, and with no formal education beyond the elementary level. The typical member of the white-collar elite will probably be of urban, middle class background, and of course a university graduate. These differences in social pedigree, formal education and culture tend to encourage differing perceptions of social and political problems notwithstanding the absence of sharp inequalities in the material condition of the two groups.

A second and much more important factor in elite polarization is that arising directly from functional differences between the two groups. Members of the party and state bureaucracy are dependent for their position and privileges on the centralized command system and the whole apparatus of political patronage which accompanies it. Any threat to the bureaucratic principle is a direct threat to those whose authority rests largely on the qualities of proven loyalty and obedience to political superiors. And in this category must be included the managers or directors of industrial firms, since under a command system they operate mainly as administrators — that is, middle level functionaries in the state apparatus. This immediate dependence on a higher chain of command means that the enterprise director is an entirely different animal from the manager of a capitalist firm, with altogether different tasks to perform and requiring different personal qualities to ensure success. The notion of the enterprise director as the spearhead of a potential managerial revolution is completely ludicrous in the context of socialist society; in fact the managers have generally allied themselves with the opponents of economic reform, since their political and administrative qualities would be of no use in a non-bureaucratic setting. Like most other members of the party and state administration their particular skills and attributes are highly specific to this *one particular version* of industrial society, and are not readily transferable to some alternative version. This entire group thus has an obvious stake in the preservation of the existing order, in a way that the intelligentsia does not. The latter have the kinds of skills which are at a premium in any type of modern society irrespective of its political make-up. And it is because the intelligentsia themselves are clearly aware of this fact that their virtual exclusion from political power is such a serious point of tension in the socialist system.

One further contributing factor here is that the socialist white-collar intelligentsia immersed as they are in the mainstream of European science and culture, are in a position to contrast their lot with that of their west European counterparts — who do not on the whole appear to regard themselves as subordinates to a morally, socially and culturally inferior political class. Now if it were the case that the socialist intelligentsia did *not* in fact feel some sort of collective resentment over their political subordination, then the notion of equilibrium, as here employed, would be rendered useless. For the basic assumption on which this notion rests is that a social group or class which feels itself

raised to a position of strategic social importance, will wish to acquire
political authority for itself and to remove it from those who lack the
technical and moral qualities which are felt to be the one legitimate
source of all power. If such a group *did* emerge in a society but
developed no conciousness of its own moral superiority, and was
content to have its hands kept off the levers of political power, then no
general claim could be advanced that disequilibrium in the stratification
order is a major source of tension and of potential system change. But
at any rate, as far as the particular case under review is concerned the
assumption is a plausible one, in so far as the socialist intelligentsia does
appear to have something approaching a common moral identity, and a
sense of its own latent power being held in check illegitimately.

Two factors contributing to this moral distinctiveness of the intelligentsia may be singled out for special comment. The first concerns the
quasi-colonial status of the east European countries. The intelligentsia
in most of these countries has historically acted as the standard bearer
of national consciousness. The literary and creative elements in particular have played a key role in preserving the sense of nationhood and
cultural unity during periods of foreign domination and shifting
political boundaries. There is perhaps more than a grain of truth in the
elitist view that under these critical conditions the intelligentsia *is* the
embodiment of nationhood and the watchdog of cultural and moral
unity. The present fact of Soviet domination throughout eastern
Europe ensures that the intelligentsia will continue to act as guardians
of national identity within the limits imposed by political surveillance
and official displeasure. Moreover, the role and standing of the intelligentsia contrast markedly with that of the political bureaucracy, who
are readily identified with the Soviet regime and whose very survival is
guaranteed largely by the presence or threatened appearance of com-
radely tanks from the East. Thus it is not merely the intelligentsia's
claim to functional importance which encourages a moral bond, but
their symbolic role as guardians of national consciousness and the
figureheads of independence.[14]

A second factor reinforcing this same tendency concerns the role of
conflict as a unifying social force. Collective identity of a class or
political kind emerges most strongly among members of a nominal
group which is caught up in a process of continuing conflict with some
other clearly demarcated social group. In the absence of such ongoing

conflict the potentialities inherent in purely formal or structural similarities do not generally transcend the latency stage. A striking difference between the professional middle classes of capitalist society and
their socialist counterparts in this respect is that the former are not
confronted by powerful and clearly definable opponents analogous to
the communist party bureaucracy. It is doubtless partly on account of
this that the western members of what Galbraith has dubbed the
'educational and scientific estate' significantly lack that sense of a
shared moral identity implied by the self-designation 'intelligentsia'. In
other words it is the close-knit and politically combative nature of the
hegemonic party itself which helps to account for the special character
of the socialist intelligentsia. It is thus on the basis of this combination
of social, functional and moral differences between the two groups that
one can describe the elite structure of socialist society as highly differentiated or polarized.

The contrast with modern capitalist society is instructive. Elites in
this system have a much greater degree of uniformity, both in social
and functional terms. In the first place, those recruited to elite positions are drawn from a far more restricted social circle than are their
socialist counterparts. Upward mobility into these positions occurs on
such a minor scale that it can always be accompanied by an intensive
programme of assimilation into elite culture. The effect of all this is to
preserve a remarkable degree of social homogeneity among those who
staff positions of power and privilege in western society. Secondly, and
more importantly, there is no functional separation between different
elite groupings, arising from different principles of elite recruitment and
legitimacy. As already acknowledged, there are two distinct sets of
principles which serve to underwrite privileged positions in capitalist
society; one associated with occupational achievement, and the other
with private property. The crucial point is, though, that these two sets
of legitimating principles do not give rise to separate and discrete
groupings, one based solely on wealth and the other on the division of
labour. A key characteristic of almost any given elite group in capitalist
society is that it will have a social mix exemplifying both sets of
principles. Political leadership for example is not the sole prerogative of
men of property, nor is the industrial elite comprised only of men of
qualifications — or vice versa. In fact it is highly artificial to attempt to
draw sharp distinctions between a propertied bourgeoisie on the one

hand and a professionally qualified middle class on the other. To begin with, those who inherit family wealth no longer constitute anything resembling a leisure class. Typically, those born into wealth will now use it to secure for themselves or their children educational privileges designed to ensure equally privileged entry into one of the professions. This is one way in which fusion has taken place between the two different bases of reward. The other way is through the opportunities available to the professionally qualified to become property owners themselves. The most striking instance of this is the case of industrial managers and executives becoming major shareholders in the companies they control. But share ownership is becoming increasingly common among the professional middle classes generally, as indicated by the rapid growth of unit trusts. The two parallel developments then, have forestalled the emergence of two clearly demarcated elites, each seeking to establish legitimacy by reference to mutually exclusive principles of status and reward. When those born to wealth are gainfully employed, and the professionally skilled have access to unearned rewards, then property and qualifications can be accepted as complementary bases of privilege and not as antagonistic principles. Those who insist that the distinction between ownership and non-ownership of property is still the major source of cleavage in the stratification order of capitalist society appear not to have grasped the significance of current developments.

One signal indication of the extent of elite fusion is the common allegiance of both propertied and qualified groups to the same political symbols and bourgeois parties. To be sure, the professional middle classes have become fully integrated into the ruling order not simply through their influence on the party system but, more tellingly, through their ability to dominate a power structure based on pluralism. Bourgeois democracy is in fact a system which is highly responsive to the demands of an educated middle class in so far as it ensures greatest political leverage to those who command the most privileged positions in the marketplace. This fact that western members of the educational and scientific estate have become so thoroughly assimilated into the power structure is, as hinted at above, one important reason for the lack of that sense of moral and social distinctiveness which is the hallmark of an intelligentsia.

The claim that modern capitalism has a unitary elite structure seems to have an important bearing on the whole problem of system contradiction and its relation to internal change. In brief, it may be suggested that system contradictions are most likely to generate pressures for change when elites are polarized, so that the unitary nature of elites under capitalism would give it rather more stability than could be predicted from the theory of system-crisis taken on its own. One reason for this is that a unified elite is able to respond more effectively to potential threats to the system. They can usually introduce ameliorative measures which avert or stave off impending crisis without dismantling the system itself in any serious way. A polarized elite, on the other hand, is much less responsive to the threat of crisis mainly because any adaptations will tend to bring advantages to one group and disadvantages to the other. Consider, for example, the readiness and facility with which capitalist society adopted Keynesian economic reforms, thereby counteracting the tendencies towards cyclical crisis – a move which among other things converted unemployment from a potential political threat to a 'social problem'. Contrast this adaptability with the relative inability of socialist states to implement the economic reforms designed to overcome their internal contradictions. Why, we may ask, was Keynes acceptable but not Liberman? The answer is that Libermanism threatens to alter the balance of authority between the political bureaucracy and the white-collar intelligentsia; whereas the interests of elites under capitalism are not sufficiently differentiated for Keynesianism to be construed in politically divisive terms. The notion of system contradiction must thus be set against the background of elite structure when assessing the potential for system change. This is a recommendation which is also implied in the Marxist notion that 'a split in the ruling class' is a necessary precondition of radical social transformation. And on this score the survival value of capitalism should perhaps be rated somewhat higher than the proponents of all the various crisis theories would encourage one to expect.

IV

Finally, then, we may turn to the question of whether the elites in socialist states are likely to become less polarized and to move towards a more unitary structure. Predictions that such a development must inevitably occur are frequently met with in the literature on Soviet systems. The argument is that the political bureaucracy cannot effectively control society if its own functionaries are less well equipped technically than members of the intelligentsia. Therefore the tendency will be for the party to ensure that new recruits to the bureaucracy will be men with the same kind of education and training as the intelligentsia. The end result of this process is that the apparatchicki will be virtually indistinguishable from the white-collar specialists; the two groups will have become fused even though the system of centralized command will remain more or less intact. Now there certainly is evidence that leaders of the bureaucracy have become concerned about the relatively low technical standards of the men who staff the apparatus, and that efforts are continually being made to improve these standards. The dilemma facing the leadership, however, is that any devaluation of political criteria in favour of technical criteria carries with it the risk of secularizing the party. If the party apparatus came to be controlled exclusively by men more noted for their paper qualifications than for their ideological loyalty, then this would be tantamount to ultimate political victory for the white-collar intelligentsia. One reason why the present political leadership would probably resist such a development is that a transfer of power of this kind would be likely to undermine the party's total domination of society. The *raison d'être* of the hegemonic party is to preserve political control in the hands of a social group which could not legitimate its power and privileges by reference to the same criteria which govern the distribution of rewards among the population at large. The skills and attributes of the political bureaucracy are useful mainly for the maintenance of the apparatus which is its own creation; they are not skills which are intrinsically necessary to an industrial society. This is perhaps another way of saying that the political bureaucracy cannot be regarded as the ascendant class within its own society. And where the political class is not also the ascendant class, its survival can only be guaranteed by a hegemonic party exercising total dominion over men and ideas. The tight censorship upon the circulation of knowledge and creative ideas is indicative of a ruling class which is uncertain of its own legitimacy, and for whom even poetry can be construed as a potential threat to political survival.

A political class which is also the ascendant class has much less need to police the thoughts and activities of subordinate groups. The European bourgeoisie, for example, has generally regarded itself as politically secure and as having a 'natural' command of all the centres of power. This confidence in its own legitimacy was a precondition for the flowering of bourgeois liberal ideology, with its institutionalized support for civil liberties, including formal rights of political dissent and the free circulation of knowledge. The granting of such rights is felt to be possible only because no other class or group in the society is seen as a serious natural contender for political power. In this situation, the coercive machinery of the state can usually be kept in the background of social life, as a means of last resort, rather than as an instrument of day to day political survival.

What all this suggests, then, is that if the communist party apparatus was to undergo a process of what Weber would call 'usurpation' by the white-collar intelligentsia, the very rationale of a hegemonic party would be thrown into question. For once the ascendant class had become the political class, it would have no obvious need to protect itself by the strategy of total surveillance and the control of knowledge. It seems unlikely however that the present party leadership is unaware of the possible consequences of secularization. And unless one believes that ideology has no bearing on men's actions, it is difficult to envisage the leadership allowing the principles of recruitment to be changed in such a way as might weaken the party's grip on society – thereby, as they perceive it, putting at risk the future of communism.[15]

As long as the attainment of the party's historic mission is felt to depend on men with distinctive attributes of loyalty and obedience, then the party apparatus is likely to continue to choose its own successors with care. And men whose primary commitment is to the political bureaucracy, whose rewards and privileges, authority and influence are dependent on this commitment are, by this very fact, a clearly demarcated social group, whatever purely technical qualities they may have in common with other men. It is this functional difference between the bureaucracy and the intelligentsia which lies at the root of the cleavage between the two elites, and which mere improvement in the former's technical qualities will not eradicate.

V

In summary, this has been an attempt to show that Marx's concept of system contradiction can be usefully employed in the comparative analysis of industrial societies. The proviso entered here was that system contradictions have to be understood in relation to certain aspects of the stratification order — and more particularly to elite structure and the distribution of power. It was argued that socialist society is characterized by disequilibrium in the stratification order — a condition stemming from the fact that the seizure of power was carried out in the name of a class which was totally subordinate in society. The effect of this was to put political power in the hands of bureaucratic class, rather than an ascendant class, so creating a cleavage at the apex of the social system. This cleavage in the elite structure tends to exacerbate tensions arising from weaknesses in system integration, and makes adaptations to system deficiencies difficult to accomplish.

This situation was contrasted with that of modern capitalism, a society in which power in all its dimensions is monopolized by the same class. The unification of elites that this condition entails, means that the dominant class is usually able to respond effectively to potential system crisis.[16] At the same time, this does not permit one to dogmatize about the political invulnerability of modern capitalism. The seizure of power must always be accepted as an empirical possibility; but any judgement on the likelihood of this event, and of the kind of system that would result from it, may ultimately depend on whether one accepts the Leninist or Marxist view of the political capacities of a totally subordinate class.

NOTES AND REFERENCES

1. David Lockwood, Social Integration and System Integration, in: George K. Zollschan and Walter Hirsch (eds), *Explorations in Social Change* (London: Routledge, 1964).

2. One must here surely agree with Lockwood that 'there is nothing meta-physical about the general notion of social relationships being somehow implicit in a given set of material conditions' (Lockwood, op. cit. p. 251).
3. *Capital* (Moscow 1961), III, p. 428.
4. *Capital*, III, p. 429.
5. *Capital*, III, p. 431.
6. Loc. cit.
7. Shlomo Avineri, *The Social and Political Thought of Karl Marx* (Cambridge 1968), pp. 181-182.
8. Cf. Plekhanov's prediction that the premature seizure of power in the name of the proletariat would result in a system of "Peruvian tutelage".
9. Cited by Thomas A. Baylis, 'The New Economic System: The Role of the Technocrats in the DDR', *Survey*, LXI (1966), p. 141.
10. The struggles over economic reform cannot be understood in terms of the clear-cut categories of a morality play. Western social scientists tend to explain opposition to the reforms solely in terms of the bureaucrats' defence of their own power and privileges, whereas the advocates of reform are seen merely to be acting in the national interest. The situation is more complex. *Both* groups invoke notions of the public good which also conceal claims to power.
11. Initially the most advanced state in the socialist bloc, Czechoslovakia had by 1963 become 'the only industrial country in the entire world to register a decrease in industrial output, national income and real wages'. Harry G. Schaffer, Czechoslovakia's New Economic Model, in: George R. Feiwel (ed.), *New Currents in Soviet-Type Economics* (Scranton 1968), p. 466.
12. For a trenchant affirmation of this view see the analysis of modern society produced by the Czech Academy of Arts and Sciences under the editorship of Radovan Richta, *Civilization at the Crossroads: Social and Human Implications of the Scientific and Technological Revolution* (Prague 1967).
13. Cf. Ota Sik, *Plan and Market under Socialism* (Prague 1966).
14. While the use of the blanket term 'intelligentsia' does not of course imply a completely homogeneous group it is probably misleading to insist upon drawing sharp internal distinctions – e.g. between scientific and creative categories. In critical situations such distinctions appear wholly artificial. It is instructive to note that even in the Soviet Union political protest against the trial and imprisonment of dissident writers has not been confined to the literary intelligentsia but has included many members of the scientific and technical elite. For documentation on this point see the detailed lists of signatories to protest petitions reproduced in *Problems of Communism*, XVII (1968), pp. 39-73.
15. Even in east Germany, where technical expertise and political authority are especially closely linked, there is a clear separation of the two spheres at the apex of power. As Baylis's study shows, the technical specialists control the Council of Ministers, but the apparatchiki still dominate the Politburo. "The peculiar division of labour between the 'political' Politburo and the 'economic' Council of Ministers may be seen as reflecting the present unstable equilibrium of east German politics". Moreover, in critical situations, "the apparatchiki are in a position to enforce political requirements at the expense of economic ones [. . .]"

(Baylis, op. cit. p. 151).

16. Bauman's view that capitalist states in the pre-welfare period were inherently vulnerable to revolutionary seizure seems to be based more on predictions of collapse than on the event itself (Zygmunt Bauman, Social Dissent in the East-European Political System, *Europ. Journ. Sociol.*, XII (1971), 25-51. The European historical record contains in fact remarkably few instances of the successful overthrow of capitalism. The Soviet Union and Yugoslavia provide the only examples of revolutionary transformation from capitalism to socialism, and in both cases the *ancien régime* was already in a state of imminent collapse as a result of war.

By contrast, the brief post-war history of eastern Europe suggests that socialist states are considerably more vulnerable to the threat of internal dissolution. The survival of most of these states in their present form is guaranteed mainly by the authority of an external power. The typical European bourgeois state, on the other hand, has been required to accommodate to internal pressures in order to preserve its stability, since, with few exceptions, it has been unable to summon the aid of a greater sovereign power when threatened by internal revolt. Thus any proper assessment of the comparative stability of the two systems requires us to "think away" the Red Army when judging the viability of the ideal-typical socialist state.

7

STABILITY OF STATIST REGIMES: INDUSTRIALIZATION AND INSTITUTIONALIZATION

Russell Hardin
University of Maryland

At the end of the Second World War Communist governments came to power in many nations of Eastern Europe including even a part of old Germany. More than a quarter century later, Western scholars still commonly claim that it is only the Soviet army which keeps those governments in power, that left to their own devices they would prove to be highly unstable.

As Parkin (1972) acknowledges, such a claim is undemonstrable so long as there is a strong hint that the Soviet army might intervene in support of those governments. Nevertheless, he presents a sophisticated argument for why we should believe that the present governments of Eastern Europe are unstable. I wish to present a contrary argument for why we should suspect that those and many other relatively young governments are likely to be quite stable. In general, the felicitous coincidence of demographic and historical change can provide statist regimes with extraordinary opportunities to institutionalize themselves – if they can stay in power and expand economically through a period of rapid demographic growth ending in a relatively stable population, as indeed most of the regimes of Eastern Europe and several other nations have done.

The elements of the argument are as follows. In the absence of external interference, the clue to stability for a statist regime in an industrial state is the state bureaucracy, whose personnel comprise a large percentage (sometimes a majority) of what Dahrendorf (1959) calls the 'service class'. The loyalties of these personnel will be substantially influenced by the regime which inducts them into service. If a statist regime, which expands the state bureaucracy relative to the total workforce, is in power during a decade or two of rapid growth in the size of the non-agricultural workforce, it will have inducted the overwhelming majority of all state bureaucrats into service. If rapid demographic growth has then ended, the costs of altering the loyalties of the bureaucracy to suit a new regime thereafter will be enormously higher.

The first two elements of this argument are clearly subject to dispute, and I will defend them at some length below. The third element is a simple algebraic relationship whose validity is clear. The strength of the final element depends on the validity of the others. The whole chain is undoubtedly too neat to be simply true, and in the argument for its truth below some of its neatness will be lost. In particular, there are sources of conflict within the state bureaucracies — especially conflict between preservation of the bureaucratic organizations and regimes and pursuance of other values. However, such conflicts are likely to be too diverse to define an efficacious political movement. To turn Jane Austen's characterization of woman around, the parties to these conflicts will be too diffuse, not strong and concise enough for a political opposition.

THE BUREAUCRATIC, OR SERVICE, CLASS

Parkin (1972) bases his conclusions about the instability of the Eastern European regimes on what he takes to be the importance of the intelligentsia and what he expects their commitments to be. The argument here is similar, at least in structure. However, it is based on what seems to me to be the much greater importance and likely commitments of that entire class which Dahrendorf (1959, pp. 93-96; 1967, pp. 310-18) and Renner call the 'service class', to which the majority of the intelligentsia belong.

Parkin and Dahrendorf are both concerned to revise Marx's analysis of classes to fit the conditions of contemporary industrial states. Dahrendorf (1959, pp. 36-71, 117-54, and in summary, 136-41) argues that it is not simple ownership of property which is necessarily important, but rather the means of controlling the use of the property. 'A theory of class based on the division of society into owners and nonowners of means of production loses its analytical value as soon as legal ownership and factual control are separated' (p. 136). Therefore, Dahrendorf has 'derived classes from positions in associations co-ordinated by authority and defined them by the "characteristic" of participation in or exclusion from the exercise of authority' (p. 151). And he contends that, 'In order to introduce change into bureau-cratized social organizations, one has to convince, if not to transform, the service class first', i.e. those who exercise authority in those organizations (Dahrendorf 1967, p. 315).

To ascertain the membership of the service class in a nation, we would need occupational data which indicated authority relationships. For nations whose employment statistics are reported according to, or are readily translated into, the International Standard Classification of Occupations (ISCO), it is at least possible to isolate 'professional, technical and related workers' (major group 0 in ISCO), and 'administrative, executive and managerial workers' (major group 1). The percentages of the whole workforces in these occupations were near 11 percent for many industrial nations at their censuses nearest 1960. In increasing order the proportions for the following nations ranged from nearly 10 to slightly over 12 percent: Denmark, the Soviet Union, West Germany, Belgium, Norway, Sweden, the United Kingdom, France, and the Netherlands. For Canada and Israel the proportion was about 16 percent; for the United States, 19 percent (OECD 1971, p. 101). Comparable data are not available for East Germany, economically the most advanced Communist state, but it must rank fairly high in this list. The East German intelligentsia numbered nearly 7 percent of the workforce in the 1964 census. Since then, the 'Hoch- und Fachschul-kader' of university and technical institute graduates have replaced the 'Intelligenz' in official statistics, and they were up to about 11 percent of the socialized workforce by 1970 (*SJDDR* 1970, p. 66). Presumably almost all of these would be included in ISCO major groups 0 and 1, which would additionally include many persons without higher education.

Clearly an important difference between a statist regime and a typical western government is that the former may be the technical employer of the overwhelming majority of its nation's service class, whereas the latter will employ substantially fewer than half. Hence, the former can deliberately mold the outlook of those in authority in more or less the whole range of significant social organizations.

INSTITUTIONALIZATION AND
CONFLICT

Survey data such as those in Almond and Verba (1963) frequently yield mean opinions across society. Such means do not take into account the greater structural relevance of some people's opinions over those of others. For example, 'the average level of popular commitment to democratic values presumably did not change substantially in Italy between 1944 and 1947, but the commitment of the Italian government did change quite radically. Arguments about political culture notwithstanding, it would seem that the latter consideration is more important than the former in explaining much of the change in Italian politics over the past generation. More generally we can say that a 'value will have more effect in a society, the higher the correlation between power and commitment to the value in that society' (Stinchcombe 1968, p. 183). Or more narrowly, 'it is logical to define the degree of institutionalization of value' within an organization as 'the correlation between commitment to that value and power', or rank, within the organization (p. 183).

A radical change in the values institutionalized within an organization involves either a change in the commitments of relevant personnel or an exchange of those personnel. A regime bent on political change in a nation must institutionalize new values in many old organizations, as well as perhaps institutionalize new organizations of social control. Changes such as those which occurred in Eastern Europe after the

Second World War required nearly exhaustive exchanges of the most powerful personnel in the most important social organizations.

Among the most important of the values to be more or less institutionalized within an organization is the organization itself *as* a value. Indeed, this is the central concern of Selznick (1957), from whom Stinchcombe's notion (above) of institutionalization is derived. Selznick uses the word in two senses:

(1) the institutionalization of values *in* an organization (pp. 60, 152-53), and

(2) the institutionalization of an organization *as* a value (pp. 5-22 and passim).

He does not explicitly distinguish the two senses, perhaps because he is principally interested in the second of these, with the notion of the organization 'as a social institution' (p. 6). This notion takes cognizance of the historical and social context of the organization which has been institutionalized, i.e. infused with value. In this sense,

> Institutionalization is a *process* [which] happens to an organization over time, reflecting the organization's own distinctive history, the people who have been in it, the groups it embodies and the vested interests they have created, and the way it has adapted to its environment (p. 16).

Eventually, the value of *the organization itself* can come to be correlated with power within an organization, and hence be as highly institutionalized as any other of the organization's values.

Institutionalization of a multiplicity of values within an organization raises the possibility of conflict among them. The literature on political parties is littered with discussions of the dilemma sometimes engendered by the simultaneous desires to gain office and to support particular policies. The history of enduring labor unions is often written as the history of a success of organization followed by a loss of ideals. In his study of the TVA, Selznick analyzes a similar devolution. He argues that in the TVA's efforts to guarantee its survival, it sought the support of a constituency whose subsequent participation in the TVA's 'grass roots' administration 'resulted in a serious weakening of the TVA's capacity to be a firstline, committed conservation agency' (Selznick 1966, p. xii).

> The leadership, by the very nature of its position is committed to two conflicting goals: if it ignores the need for participation, the goal of co-

operation may be jeopardized; if participation is allowed to go too far, the
continuity of leadership and policy may be threatened (p. 261).

One need only discover that the TVA is now one of the world's largest
consumers of strip-mined coal to know how severely that model of
idealistic democracy has compromised between its goals. Moore's
history of the Bolsheviks delineates a similar compromise at a national
level: the survival of the party meant the abrogation of many of the
goals, especially freedom and equalitarianism, which it had been formed
to support. In his paperback epilogue Moore (1965, pp. 428 and 430)
discusses the Stalinist terror: 'One cause that was slighted in *Soviet
Politics* was the necessity for speed in transforming backward agrarian
Russia into a modern industrial state, a task that had to be carried out
in the teeth of a generally hostile world.' As happened repeatedly, 'the
means swallowed up and distorted the original ends'.

Such intraorganizational conflicts are not so general as class conflict
as understood by Marx, or even by Dahrendorf or Parkin. In Barry's
(1965) terms, they cannot be called conflicts of interest, as a union-
management dispute appears to be, because they cannot be translated
into the terms of a generalizable value such as money. Rather, each one
is rooted in its particular — perhaps peculiar — values. Hence, an
explanation of one of them does not have the enormous scope of an
explanation of conflicts of interest. Members of other organizations are
commonly not likely to identify with such particular conflicts. Indeed,
it may even happen that such conflicts inhere in the value systems of
individual persons, so that the organizational dilemma over two conflicting institutionalized values need not define two factions, each
supporting its preferred value. Dahrendorf presumably would argue that
such conflicts are not so consequential for political order as is class
conflict. Typically that conclusion is probably correct, although one
can easily enough imagine such a conflict which could lead to social
catastrophe.

Perhaps the largest literature on conflicting value commitments
within organizations deals with conflicts between commitment to preservation of an organization as it now is and commitment to virtually
any other given goal of the organization. The cases in the studies cited
above fit this pattern vaguely enough. Writing generally, Starbuck
(1965, pp. 473-75) suggests that in new organizations, members 'tend

to be attracted by either goals or task structure. They tend not to be attracted by the social structure' of their organizations. But, 'As an organization ages, its members' central commitments undergo a shift in emphasis toward the organization's social structure.' Consequently, young organizations are most likely to change their social structure; old organizations are most likely to change their goals. The reasons for the shift are those tendencies which Selznick (1957) elaborates under his notion of the institutionalization of the organization as a value. One might be rudely tempted to draw an analogy with marital success: it is romantic attachments which hold young marriages together, and social attachments which sustain old marriages.

Of course, organizational aging is not the only source of such conflicts. Gouldner (1957) factor analyzed a college faculty into cosmopolitans, who were committed to their professions, and locals, who were committed to the college. These commitments did seem to define factions which were in manifest conflict, whereas Starbuck's aging thesis could simply imply conflict inherent in each individual member's commitments over time.

The peculiarly limited scope of such conflicts suggests, however, that we cannot generalize from such studies to other organizations without great care. Against the generality of Gouldner's finding, Blau and Scott (1962, p. 71) suggest

> that a commitment to professional skills will be associated with low organizational loyalty only if professional opportunities are more limited in the organization under consideration than in others with which it competes for manpower. In other words, only if it is the structure of the organization rather than the structure of the profession that restricts opportunities for advancement do we expect professional commitment to be accompanied by a cosmopolitan orientation.

At best it is an open question to what extent the values for whose realization major organizations have been created will become, in a sense, the principal victims of those organizations, both in communist and in market or democratic societies. There is perhaps no organization for which it seems indisputably clear that its structure is causally related to its values (or at least to the means of realizing its values) to such a degree as to make the values almost uniquely realizable through *its* structure. Perhaps armies come close, but as dozens of nations have learned in the past decade or so, an army only marginally capable of defending a nation can be fully capable of taking over the nation's government and suppressing many of its values other than survival in the event of foreign attack. At another extreme, individual enterprises perhaps also come close — although in modern states, survival, surely an important value, is occasionally beyond the individual enterprise's control.

At an intermediate level, the collective farm perhaps also comes close. To alter collective farms very much would be to alter drastically the task structures of most of their administrative and technical personnel, so that many of these could be expected to resist major changes. To a lesser degree, perhaps, the broader social structure of the farms could not be altered without at least some grave regrets on the part of the farmers and their families, and opposition from at least some of them.[1] One of the goals of farms is the production of food: within broad limits (e.g. wheat and dairy farming must be large scale to be economical) efficient realization of that value seems so thoroughly dependent on land quality, fertilizer, and capital investment that it cannot convincingly be shown to depend on the distinction between independent and collective social organization of farmers. Hence, collective farms seem naturally to institutionalize the value of collective organization of farming, while they do not conspicuously institutionalize other values in conflict with this one.

Again the conflicts between particular values institutionalized within an organization are much more diverse than class conflicts. Hence, they are both less subject to sociological generalization and less likely to become the basis for widespread political opposition. This is an issue to which I will return after discussing processes which suggest that government bureaucracies in many new industrial states have become highly institutionalized over the past two or three decades.

PROCESSES OF INSTITUTIONALIZATION

Analytically, one can specify two ways in which the correlation between commitment to a regime value and power can increase: either the power of the committed can increase relative to the power of the uncommitted, or the commitment of the powerful can increase relative to the commitment of the non-powerful. Surely both these occur. Commitment to the right values leads to greater power through promotion up the hierarchy of the bureaucracy; and power (or rank) within the bureaucracy leads to greater commitment.

Commitment Leads to Promotion

There may be a considerable degree of self-selection out of and into the state bureaucracy. Because of self-selection into the bureaucracy, the general level of commitment of bureaucrats is likely to be higher than among the workforce in general. And if there is self-selection out of the bureaucracy, bureaucrats who are most strongly committed will be most likely to stay on long enough to be promoted into the highest ranks. This latter effect must have been quite pronounced in many nations, especially East Germany, but also Cuba, South Africa, North Korea, and perhaps China, Greece, and others, from which numerous bureaucrats have emigrated.

Besides self-selection, there are almost certainly processes of selection by superiors which promote the highly committed faster than the less committed. Stinchcombe (1968, p. 109) and Selznick (1957) suggest that, in selecting successors who share their values, power-holders act both from conscious policy and from natural affinity. The argument from natural affinity is eminently believable, but its import on any broad scale may well be beyond demonstration. Conscious policies, however, frequently at least enter the public record. For instance, an absurdly large part of the literature on Communist politics is a record of Communist selection policies (one suspects motes in the eyes of the Western beholders). A brief outline of that record in the case of East Germany is instructive.

In East Germany, the first and perhaps most important selections were presumably made by Russian Communists. And the first broad scale selection policy was formulated by the Four Powers and realized under the Soviet Military Authority in Germany (SMAD). That policy was stated in essentially negative terms: to eliminate all Nazis and Nazi sympathizers from significant public offices. But it had substantial positive results.

The Nazi administrators had to be replaced, and in decisive Soviet style the exchange was carried out almost instantly. In the twelve central administrations appointed by the Supreme Soviet Commander in 1945,

> an effort was made to obtain the services of all capable anti-Nazis irrespective of their political views . . . The success of the recruitment was cumulative; as the Germans became aware of the seemingly unbiased method of selection they came forward to join these organizations in increasing numbers. Between July and October 1945 a complete administrative organization of considerable efficiency came into being (Nettl 1951, pp. 114-18).

But over the next decade or so, mere administrative efficiency would have been inadequate to the tasks of the new authorities. For,

> The task of building values into social structure is not necessarily consistent, especially in early stages, with rules of administration based on economic premises. Only after key choices have been made and related policies firmly established can criteria of efficient administration play a significant role (Selznick 1957, p. 60).

The Four Powers understood this principle well enough. In their Directive number 24 of 12 January 1946 'concerning the removal of Nazis and those opposed to Allied programs from offices and responsible positions', they noted that 'It is important that leading German officials at the heads of provinces, governmental districts, and localities be proven opponents of Nazism, even if this implies the appointment of persons whose capacity to fulfill their functions is less ('Amtsblatt des Kontrollrats in Deutschland', *Ergänzungsblatt* No. 5, Berlin, 1946, p. 115; cited in Doernberg 1968, p. 110). Once the Nazis had been eliminated and the basic organization of government functions had been achieved, the criteria for subsequent recruitment and promotion included evidence of commitment to Communist and Socialist organizations and policies. And a general policy to give preference in the educational system to individuals from working class and farm backgrounds was openly introduced even before the German Democratic Republic (GDR) was established as an independent state in 1949.

This last policy, of course, expressed one of the values peculiar to the regime. In negative terms, that value was to destroy the culture of inherited privilege attaching to the upper and upper middle strata of

German society. In positive terms, it was to give everyone an equal opportunity for education, career choice, and so forth, in a socialist society. There is now apparently general agreement that the policy has successfully spurred a considerable degree of equalization of such opportunities. One suspects that the policy would have been adopted even if it had not implied a reorientation of the educated stratum in the future. In so far as it probably did imply such a reorientation, the policy was perhaps therefore in part an instance of selection from natural affinity.

Hence, whether deliberately or coincidentally, the East German authorities selected the future members of the GDR service class in a fashion which Selznick (1957) suggests might be wise in any new organization:

> It may at times be useful to recruit whole staffs from a particular social milieu, in order to increase the chances that a given set of policies will become meaningful and effective guides to behavior (p. 57). By choosing key personnel from a particular social group, the earlier conditioning of the individuals can become a valuable resource for the new organization. Conversely, of course, just such conditioning is in question when a particular source of personnel is *rejected* (p. 105).

By the end of 1964, more than 85 percent of the GDR 'Hoch- und Fachschulkader' were people who had done their study under the Communist government and whose selection for higher education had partly been based on their social backgrounds.

Promotion Leads to Greater Commitment

There is a vast range of findings to suggest that accession to positions of higher rank in an organization tends to induce greater commitment to the organization. For instance, a large study of the United States Federal Service reveals that 'Among governmental workers, the prestige of the federal service is lowest among clerical personnel, but rises with increased rank' (Peabody and Rourke, 1965, p. 811). There is also evidence which suggests that having '*an orderly career* in which one job normally leads to another, related in function and higher in status' leads to strong work attachments (as well as strong ties to society, etc.; Wilensky, 1961, p. 521, who cites other references).[2] Similarly, Fullan

(1970) argues that a reason for the generally recognized difference between the attitudes of workers in manufacturing and in process production factories is that for the former there is no prospect of promotion, whereas for the latter promotion is an expected feature of employment. Fullan concludes that 'the institutionalization of mobility increases the integration of the worker in the company' (p. 1030; see also Stone, 1952).

Apparently the most extensive study of promotion mobility and attitudes is that included in the government sponsored study of American soldiers in the Second World War. Stouffer et al. (1949, especially ch. 3 and 5) conclude from various surveys of soldiers that:

(1) for a given longevity, the higher a soldier's rank, the greater is his job satisfaction, commitment to the army, etc. (p. 93 and ch. 5);

(2) and inversely, the longer a soldier's longevity at the rank of private, the less his job satisfaction, commitment to the army, etc. (p. 89).

The first of these findings is by far one of the strongest in the whole study. The second is, per se, also strong, but it is not broad enough to test attitude toward rapidity of promotion in a fashion that would be suggestive for present purposes. On the latter issue, Stouffer et al. also find 'that job satisfaction was highest in the Air Force, intermediate in Service Forces, and lowest in Ground Forces'. This ordering is the same as the ordering for promotion opportunities from greatest to least (p. 257). Both orderings were very strong, but one might reasonably suspect that other factors were too important to allow clear conclusions about the effect of promotion on the correlation.

THE DEMOGRAPHY OF INSTITUTIONALIZATION

In a brief aside, Stinchcombe (1968, pp. 187-88) suggests that 'the strength of the relation between communism and government stability' is due to 'the high degree of institutional integration in communist societies. By a series of devices, many of them quite unsavory, the communists manage to make the correlation between commitment to communist ideology on the one hand and power on the other highly positive in all institutional areas.' Surely the numerically most important device in most of the Communist states (perhaps excepting East Germany, in which emigration was numerically about comparable in its effect), and one which presumably would not be found unsavory, was controlled economic expansion in the fortunate circumstance of demographic growth. That is, the rapidity with which these regimes have achieved political stability is partly a result of controlled economic expansion, which involves rapid expansion of administrative bureaucracies, which causes high rates of recruitment to and promotion within the bureaucracies, and which increase regime support while diluting the significance of recalcitrant holdovers in the bureaucracies.

There are two implications of rapid expansion of the bureaucracy:

(1) the new regime will have selected a very large percentage of all incumbent bureaucrats at the end of a very short period (plausibly a near majority within a decade even if no holdovers are forcibly retired); and

(2) there will be rapid promotion throughout the bureaucracy so that the rate of promotion per se may increase commitment at higher levels.

For largely demographic reasons coupled with secular changes in their economic structures, many industrial states today enjoy much higher rates of bureaucratic expansion and promotion than did Great Britain, West Germany (in today's boundaries), or France during the century and a half of rapid industrialization following the French Revolution. Opportunities for service class promotion in Japan, the Soviet Union, Poland, and East Germany during the 1950s were roughly double those in the United Kingdom (with its nearly stable workforce), about 60 percent higher than those in the United States, and roughly one-third higher than those in Czechoslovakia, West Germany, and Italy (Hardin, 1972, p. 2). From the studies cited above, it seems reasonably likely that high rates of promotion have been conducive to the development of affect among the service class for the political institutions of many of these states. Furthermore, the expansions coupled with natural turnover meant that as of 1960, about 40 percent of incumbent bureaucrats in Japan, the Soviet Union, and Poland had been recruited in the previous decade. With the additional effect of emigration before the Wall (erected in 1961), more than 70

percent of East German bureaucrats in 1960 had probably been recruited during the 1950s (figured from Hardin, 1972, p. 27).

The sources of the expansions in these nations have been

(1) demographic growth, especially among those of working age;

(2) the decline of agricultural employment, largely through inter-
generational mobility off the land;

(3) the virtual elimination of unemployment; and

(4) the increased participation of groups not previously very active
in the workforce, by far the most important group being women.

The last of these is especially interesting, because women are the last
remaining source for substantial expansion in most Western industrial
states (excepting Canada with its high demographic growth rate) unless
and until reproduction rates change drastically and barring a preliminary surge in unemployment. In Eastern Europe (excluding East
Germany) and in Japan there are still substantial residuals in agriculture
and in demographic growth, whereas in most of these states there are
few unemployed women left.

CONCLUSIONS

In summary it appears that under some circumstances statist regimes
have inherent structural advantages. The very effort to expand the
functions of the state to control particular social distributions helps a
statist regime to institutionalize itself. On the other hand, the effort to
limit such expansion prevents a conservative regime from enjoying the
benefits of increased institutionalization from expansion. Hence, the
process of expansion per se implies a tendency to self-preservation of
the expanded role.

The statist regimes in Eastern Europe and the moderately statist
regime in Japan have benefited from the historical fact that they have
come to power at a time when those nations still had massive labor
reserves in agriculture and after they had undergone what might be
called the first demographic revolution of modernity but before or soon
after the second. That is, they have come to power at a time when their
populations were growing rapidly as a consequence of sharp reductions

in the mortality rate, but before the diminishing effects of a falling birth rate have begun to be heavily felt among their populations of working age.

Communist policy in most of Eastern Europe has therefore substantially contributed to the institutionalization of state bureaucracies partly through the inadvertant fact of the age structure of Eastern European populations. Because the Communists undertook state administration of active social reconstruction, they have had an extraordinary advantage in institutionalizing themselves with their programs of economic expansion and modernization, and perhaps even with their tendency toward aggregation and centralization. Had Communists come to power much later in the development histories of these nations, they presumably would have faced much greater difficulties simply because expansion would have been less nearly automatic and would necessarily have been much more limited. Similarly, were a party of the radical left to come to power in present day West Germany or Britain, it would face profoundly less propitious circumstances in part just because substantial expansion of the bureaucracy would not be feasible within the severe constraints of the lack of large agricultural labor reserves and the stability of the populations in those nations. That stability cannot be affected for a generation.

Contrary to the above argument, the more popular thesis in the West is that, as compared to regimes in advanced Western states, the regimes of Eastern Europe are unstable. One of the most sophisticated recent versions of that thesis is Parkin's (1972) analysis of 'system contradiction and political transformation', which is 'an attempt to show that Marx's concept of system contradiction can be usefully employed in the comparative analysis of industrial societies' (p. 61).

Despite the loss of subtlety which a summary entails in this instance, Parkin's analysis (1972, p. 50) is compelling even when briefly stated. He argues that

> In socialist society the key antagonisms occurring at the social level are those between the party and state bureaucracy on the one hand and the intelligentsia on the other. The power of the former rests upon their control of the political and administrative apparatus of the state . . . The social power of the latter group inheres in its command of the skills, knowledge and general attributes which are held to be of central importance for the development of productive and scientific forces in modern industrial society.

Hence, the intelligentsia in socialist states is 'the ascendant class' — ascendant because it is not yet dominant politically even though structurally it should be.

Elite recruitment in all industrial states tends primarily to be tied to the division of labor. In capitalist society an alternative basis for recruitment to the elite is property ownership; in socialist society an alternative is party office (Parkin, 1972, pp. 53-54). In the West the two sources of recruitment are highly intertwined, so that the elite is reasonably 'unitary'; in the East the two groups are quite distinct and antagonistic, and the conflict, or 'split in the ruling class', is a contradiction which presages political change (pp. 57-59).

There are analytical objections which one might raise to the argument in this cursory form, but those who turn to the original will find that Parkin has carefully met the most cogent of these. In the end he would perhaps agree that his thesis must stand or fall on the quality of his factual assertions about particular societies, East and West. Some of his most important assertions (e.g. the 'class consciousness' of the Eastern European intelligentsia) are based on subjective appraisals of limited evidence, very much as are some of the assertions in the present paper (e.g. under 'processes of institutionalization'). I will address only the two most important of Parkin's factual assertions, which are common to many of the analyses of Eastern European instability. These concern the importance of the Eastern European intelligentsia, and the extent to which the intelligentsia are quite distinct from and in conflict with the political bureaucracy.

How Distinct are the Intelligentsia and the Bureaucracy?

To begin with the latter issue, either the intelligentsia or the political bureaucracy constitute a very small group, or the two must massively overlap. If the bureaucrats at issue are the few 'apparatchiki' at the highest levels of party and government (see Parkin, this volume, note 15), there would seem to be no profoundly serious contradictions in these states since it should be easy to find more than enough committed Communists among the intelligentsia for recruitment into the next generation's apparat. If that has not yet happened, it is plausibly a demographic effect (those of the intelligentsia educated under the

Communists are considerably younger than the apparatchiki), and partly perhaps no more than an accidental fact much like the fact that the United States has had few intellectual presidents (since the era of Jefferson-Madison-Adams there has been only Wilson, and the future is not promising). But one need not fully share Weber's blend of pessimism and positivism to think that much of the point of 'rational administration' through bureaucracy is that it can survive the reign of dullards. Certainly intellectuals, as Western academics and scientists amply demonstrate, can prosper while employed in organizations run by dullards. If a few dullards at the very top were adequate to define a broad gauge class conflict, most states would surely suffer Jefferson's prescription of a revolution every generation.

If it is the intelligentsia which are a very small group, it is unlikely that they are ascendant. If that is too short an answer, there is a fuller answer implicit in the discussion below of Parkin's interpretations of the importance of the Eastern European intelligentsia.

Finally, if both the bureaucrats and the intelligentsia are large groups, then they must heavily overlap, especially in the most advanced states. Hence, as with their Western counterparts, the Eastern European intelligentsia must have been massively 'assimilated into the power structure'. The strongest case for this claim is probably East Germany, but it is probably also true that if the intelligentsia are potentially powerful anywhere in Eastern Europe, then especially in East Germany. Since these two factors are likely so highly correlated, to argue here from East German experience is perhaps not a too grievous abuse of the logical canon that one should argue from the worst case (presumably Romania or Bulgaria in this context), the more especially since East Germany is the most demographically 'advanced' of the Communist states.

Among the 11 percent of the GDR workforce in the 'Hoch- und Fachschulkader' in 1970, 4 percent had university degrees, and the remainder had technical institute degrees (*SJDDR*, 1970, p. 66). The East German educational level is now higher than that of many, perhaps most, advanced Western states (probably including West Germany). Those educated persons now dominate the higher and highest reaches of the administrative elite in government and in industry, and they are increasingly represented in the Socialist Unity Party and in its Central Committee (Richert, 1967, p. 222; Ludz, 1970, p. 22; 1968, pp. 147

and 178-81). If there are conflicts between the values of the intelligentsia and those of the bureaucracy, then they are conflicts which inhere in the complex value systems of numerous individuals and they are not so generalizable in scope as to define precisely two politically significant factions or classes.

As a final note in this context, it is interesting to compare the old Russian and Polish intelligentsia with the old German 'Intelligenz'. The Russian intelligentsia was a group apart from the remaining social order. Its members are 'déclassé'. They were a counter-elite 'who almost by definition were disassociated and not infrequently alienated from the governing circles' (Black 1964, p. 182). Their greatest moment was 1917. The Intelligenz developed in a fashion very nearly the opposite of that of the Russian intelligentsia. The Intelligenz was virtually co-opted by the governing elite, as one might expect from the fact that it was defined by the set of roles presumed necessary to the maintenance of society and requiring fairly high level education in the universities of the princes. In classical German usage from the eighteenth century, the Intelligenz is the stratum of the scientifically educated (in the broad sense of the German 'wissenschaftlich'), which included principally the medical and legal professions and teachers. Politically they had more in common with the 'Beamten' (government officials) who flourished under the Prussian hegemony than with literati or revolutionaries.

In the Soviet Union and the GDR, Communists have used the words 'intelligentsia' and 'Intelligenz', but their meanings have widened to include simply all those who have and use higher education at a time when almost all leading personnel in economic, political, and cultural life have higher education. Indeed, in East Germany the term Intelligenz is apparently even being dropped in the last few years in favor of the more explicit and more prosaic term 'Hoch- und Fachschulkader', i.e. 'university and technical institute cadre'. There are residuals of the classical intelligentsia in Poland today, and there are evidently similar persons throughout Eastern Europe, especially in Czechoslovakia. However, most of those commonly labelled as among the intelligentsia could more appropriately be called 'Hoch- und Fachschulkader'. Increasingly, these are the mainstay of the bureaucracy.

How Important are the Intelligentsia?

Parkin (1972, p. 55) argues that the intelligentsia 'have the kinds of skills which are at a premium in any type of modern society irrespective of its political make-up'. This is a claim which may be based more on hindsight than on foresight. Brilliant scientists may be few in number now and forevermore, but the general run of worthy intelligentsia may be on the verge of becoming too numerous for their own good.

The commercial wit of the Peter Principle notwithstanding, Thompson (1969) argues cogently that the general level of talent and intellectual capacity of American government bureaucrats far transcends the general level of demands made on them by their jobs. The acute shortages of engineers and other educated persons in Western States in the recent past seems now to have been merely a demographic and economic transition, partly exacerbated by the inefficiency of the market in regulating the production of BS and PhD degrees. The soul-deadening glut of degree-holders of the more recent past and present in several nations may seem a generation hence to have been the more typical and pervasive problem. It seems likely that the nations of Eastern Europe will soon make similar transitions, albeit perhaps with somewhat less inefficiency. Indeed, the East German and Czecho-slovakian bureaucracies might well already be subject to Thompson's thesis.

Outside science, industry, and the bureaucracy there is another group which shares more with the classical Russian 'déclassé' intelligentsia than with the German 'Intelligenz'. This group comprises the 'literary and creative elements' which Parkin (1972, p. 56) and numerous other Western analysts reckon to be of profound symbolic importance in the East. Here again, facts are subjective. However, I simply doubt that all the novelists in the world (and Gulag) amount to more than a handful of political beans. Worthy novelists and other artists have as great a chance of being déclassés in the West as in the East, and as great a chance of being co-opted in the East as in the West. Anyone interested in political change should probably follow the example of bureaucrats everywhere and ignore them.

Another summary at this point would seem like a bludgeon, so I will spare the reader. Merely note again that the conflicts which define significant classes that bring about radical political change are not the conflicts of limited scope over diverse, particular values which commonly inhere within organizations and individuals. The structural source of power East and West is principally in the governmental and industrial bureaucracies, and the intelligentsia share in power to the extent they fill managerial positions, i.e. roles of authority. Bureaucratism may be as pervasive and as pernicious to socialist (and other) values as Mao and Trotsky and a host of others would have us believe. But it is not easy for the holders of these diverse other values to mount an opposition, much less to see themselves as a united class in conflict with 'the bureaucrats', who are chiefly themselves.

NOTES

1. According to a West German critic of East German collective farming, among the social advantages of socialized agriculture are shorter, more nearly stable work hours; better work conditions, especially for women; de facto guaranteed minimum income (through government loans if necessary) and greater security in general; and freedom to take vacations. Disadvantages are lack of independence and the virtual impossibility of achieving exorbitant income (Blohm 1969, pp. 394-403). In general, comparing East and West German farmers, there is in East Germany 'without doubt a far-reaching approximation of the social condition of the members of [collective farms] to that of wage-workers in [sozialized industry]' (p. 392), whereas in West Germany *'the income disparity within agriculture* [is] considerably greater than the income disparity between industry and agriculture' (p. 395).

2. Wilensky's (1961) notion of an orderly career and, hence, his finding might well be thought more relevant to an understanding of present Communist societies and Japan than of American society. That is because much of Crozier's (1964, pp. 278-79) characterization of the French Civil Service probably applies even more strongly to the entire administrative bureaucracy in most Communist nations.

In comparison with business, [Crozier writes] 'the Civil Service was the world of open competition and of equality of opportunity.'

But unlike other western countries, and especially America,

> equality of opportunity was not understood in France as the ability to compete on equal terms on an open economic and impersonal market, but as the possibility of striving individually for selection within a very impersonal but also hierarchical educational system.

REFERENCES

Gabriel Almond and Sidney Verba (1963), *The Civic Culture* (Princeton: Princeton University Press).

Brian Barry (1965), *Political Argument* (New York: Humanities).

Cyril E. Black (1964), 'The nature of Imperial Russian society', in: Donald W. Treadgold (ed.), *The Development of the USSR* (Seattle: University of Washington Press).

Georg Blohm (1969), 'Kritische Betrachtungen zu den agrarpolitischen Massnahmen in Mitteldeutschland', in: Edgar Tümmler, Konrad Merkel and Georg Blohm, *Die Agrarpolitik in Mitteldeutschland und ihre Auswirkung auf Produktion und Verbrauch landwirtschaftlicher Erzeugnisse* (Berlin (West): Duncker und Humblot).

Peter M. Blau and W. Richard Scott (1962), *Formal Organizations* (San Francisco: Chandler).

Michel Crozier (1964), *The Bureaucratic Phenomenon* (Chicago: University of Chicago Press).

Ralf Dahrendorf (1959), *Class and Class Conflict in Industrial Society* (Stanford: Stanford University Press).

Ralf Dahrendorf (1967), 'Recent changes in the class structure of European societies', in: Stephen R. Graubard (ed.), *A New Europe?* (Boston: Beacon).

Stefan Doernberg (1968), *Kurze Geschichte der DDR* (Berlin (East): Dietz).

Michael Fullan (1970), 'Industrial technology and worker integration in the organization', *American Sociological Review*, 35: 1028-39.

Alvin W. Gouldner (1957), 'Cosmopolitans and locals', parts I and II, *Administrative Science Quarterly*, 2: 281-306; 444-80.

Russell Hardin (1972), 'Promotion mobility in industrial states', University of Pennsylvania, typescript.

Peter C. Ludz (1968), *Parteielite im Wandel* (Cologne and Opladen: Westdeutscher Verlag).

Peter C. Ludz (1970), *The German Democratic Republic from the Sixties to the*

Seventies (Cambridge, Mass.: Harvard University Center for International Affairs).

Barrington Moore Jr (1965), *Soviet Politics: the Dilemma of Power* (New York: Harper and Row (first published, 1950)).

J. P. Nettl (1951), *The Eastern Zone and Soviet Policy in Germany 1945-50* (Oxford: Oxford University Press).

OECD (Organization for Economic Cooperation and Development) (1971) *Occupational and Educational Structures of the Labour Force and Levels of Economic Development,* Vol. II, *Further Analyses and Statistical Data* (Paris: OECD).

Frank Parkin (1972), 'System contradiction and political transformation', *European Journal of Sociology,* 13: 45-62. *Reprinted this volume, Chapter 6.*

Robert L. Peabody and Francis E. Rourke (1965), 'Public Bureaucracies', in: James G. March (ed.), *Handbook of Organizations* (Chicago: Rand McNally).

Ernst Richert (1967), *Sozialistische Universität: Die Hochschulpolitik der SED* (Berlin (West): Colloquium).

Philip Selznick (1957), *Leadership in Administration* (Evanston, Illinois: Row, Peterson).

Philip Selznick (1966), *TVA and the Grass Roots* (New York: Harper (first published 1949)).

SJDDR (Statistisches Jahrbuch der DDR) (1970), (Berlin (East): Staatsverlag der DDR).

William H. Starbuck (1965), 'Organizational Growth and Development', in: James G. March (ed.), *Handbook of Organizations* (Chicago: Rand McNally).

Arthur L. Stinchcombe (1968), *Constructing Social Theories* (New York: Harcourt, Brace and World).

Robert C. Stone (1952), 'Mobility factors as they affect workers' attitudes and conduct toward incentive systems', *American Sociological Review,* 17: 58-64.

S. A. Stouffer, E. A. Suchman, L. C. Devinney, S. A. Star and R. M. Williams Jr (1949), *Studies in Social Psychology in World War II,* Vol. 1, *The American Soldier: Adjustment during Army Life* (Princeton: Princeton University Press).

Victor Thompson (1969), *Bureaucracy and Innovation* (Alabama: University of Alabama Press).

Harold L. Wilensky (1961), 'Orderly careers and social participation: the impact of work history on social integration in the middle mass', *American Sociological Review,* 26: 521-39.

III

EVOLUTIONARY PERSPECTIVES ON MORPHOGENESIS

8

THE ROLE OF INSTABILITIES IN THE EVOLUTION OF CONTROL HIERARCHIES

HOWARD H. PATTEE
State University of New York at Binghamton

The main aim of this paper is to emphasize a creative mode of evolution that is largely neglected or even purposely excluded from most models and theories of control in complex organizations. I shall argue that this so-called *creative mode* is a necessary complement to the more commonly accepted *optimization mode* of evolution. I associate this creative mode with a type of failure of description which optimization cannot correct, and therefore with the generation of new levels of hierarchical systems. The optimization and creative modes are useful for interpreting the global structure and evolution of hierarchical organizations at all levels, from cells to societies.

These two modes are complementary in the sense that *both* are necessary for understanding the origin and evolution of control hierarchies, and yet the two modes are mutually exclusive if one tries to combine them into a single description. In other words, the two modes have contradictory assumptions. In particular, the optimization mode is essentially continuous and rate-dependent, whereas the creative mode is essentially discrete and rate-independent.

This type of descriptive complementarity is a well-established conceptual framework that is often associated with Bohr's principle of complementarity in physics, although it has much older expressions (e.g. see Jammer, 1974). My first awareness of complementary descriptions came from my early training in physics, but the ideas presented here are more directly traceable to what I have learned of biological organization and its characteristic structure-function duality at all levels.

GRADUAL OPTIMIZATION

What I mean by the optimization modes of evolution are processes in which some metrical observable quantity can be interpreted as a figure of merit for some function of the organization. In other words, the optimization mode requires a defined function or goal of the organization with a measure of success possessing enough of a convergence or *continuity* property to define a relative optimum. For example, in the theory of biological evolution, we assume that mutation and natural selection provide the mechanisms of optimization of all functions, the most global of which we call fitness. Biological evolution is, of course, far too complex to model or even to define in any detail, but we still recognize this aspect of the theory as representing an optimization process. In simpler systems that are sufficiently well-defined we may actually solve optimization problems by prediction or design rather than by trial and error. Our ability to predict, however, depends on the formal properties of our model of the system as well as on the rules for our interpretation of the formalism. For example, a formal predictive model must be sufficiently continuous to define rates or derivatives and therefore to express dynamical equations that connect present states of the system with future states (e.g. Bellman, 1969; Kalman et al., 1969). Equally necessary is the interpretive condition that the formal structure of the states of the system are topologically mappable into the functional or adaptive observables. This is a much more difficult condition to express since the interpretive aspect is not completely formalizable (e.g., Rosen, 1962). However, for this discussion, we may rely on the condition for predictive models that Hertz (1894) expressed so succinctly, that '... the necessary consequents of the images in thought are always the images of the necessary consequents in nature of the things pictured'.

FAILURE OF THE IMAGE

Now the essential observation that justifies my introduction of what I call the creative mode as a complement to the dynamical optimization mode is that Hertz's condition cannot always be met. That is, even relatively simple dynamical models have singularities where the description fails and where the consequents of the images are no longer the images of the consequents. Poincaré expressed a very similar idea in his definition of dynamical instability as a condition where unobservable causes have observable effects. This failure of description is also the basis of Thom's (1974) topological method of description that associates morphology with the discontinuities or catastrophes in the trajectories of dynamical systems. Again, the essential point is the failure of the dynamical image. That is, the evolution of such a dynamical description, even if it is 'structurally stable', may exhibit a complete indeterminacy at a discontinuity.

CHANGE OF RULES

The more complex a system becomes, the more possibilities exist for these exceptional configurations where one dynamical description fails. Especially important in biological and social systems are processes of growth, and the production of new interactions that generate new degrees of freedom and rules of constraint. In effect this must be treated as an entirely new system with an alternative dynamical description. We then must consider a new hierarchical level in our model, that is, a level that is used to predict which description is appropriate under an observed set of conditions (Burns and Meeker, 1973).

The generation of this new decision level of description I associate with a creative mode. This terminology can be criticized as being excessively teleological, and so one might prefer to call it the *syntactical* or *control mode*, or simply the *non-dynamical mode,* just as we speak of non-linear dynamics as applicable to those systems that are not describable by linear dynamics. But the situation is not entirely analogous. What I want to emphasize is that the control mode is at a higher level than the dynamical or optimization modes, since it serves to define the *choice* of dynamics or what is to be optimized at the lower level. In this respect, it is like a meta-language, or a choice of syntax rather than a description within a given language. The control mode generates rules or constraints under which a given dynamical system may be optimized. It is also distinguishable from the dynamical mode by its *rate-independence,* or at least by a kind of time dependence that is not integrable within the time measure of the dynamical equations. Such constraints are called non-holonomic, and as we would expect from this discussion, we find that most dynamical structures which appear to have a definite *function,* from enzymes to machines with moving parts, are only representable as non-holonomic constraints (e.g., Pattee, 1967; Neimark and Fufaev, 1967).

A constraint in physics is already an alternative description to the dynamics of the system. Simple constraints are statements of added conditions on the motions of a system that are imposed by fixed structures such as a table top or the walls of a box. Such constraints permanently remove degrees of freedom (the table top) or permanently limit the range of degrees of freedom (the box).

Non-holonomic constraints are also structures that may limit the number or range of the degrees of freedom, but they also restrict the allowable dynamical trajectories in real time. The classical example of a non-holonomic constraint is a thin disk rolling without slipping on a plane surface; but in this paper I am thinking more of flexible constraints, like enzymes or structures with moving parts, like ratchets or switches, that have a non-integrable sequence-dependence that cannot be reduced or solved without using the time-dependent dynamical equations of the entire system.

The essential point is that function requires constraints, and constraints require auxiliary descriptions that are not reducible to the rate-dependent dynamical description of the system. This only serves to confirm our feeling that dynamics, structure and function require complementary descriptions at different levels.

Before giving more details and examples, then, let me summarize. The evolution of complex organizations requires at least two complementary modes of description. By far the best understood mode we have called the optimization mode. This mode is formalized by dynamical models in which *continuity* and *rate-dependence* play an essential role. We are most familiar with this mode since it evolved from differential equations of classical physics. It is often assumed that if a complex system could be correctly described in atomic detail by this dynamical mode, then we would have 'reduced' the system to physics. The evolution of the system would then be determined by integrating the dynamical equations.

The fact is, however, that the dynamical description will not hold everywhere for a variety of reasons, such as singularities, catastrophes, new interactions, and non-integrable constraints. Instead of trying to avoid these failures, I am focusing attention on them as a necessary condition for generating a new level of description. This generation process is not an optimization in the dynamical sense, but it is a change in the constraints, rules or interpretations of a dynamical description, and therefore, I call it a *syntactic* or control mode. To explain this mode in more detail and to show how the evolution of complex control hierarchies require both the dynamic and syntactic modes, we must look at what we mean by *failure*.

SYSTEM AND DESCRIPTION FAILURE

We often think of functional organizations, whether they are committees, football teams or artificial machines, as having only one way of working optimally, but many ways of failing. This is because we generally use a dynamical or optimization mode of description for machines, which defines failure and tells us what improvement can be made. If adequate function is not achieved, we call the machine itself a failure while its description or rules of operation might still be considered a success. In other words, we would say that the machine works *in principle* but has some practical difficulties. To the extent that we think of living organisms or societies in the optimization mode or as mechanistic organizations, the concept of failure can similarly be associated with the non-optimal function of the ideal organization. In this sense, failure is the opposite of optimization, and both are measured in terms of the ideal model or description of the system. This usage puts failure on the same 'objective' level as optimization.

However, failure is not a concept that we can always objectively associate with organizations. Very often it is our model of the organization that fails. The motion of atoms or of planets, for example, is not subject to failure. On the other hand, our descriptions of these systems may have indeterminate singularities, as we have seen. In this case, we would have to say that the machinery of nature is a great success while our descriptions or rules are a failure (cf. Minsky 1967).

We are, therefore, using here two meanings for *machine* and two meanings for *failure,* and it is essential to distinguish carefully between them since in some sense they are opposites. By the 'machinery of nature' we mean the failure-proof laws that we assume underlie the predictable behavior of matter. When we find certain types of natural events unpredictable we assume that our description or theory of these events are failures, but not the events themselves. For example, man first observed X-rays and superconductivity as events that existing theory failed to predict, not as failures of natural laws. On the other hand, while we assume that the rules of arithmetic are not subject to failure, it is clear that a physical machine designed to execute these rules may fail all too often.

This duality of error in descriptions and error in operation occurs at all levels of organization. For example, in computer programs it is possible to have an error in the program itself or an error in the machine executing the program. Furthermore, at higher levels it is also possible to have an error in the choice of algorithm which is being programmed or even an error in the choice of problem that the algorithm solves. Similarly in social and political organizations we try to distinguish between the failure of a policy and the failure to properly execute a policy. In other words, we try to distinguish between error in our models of social activity which leads to incorrect policies, and error in social constraints which lead to failure of policy implementation.

The central concept in my theory of the evolution of power and control hierarchies is that new levels of organizations develop from an interplay of dynamical optimization and descriptive failure. Failure of description is related to the inadequacy of a syntactical structure, e.g. a model or a policy, at some essential decision point. This is a rate-independent discrete type of failure, rather than a power failure, i.e. a failure of quantity, rate or function. It is like missing a train by taking the wrong turn, rather than by going too slowly to the station.

The reason for the predominance of the optimization modes of thinking is probably the result of their more precise formulations than the syntactic modes. However, we must always bear in mind that this precision is based on a tacit understanding of syntactical modes underlying the formulation of optimization problems. The existence of syntactical rules and structure constraints are a prerequisite for any descriptive or measurement process, and if the results of description or measurement appear clear and simple, this is largely the result of the choice of syntax rather than the result of dynamics. Similarly, if quality of function can be associated with a continuous variable, then optimization can be simply represented, but the nature of this association that simplifies optimization must depend on complex syntactical constraints.

The appearance of formal, objective dynamical models of social systems as well as simple physical systems is therefore largely an illusion; for every formal model must be expressed in a language formed by syntactical constraints and must be interpreted (if it is never to be of any use) through informal concepts and constraints of measurement and function for which no formal description exists.

EVOLUTION OF CONTROL IN CELLS

I said at the beginning that the complementarity of continuous dynamical modes and discrete syntactical modes is the essential relation needed to understand the evolution of control hierarchies at all levels from cells to society. So let me give some specific examples to help justify this assertion. First let us look at the control levels in the cell. We cannot understand the genetic DNA as only a continuous dynamical structure any more than we can understand the words on this page by their physical properties. The meaning of the gene requires the syntactical rules of the genetic code and the constraints of the ribosomes that construct the enzymes that control the rates of growth and metabolism. At the same time, neither can we understand the folding, specificity and catalysis of enzymes by any syntactical rules in the cell. The DNA can describe the enzyme only up to the linear sequence of amino acids that are joined by the construction apparatus. The process of folding the linear sequence into a functioning constraint, the recognition of the substrate, and its catalysis are dynamical processes for which no description exists in the cell. A naive reductionist would argue that these events — the folding, specific binding of substrate, and catalysis — are simply the results of the dynamical laws of physics and chemistry. But it is not that simple. These universal laws certainly hold and operate, but the rules of the non-holonomic constraints of the enzymes' structures also hold and operate, *and these constraints are not a dynamical property but the result of the syntactical mode of the genetic description.* It is legitimate to say that these syntactical constraints control or harness the dynamical laws (Polanyi, 1968; Pattee, 1972).

Next we must ask how evolution takes place in cells. What role does optimization play? What role does failure play? How do the dynamical and syntactical modes interact to generate new hierarchical control levels?

First it is clear that mutations in the structure of DNA are necessary for evolution. From the dynamical or physical point of view a mutation may be described as a statistical fluctuation but not as a failure. To be a failure (or a success) a mutation must at least alter the *meaning* of the genetic description, and meaning depends on rate-independent syntactical constraints. In other words, a mutation must alter the cell's model of itself if it is to have any operational effect on the life of the cell.

The neo-Darwinian theory of evolution considers the mutation as a source of variations or trials which are optimized by natural selection. This is certainly a good theory in so far as it can explain the gradual optimization of the functions of, say, organs like the eye that essentially achieve the physical limits of sensitivity and resolution. Optimization can only improve the execution of a function or policy.

What optimization does not explain is the origin of functions or

policies themselves. In fact, optimization cannot account for the ultimate choice of what properties are selected (i.e. policy) any more than
it can account for the origin of the genetic code and the constraints
under which any optimization must take place (Waddington, 1969;
Danielli, 1975). Optimization can account for improved techniques for
winning a game, but it cannot at the same level account for the rules of
game.

THE EVOLUTION GAME

What are the forces of evolution? When a complex system changes its
organization what types of forces cause it to do so, and what types of
changes are available to it? We can classify the forces as the challenges
of nature and the competition among species. A limited concept of
evolution is that each species will adapt to these forces by trial and
error so as to optimize separate functions as well as its overall fitness.
However, the dynamical mode of optimization above is not adequate
here because the payoff of the evolution game is not a metrical
quantity. As Slobodkin (1964) expresses it, evolution is a game where
the only payoff is to stay in the game. Or to put it another way, an
organization can dynamically optimize its function only so far under a
given set of constraints. If that optimum value is not good enough to
remain in the game, then to survive, the organization's only alternative
is to change the game. I express this by saying that when dynamical
optimization fails, it is not a failure to reach some well-defined objective goal, but a failure of the syntactic models and constraints which
define the optimization process. Biological and social structures are not
objective in the sense of physical laws. They are coherent systems
obeying dynamical laws and syntactical rules that are distinguished
from isolated physical systems by their ability to change their internal
constraints and thereby change the rules of the game.

   The long evolution of living organisms has built into them many
levels of syntactical and dynamical back-up systems so that a failure of
a dynamical control system in one situation results in a syntactic shift
to a more appropriate dynamical model. This is what Warren McCulloch

has called the redundancy of potential command, and what I am emphasizing in this concept is the biological necessity for both dynamical and syntactical modes, not only to implement this type of control but to evolve it in the first place (Pattee, 1972).

THE EVOLUTION OF CONTROLS
IN SOCIETY

Cells are obviously much simpler than societies, and already I have grossly over-simplified the cell in many respects. However, one aim of any theory is selective simplicity — especially a theory of control of complex systems, since there is little use to a theory that is as intricate as the system itself. In fact it is the major prediction of my model of the evolution of control that the instabilities of complex dynamical behavior are the source of the simplifications from which hierarchical controls evolve. The essential requirement of any administrative organization is a selective filtering out of complex details at the dynamical levels so that wise syntactical rules and control decisions can be generated.

However, as I stated at the beginning, my aim in this paper is to show that even the simplest useful concept of a cellular or a social system must be formulated using complementary dynamical and syntactical descriptions, and that the evolution of new levels of controls in biological and social organizations cannot be understood by only a dynamical model no matter how detailed.

The popularity of dynamical models is now growing rapidly, largely because of the powerful computers that are available for simulating very complex systems involving large amounts of data. In fact, the power of computer forecasting in this dynamical mode already poses serious problems of control in society, since within this rate-dependent mode the computer can out-think the human brain in terms of speed, data capacity, and parameter optimization. This means that if enough people believe that the dynamical simulation is an adequate type of model of society, then they must also believe that the predictions of the computer will be a sound basis for policy-making and control.

It is this apparent machine-like determinism or finality of dynamical models that frightens the instinctly creative person who knows that predictions and novelty are somehow incompatible. Indeed it *is* frightening to imagine a generation of computer-minded leaders who really have faith in the computer as an oracle simply because it thinks dynamically faster and more accurately than the brain. Critics of our technical society (e.g. Latil, 1953; Ellul, 1964) see the determinism of computer-controlled dynamics as essentially malignant, since they have not fathomed how human control over this dynamics can ever be re-established once belief in technical forecasting is affirmed.

It is of course also the case that the syntactical mode by itself can produce an uncontrolled growth of well-formed, timeless expressions without in any useful sense creating something new. Such uncontrolled growth of expressions can be found in certain branches of mathematics, philosophy and almost any formal discipline that has not discovered the necessity of the complementary dynamical, real-time mode. Fortunately such uncontrolled linguistic activity behaves more like a benign tumor than a malignancy.

The computer as well as most of man's other artifacts has the dynamical machinery and syntactic controls lumped in separate compartments. When failure occurs in any compartment of such an open or loosely connected hierarchy it is necessary to add a new level control — the repairman — who provides external policies and parts. Living systems and social organizations are characterized by closure of their dynamic and syntactic modes so that a local failure at any level leads to the transfer of control or function to an adjacent level. The units of biological and social organization, namely the cell and the individual, are incredibly coherent in the closure of the internal hierarchies and hence resilient to external stress and to local, internal failures. Both units possess the ultimate repair mode, self-replication, which itself requires a closed network of dynamical and syntactic structures (e.g. von Neumann, 1966).

Our theories and simulations of these natural systems, on the other hand, tend to emphasize precision at the local level and to exclude the richness of the interlevel controls. For example, the two most common mathematical languages which we use for modelling are continuous differential equations and discrete automata theory. They are certainly precise and highly developed languages of great power, but partly because of their independent development they are practically isolated from each other. Theories or models are generally expressed in a rate-dependent dynamical language or a discrete switching language and these two are seldom combined, although some attempts to do so have been made (e.g. Kalman et al., 1969). On the other hand, in even the most elementary levels of the living cell, both the discrete, rate-independent, sequential modes of the genetic instructions and the rate-dependent enzymatic reactions are intimately related at all times. Similarly, in the development of multi-cellular organisms the discrete cellular events like division, differentiation and selective death are inextricably associated with continuous processes of growth, motility and metabolic control. Finally, at the highest level of organization in the individual, the brain, there is growing evidence of the highly parallel interactions of the discrete nerve-pulse networks and the continuous chemical networks (e.g. Pattee, 1974), although as yet our knowledge of brain organization is relatively poor.

CONCLUSION

Control hierarchies are complex organizations with levels of homeo-static interactions that preserve the organization under a variety of challenges. However, no matter how well-integrated or 'fail-safe' such controls may appear to be, such systems will possess instabilities that strongly affect their global behavior and evolution.

In biological systems such instabilities may be the precursors of the novelties of archetypal forms in evolution, including perhaps, the origin of life itself (Pattee, 1973). In social organizations such global instabilities may trigger revolutions which drastically redefine the game rules as well as the material controls. And finally, in intelligent problem solving such singularities may be the essential matrix that generates the sudden illumination of a solution − a solution that could not be reached by a gradual optimization, but required a complete change of representation or image.

From these examples and arguments, which I have stated only briefly here, I conclude that theories of the behavior of complex organizations need to be expressed in more than one formal language. That is, a *predictive theory of organization must have at least two complementary modes of description: one corresponding to the rate-dependent dynamical or optimization mode, and the other corresponding to the rate-independent syntactical or creative mode.* The latter mode must provide a tacit decision process generated from the coherent interactions of the dynamical and syntactical modes. In one, limited sense, such a double description is implicit in all models, since the formal language of the explicit model must always be interpreted by a meta-language, which is most often our natural language. But this is not enough, since the formal language system and our natural language interpretation are as artificially separated as the hardware and software of the computer. In this situation the natural language plays the role of the 'universal repairman'. That is, if a formal theory fails, we first try to patch it up by local reinterpretations. If that is inadequate, we may define some new variables or modify the equations. Finally, if nothing works, we say the formal language is inadequate and try another language. In all these cases, we are assuming that a local failure means that something is objectively wrong. What I want to emphasize is that even in good models this type of description failure is inevitable and may only foreshadow the generation of new levels of constraint in the organization. Unless the consequents of an organization's inevitable dynamic singularities are represented by some complementary image in our models of complex systems, we should not expect our model to give us an image of the behavioral consequents of the system's evolution.

REFERENCES

R. Bellman (1961), *Adaptive Control Processes: A Guided Tour* (Princeton: Princeton Univ. Press).

T. Burns and L. D. Meeker (1973), 'A mathematical model of multi-dimensional evolution, decision-making and social interaction', in *Multiple Criteria De-*

cision Making, Cochrane, J. and Zeleny, M. eds. (Columbia, S.C.: University of South Carolina Press).

J. F. Danielli (1975), 'A structuralist approach to social biology', Dialogue discussion paper, Center for the Study of Democratic Institutions, Santa Barbara.

J. Ellul (1964), *The Technological Society* (New York: Alfred A. Knopf, Inc.).

H. Hertz (1894), *The Principles of Mechanics* trans. by D. E. Jones and J. T. Walley (London, 1899; New York: Dover Pub. Inc. 1956).

M. Jammer, (1974), *The Philosophy of Quantum Mechanics* (New York: John Wiley & Sons, Inc.).

R. E. Kalman, M. A. Arbib and P. L. Falb (1969), *Topics in Mathematical Systems Theory* (New York: McGraw-Hill Book Co.).

P. Latil (1953), *La Pensée Artificielle* (Paris: Gallimard).

M. Minsky (1967), *Computation: Finite and Infinite Machines* (Englewood Cliffs, New Jersey: Prentice-Hall, Inc.).

I. Neimark IV and N. A. Fufaev (1967), 'Dynamics of non-holonomic systems', *Translations of Mathematical Monographs, Vol. 33* (American Mathematical Society).

H. Pattee (1967), 'The physical basis of coding and reliability in biological evolution', in: *Towards a Theoretical Biology,* Vol. I, C. H. Waddington (ed.) (Edinburgh: Edinburgh Univ. Press), 69.

H. Pattee (1972), 'Laws and constraints, symbols and languages', ibid., vol. 4, p. 248.

H. Pattee (1973), *Hierarchy Theory: The Challenge of Complex Systems* (New York: George Braziller), ch. 4 and postscript.

H. Pattee (1974), 'Discrete and continuous processes in computers and Brains', in: M. Conrad and W. Güttinger (eds.), *The Physics and Mathematics of the Nervous System* (Heidelberg: Springer Verlag).

M. Polanyi (1968), 'Life's irreducible structure', *Science* 160: 1308.

R. Rosen (1962), 'Church's thesis and its relation to the concept of realizability in biology and physics', *Bulletin of Mathematical Biophysics,* **24**: 375.

L. B. Slobodkin (1964), 'The strategy of evolution', *American Science,* **52**: 342.

R. Thom (1974), *Stabilite Structurelle et Morphogenese* (New York: W. A. Benjamin, Inc.).

J. von Neumann (1966), in A. W. Burks (ed.), *The Theory of Self-Reproducing Automata* (Urbana, Ill.: Univ. Ill. Press).

C. H. Waddington (1969), 'Paradigm for an evolutionary process', in: C. H. Waddington (ed.), *Towards a Theoretical Biology,* Vol. 2, (Edinburgh: Edinburgh Univ. Press), 106.

9

THE NATURAL HISTORY OF HIERARCHY: A CASE STUDY[1]

Ronald Cohen
Northwestern University

INTRODUCTION

Hierarchical organization is a natural outcome of social evolution. Even though many societies have until recently been able to maintain low levels of hierarchy, more complex, larger-scaled systems have evolved on all continents. Given the right conditions such systems develop as a normal part of culture history. The problem for social theory is to isolate the proper mix of factors that give rise to and result from such developments, whether they apply to the near east, China, middle America, West Africa or highland Peru.

Possibly the most widely discussed correlate — sometimes seen as the basic causal factor — is that of increased population growth and/or pressure.[2] Fried[3] suggests that population pressures are associated with greater scarcities and less equitable access to resources utilization. This is expressed in greater degrees of social stratification and in distributive systems that support these inequities as well as greater degrees of hierarchical control. In effect, and most often, land becomes scarce;

people give greater and more regular tributes for its allocation; the 'owner' or person having rights of land-use allocation becomes richer and therefore redistributes more goods more often, thus sustaining greater power for himself and his group. Carneiro uses a systems approach to suggest that hierarchization and more centralized control is a logical and empirical correlate of increased population size in situations where a society remains unified and integrated.[4] Harner has repeated his work and described how population pressures are highly correlated with increased stratification and greater complexity of political organization.[5] In reviewing much of this work Alland comes to the same conclusion and chooses population pressure as the key variable from which basic organizational changes arise.[6]

Population pressures are widely seen to be the result of technological innovation[7] such as irrigation, new types of food or other exploitable resources, and geographical conditions that bring about population crowding. A more controversial variable is that of warfare. Early in such discussions Spenser saw warfare as the root cause of population pressure and increased hierarchical organization in society.[8] For him increased population created a problem in social order for which simpler forms of organization were insufficient. Scarcities produced competition, conflict, and war. Those better organized militarily won out and eventually the greater capabilities of military organization were taken over into the civil sector as the military leaders become rulers as well as warriors. Fried explicitly rejects this idea, arguing instead that successful warfare is itself a consequence of already well-established hierarchical organizations in society.[9] Only when complex structures and social stratification already exist can organized warfare arise. Thus, some writers see warfare as an important precursor to population pressure and evolution, others do not.

What is missing in most of this work is some sense of transition. By correlating factors at one level of organization with socio-cultural contexts and then comparing all of these to more complex levels, it is possible to pick out theoretically relevant variables associated with the changes. However, how this transition from one level to the next actually occurs, how institutions especially softer ones such as ideology, rules of recruitment, concepts of social stratification actually change from fewer to greater levels of complexity — all of this is very thin in the literature and in the resulting theory of human social evolution.

The solution to such problems, in my view, must come from the methods of history and ethnohistory that record actual cases in which the entire gamut of changes across the cultural map can be recorded. This is why the work of Horton is so suggestive.[10] Working independently on Kalabari materials in West Africa he has tried recently to generalize about social and cultural changes that accompany greater degrees of centralized control. Looking at less hierarchized systems, Horton summarizes the present data by showing that stateless societies expand continually to form separate fissioning communities across the landscape. This expansion is a normal outcome of internal cultural, social and political dynamics and continues to operate unless specifiable conditions prevent the process from occurring. In other words, population growth leads to lineage proliferation and segmentation. Land shortages around villages plus leadership disputes and arguments over the distribution of rights and obligations within the lineage underlie this normal break-up and expansion. Hierarchy and incipient class structure is ubiquitously available in such societies because of the concept of the higher status village founders or 'owners of the land' whose leader is village head and those lower status groups who joined the community at a later date. Such multi-origin villages are by far the most common in comparison with the relatively rare Nuer-Tiv varieties in which every one is part of the same over-arching descent structure. Horton then points out that once such small proliferating villages are presented with problems of warfare and defence they must remain in larger more compact settlements. This is an explanation for increased population pressure. It creates as well a significant reorganization and development of pre-state institutions to produce more community-wide organization, increased hierarchy, and greater power and authority for leaders. Thus, Horton bridges the gap by showing how new institutions emerge naturally from old ones, once the need arises.[11]

Summarizing theory to date we can say that increased hierarchy and greater degrees of centralized control are a function of population pressure and the growth of larger more compact communities. It is not simply that the society remains integrated, as Carneiro suggests,[12] since widely scattered nomadic groups like the Somali, Bedouin, or Tubu use descent ideology to accomplish this same goal, *without* increasing their hierarchical organization. Instead we must, as Horton suggests, look for increased population pressures and larger more compact, non-fissioning communities.[13]

The development of this population change is dependent upon a series of factors, one or all of which may bring it about. Increased technological capability produces more food to support larger denser populations. Restrictive ecologies such as river valleys, lake shores, irrigation works, growing aridity, among other factors, produce denser populations within a more restricted space. Inter-group hostility produces the same effects by forcing populations to unite for defensive purposes. All of these factors are probably interrelated systemically, so that the occurrence of one provides increased probability for the occurrence of the others.

Once such changes are set in motion society is faced with organizational problems. These are solved universally by increasing the degree and scale of social stratification and the organization of social control through increased hierarchy and centralization. Institutions that have previously supported locally autonomous groupings with low levels of hierarchy are adapted and changed to reflect and support more complex institutions. When available, ideas and practices from elsewhere are also utilized for the same purpose. Such, theoretically, is the natural history of hierarchy and political complexity.

Population pressure is the basic factor underlying the growth of political complexity. However, underlying this widely accepted notion is the less well-known one, that all political systems except centralized states are fissiparous. That is to say, they break into proliferating segments that spread the population out across the landscape, and they do so as a normal part of their social and political history. Hierarchy and centralized control are the effects of those forces that impede and inhibit this process.

The centralized state or its immediate precursors emerge from a generalized background of less hierarchy when forces in the physical and social environment make it advantageous for particular polities to remain in one place rather than splitting up as they normally do. The society that results is larger, more stratified, and more coordinated. It must, if it is to succeed, create some means by which centralized control can perpetuate itself, carry on over individual life spans, and execute authority while maintaining channels of communication and appeals from the people to their rulers. Along with such coordination, indeed often as the basic reason for its development, is the coordinated use of force by the rulers for the defence and welfare of the society.

Naturally, increased coordination and the organization of force helps to sustain in power those who command its use. The process is not necessarily a revolutionary one. If there is selective pressure for greater degrees of centralized control, then a probability exists that some groups in the environment will hit upon ways and means to respond that involves the ultimate evolution of a new societal form.

In what is to follow I wish to examine in summary form the rise of increased hierarchy and centralized control among a people who seem to have existed for centuries quite well without it. The case reveals that warfare and more compact town life are interrelated and lead to, or are associated with, the evolution of more complex hierarchies and centralized control. The case also shows that increased social stratification, the incorporation of integrative 'bureaucratic' mechanisms, and the development of social, cultural, and ideological features to support hierarchization can develop quite normally among systems in which such complexity is previously absent. The state-stateless dichotomy is not so much a polarized set of opposites as a matter of degree in which less complex institutions evolve to meet the demands of a new situation.[14]

DIFFERENTIATION IN BURALAND

The Setting

The area we are concerned with lies for the most part in Biu emirate south of Borno* in the Northeast State, Nigeria. The Bura-speaking peoples of the emirate number some 200,000 of whom about 75 percent call themselves Bura of which 25 percent or thereabouts refer to themselves as Pabir. In general the Bura live south of the major administrative center of Biu which the Pabir dominate and the area north of the town up to the borders of Kanuri and Fulani settlements. In more recent years, there has been an expansion of Bura settlement into traditionally Pabir areas, but the traditional spatial distinctions are still widely recognized.

*In 1974, with the advice of local scholars, the Nigerian government established Borno as the official spelling of the region previously known also as Bornu.

The area is administered by the Biu Local Authority under the authority of the Emir and his Council at Biu. The emirate contains five districts under a head (Ajia) and town or 'village head' (Lawan) with ward and hamlet heads under the Lawans. In two cases the districts are really semi-independent non-Bura chieftaincies, but all others are integral parts of Buraland. The system is essentially that developed in Borno and described elsewhere.[15]

The most binding feature in the area is language. Both Pabir and Bura speak Bura, a variety of the Bura/Marghi sub-branch of the Chadic language family.[16] This unites them to that broad band of peoples running from the Cameroon mountains westwards across northern Nigeria including the Hausa on the west and the Mandara and Kotoko on the east. Hausa as a lingua franca is spreading throughout the area so that many Pabir and Bura speak a common second language as well. On the other hand, many Pabir, especially officials in Biu, also speak Kanuri which is quite rare among Bura except for a few who have spent many years in Borno.

The two groups also share basic concepts and practices of social organization. Both live in polygynous patrilocal or virilocal compounds in which household organization, and most of their kinship practices, are very similar. Descent is patrilineal and there are named clans, sub-clans *(dur)*, and sets of constituent patrilineages *(nyarmbwa)*. Descendants of founding lineages are village and ward heads, and form councils along with the heads of lineages who arrived and settled later in the area.

Bura villages are traditionally small and somewhat dispersed into wards *(zara)* that are in effect localized patrilineages. These are separated from one another by *tiksha* or first planted fields closer to each compound. Thus, the basic ecological pattern disperses the population. Some wards are over a mile apart. This process is exacerbated by the constant segmentation of lineages which further spreads the settlements across the landscape. Genealogical knowledge, inter-clan unions and local shrines establish political, religious and economic alliances that cut across these proliferating settlements.

Pabir lived in larger, more stable, and more tightly packed settlements with a set of less stable hamlets surrounding the larger town, under the loose political control of the town. This control meant mostly adjudication of disputes but also some cooperation for defence in case of an attack. There were and are no *tiksha* fields between compounds and, unlike Bura, crops were grown inside the compound. Thus, compounds were built close together in a more 'urban' fashion than was the case for Bura. The towns were walled and even today older people can still trace out the exact location of the walls and gates.

Major Pabir towns had a chiefly head and title *(Kuthli),* with titled heads of other lineages who formed a council to govern the town and its surrounding hamlets. The role of chief was associated with elaborate rituals of installation and burial, a council of nobles, and the wearing of a sacred top-knot. Today, the chief or Emir at Biu is the senior of all chiefs in the area and traces his descent back 27 generations to a founder who is said to have come as a conqueror from the pre-nineteenth century Kanuri capital of Birni Gazargamu.

Both Bura and Pabir have identical ranges of occupations although Bura are widely believed to have had special blacksmith clans (e.g. Mshelia). Both groups placed much emphasis on hunting, cotton grow-ing and weaving as an export crop, and very similar food crops. Division of labour seems to have always been quite similar throughout the area and small weekly markets were widespread. Generally speaking, most settlements were self-sufficient except that salt had to be imported from the Jukun area and possibly from Lake Chad as well. Clothing was locally made and cattle were farmed out to nomadic Fulani who were supposed to obtain profit from milk and take a percentage commission if a beast was slaughtered. Sheep and goats were herded by the young boys of the settlements. Brassmithing was also practised throughout the area as a male occupation and brass and iron ornaments were used as essential parts of the bridewealth payments.

In general Pabir are Muslims, while Bura are Christians with a significant and expanding number of Muslims among them. Underneath the present distinctions of Islam and Christianity both the Bura and Pabir have a common set of strongly held indigenous beliefs and practices. Each has a village settlement shrine *(Milim)* and each house has its own compound shrine *(Haptu)* to the ancestors. Village shrines can be consulted and prayed to by non-villagers so that people from one area often travel many miles to consult and obtain help from a famous shrine elsewhere in Buraland. Within the compound and the lineages, the ancestors are felt to be participating members with the living who help and punish their descendants. Witchcraft *(mutu)* and sorcery or medicine *(thukula)* are common throughout the area, as are beliefs in the power of ghosts to come and interact — sometimes vengefully — with the living.

Summary of the Problem

Here then are a people sharing one language, many beliefs, as well as social and economic practices, and all living together within one geographic region. Conversely, they refer to themselves by different identity or ethnic labels and one group is more highly organized with more centralized, more hierarchical political structures. This differentiation is the focus of this paper. What follows is not definitive; research is still in progress. However, this is a preliminary summary of my findings and an interpretation of their meaning.

THE COLONIAL OVERLAY

The contemporary political system of the area is primarily the result of the colonial intrusion. When the British first arrived they found a series of larger towns stretched across the northern part of the area. Directly to the south were a series of locally autonomous small villages that practised a fiercely independent existence. The British chose two of the largest towns one in the Bura-speaking area (Biu) and the other among the dominantly Tera-speaking peoples (Gulani). These they tried to rule from Gujba at the southernmost extension of the Borno emirate directly to the north. Each town was to be the centre of an emerging administration that would incorporate unorganized linguistically similar groups to the south and come in turn under the jurisdiction of the larger scaled organization of Borno in an emerging provincial system.

In Western political terms such a policy made sense. However, a number of problems soon surfaced, the solution of which created the present set of arrangements and compromises. The Tera-speaking groups consistently rebelled against Gulani rule. Investigations showed that complaints of extortion, misrule, and a distorted idea of British intentions were a constant element among the Tera-speaking groups. Accordingly in 1914 the Gulani area was split up and its eastern portions given to Biu. In the meantime the latter had been given jurisdiction over all of Buraland and was emerging as the centre of the most powerfully organized division in the area.

In Biu the Mai or Kuthili (referred to as 'Emir' after about 1918) found it advantageous to work closely with the local British colonial officer. The Emir realized very soon after the British arrived that he could utilize their superior weaponry and their desire to centralize local administration in order to advance the power of Biu far beyond its extension in the pre-colonial era. Accordingly he stamped out the power of the largest rival Pabir kingdom, and utilized British 'patrols' or armed forces to subdue the independent Bura villages to the south.

Today the situation reflects this history plus the contradictory trends that have developed since that time. Missionary work among the non-Muslim Bura, political party strife in the 1950s and 1960s, and the growing desire of educated Bura for more access to local positions of authority have created and/or maintained the tensions between Bura and Pabir groups within the emirate. Many on both sides define the situation as a zero-sum game. This leads to Pabir resistance against Bura recruitment to the Local Authority and to Bura 'nationalists' stressing any or all cultural differences in order to support their demand for more Bura appointments. Pabir say instead that all Bura-speakers are one people and therefore there is no real need of a special ethnic and political status for Bura peoples.

On the other hand, the Muslim religion, Hausa language, and a more widely used northern Nigerian dress style are spreading rapidly through the area. This is especially true of language and dress patterns, both of which tend to lessen the apparent differences among groups. There are therefore forces driving Bura and Pabir closer together and others pulling them apart.[17] However, it is clear even from this short summary that colonialism was not the ultimate source of these distinctions and tensions. For this we must seek earlier and more indigenous socio-political forces underlying these later developments.

THE PRE-COLONIAL DIFFERENTIATION

Pre-colonial differentiation in the area has resulted from selective factors that have produced greater degrees of hierarchy and centralization.
It is important to note however that these changes have emerged out of
a less complex socio-political system that manifests internal variability
and a continuing capability for local adaptation.

Bura culture and society is basically adapted to continuously expanding and splitting communities that are locally autonomous. Villages are traditionally quite small and spread out. Male members and
the wives and unmarried children of each lineage segment remain,
ideally, close together while others more distantly related, or other
sub-clans live in their own *zara* or ward clusters. A 1913 census of
central Bura villages south of Biu revealed a range of 4 to 50 compounds per named village, with an average of 21.1.[18] This means that
most traditional villages had about 200 people in all; small settlements
ranged from 25 to 50 while a few large villages housed possibly as many
as 300 persons altogether.

Conflicts and pressure within either the village, the sub-clan, or the
local lineage segment, produce constant hiving off. Informants give the
same reasons over and over again. These include land shortage, especially for *tiksha* plots just outside the compound walls, desire to
escape from feuding *(ta sukur),* disease, witchcraft, and sorcery accusa-
tions or their effects. Close segments may remain related depending
upon how far they move from one another, and whether or not a
formal breaking of relationship ceremony *(gabaku)* has been performed
which allows for inter-marriage and the abrogation of common feuding
obligations and responsibilities.

Although it has slowed down considerably as roads and town-sites
have developed, the process is nevertheless a continuing one. Bura-
speaking groups are still segmenting and spreading. Sub-clan and lineage
histories indicate a somewhat random and vibratory north-south set of
movements, and the continuation of a westward spread as population
expands. This has been noticed by Newman who reports that the Bura
language is replacing Tera on the western borders of Buraland.[19] Thus,
segmentation and population expansion work together to produce a
constant pressure on population distribution which has meant a general

east to west movement of peoples in this area over the past few centuries.

Each village of Bura people is an independent unit. The people have picked up practices from neighbours, adapted to local soils and terrain. Under such conditions beliefs and customs tend to vary across the area. Groups pick up ideas and practices locally and tend to differentiate from other Bura-speakers across Buraland. In the west and south of the area there is a secret society for adult men only that resembles similar institutions among non-Bura to the south and west. In the east and south there are spirit familiars that resemble practices among the local non-Bura neighbours. Good cotton soil in the east and north of the area has created an export trade in this item that is widespread throughout the west and central Sudan.

Cross-cutting forces of localized differentiation are a range of practices that tie all of Buraland into an integrated unit. No matter whether genealogies are taken from Pabir or Bura the vast majority (over 90 percent) of all marriages are among Bura-speakers. Clan or sub-clan exogamy among the Bura has forced people to marry outside their descent groups. Quite often, and very often in the past, this meant marrying into another locality. The culture requires elaborate duties and obligations owed by in-laws to the lineages from which they obtain wives. These can take place during clearing and hoeing of farm fields, house-building and at funerals. Because most Pabir have some Bura wives these linkages can and do cut across the Pabir/Bura sub-ethnic distinction.

Annual and less frequent hunts brought together men from many surrounding villages under the authority of the owner of the hunt who had initiated it. The largest of these held every few years was advertised by word of mouth over a very wide area of Buraland, bringing men from the entire area to participate. Bura language and residence in the area seem to have been the primary criteria for participation. Such practices expressed and helped create a sense of unity and identity in the area.

Added to this were famous shrines and medicine men-diviners whose reputations were widely known. People from one part of Buraland were free to visit shrines and practitioners in any other part. Under extreme circumstance of misfortune, several elders of local lineages would be dispatched to consult a diviner, bring him back to the village, or ask for help at a particularly powerful shrine. The reputation and experience of such places and people kept knowledge and contact between Bura-speaking areas fresh and continuous, as it still does today.

Although this is but a brief summary of a complex and rich topic it is enough to document the fact that amidst local autonomy and differentiation forces of unification were operating as well. It is important to repeat that the integrative institutions and the localization referred to above cut across Pabir and Bura. Bura and Pabir inter-married, they attended each others shrines, and may on occasion (the point is less clear) have attended similar hunts.

THE PABIR VARIANT

If this was the whole story things would be complex enough. Buraland social evolution could then be seen as the result of steady population expansion and specific culture contacts that have produced continuous variation throughout the area. These variations could then be conceived as being restrained from expanding their influence by a set of contrary forces that unify the people and localize their adaptation. This is the result of a set of social institutions that foster and maintain social relations across local descent groups and dispersed villages within the wider context of Buraland itself.

However, northern Buraland has been the scene of an even more complex developmental history. It is here that selective forces have exerted harsh pressure on Bura variability resulting in the evolution of chieftaincy and more centralized political institutions.

Well before the colonial conquest two quite distinct political systems were associated with Pabir and with Bura. The Bura, like many other locally autonomous societies, practised a political system that resulted from the integration of descent with locality. Villages were sets of dispersed wards. The eldest member of the founding lineage was village head and the same principle applied to each ward. Senior lineage members, ward heads, and the village head formed a council to settle disputes and discuss major affairs. The village head in addition had to ratify the use of house sites by in-migrants, he could expel miscreants from the village, he prayed at the village shrine and he must plant his fields before anybody else could begin to plant. He announced major events and he had powers of witch-finding and spirit-seeing that allowed him to protect the village from these generally unseen enemies. Village boundaries were defined quite strictly and the jural authority of a village head could not go beyond. There are several documented cases of violence in the early twentieth century against village heads who were authorized by emirate authorities to expand their power beyond traditional boundaries.[20]

In addition to this basically spatially distributed set of descent groups the unmarried men of the entire village *(dakwi)* selected a leader of the youth who along with a leader of the adult younger women work closely with the village head. They organized village-wide festivals, communal work, and *rites de passage* ceremonies.

Annual and less frequent hunts as already noted were under hunt leaders who were given full authority for the entire period of the hunt by anyone wishing to join the fray. One man in the village, noted for his powers in fighting, was elected by the young men to the position of Kadalla Kuma or war leader. Revenge and personal injury claims were generally a descent group affair. However, if the village was being attacked, or if the entire village was to engage in paying back another one for injury done to members of several sub-clans, then the war leader sounded a special horn and the young men gathered for war. The degree of his authority varied as a function of his own skills at leadership and the severity of attacks.

In basic structural features, Pabir village organization was similar to Bura. Youth sets and hunts were present as well as ward leaderships. However, in a number of cases there was a chief or Kuthli whose authority and status greatly exceeded anything practised by the Bura village head. The Kuthli ruled a compact settlement from his large compound near its centre. There he held court with a set of titled leaders made up of princes and leading lineages of the town. His personal style was one of wealth, pomp, and supernatural power to bring welfare to his people. His court settled disputes and made decisions about defence, public works such as walls, roads, war, and the apprehension and punishment of wrong-doers. There was no revenue system as such but people always brought gifts in kind when they came to greet the Kuthli or request his adjudication services. Gifts were also brought after harvest as gratitude for his supernatural help with crops. In turn the Kuthli distributed salt, natron, and other items of long-distance trade. He also gave food gifts to court officials and exchanged symbolic gifts with Jukun, Marghi, Kanuri, Tera, and other Pabir chiefs. Through ward and age-set organizations he organized work forces to create and repair town walls, and he organized military offence and defence with the help of his courtiers. The chief's house contained the great drums of office and a long brass war horn instead of the simple cow's horn used by the Bura war leader. By the end of the nineteenth century Pabir armaments included horsed cavalry, chain mail, and other equipment associated with the more northerly Sudanic states.

The Kuthli was elaborately buried in a special upright position in a circular grave, and there was as well an elaborate installation ceremony involving a retreat to the house of the Queen Mother (Magira) in a nearby town, and a re-appearance (re-birth) of the heir as a chief. Although the data are not completely clear, the Kuthli does not seem to have been given direct authority over anything but his own town and its surrounding hamlets and outliers. On the other hand several Kuthli, especially the Wolviri (clan) rulers of Mandaragirau and Biu, were revered and even appealed to for settlement of disputes from a number of other Pabir towns. The leaders of these other towns had another title (Herima or Thlerima) which indicated semi-subordination at least in rank to these Wolviri Kuthli, and they attended Wolviri chiefly funerals and installations. Possibly there were others as well who had such senior status – this point is still to be established.

Analysis

To understand how this differentiation has come about we must fit this local development into its wider regional context.

In the fifteenth century, the Borno plains were forced to react to a traumatic change. Internicine struggles for local dominance among various groups in Kanem had forced the migration of a powerful well-organized and well-armed clan and its followers onto the plains of Borno. These Magumi Sefawa finally founded the city of Birni Gazargamu, and began a slow but steady expansion. They evolved a system of administration consonant with their Islamic religion and ideally suited to the steady incorporation of the indigenous peoples of the area who they collectively called So or Sau.[21] Some of these plainsmen adapted and were incorporated into an emergent culture known as Kanuri. Others probably ran away toward the hills and more protected regions bordering the open plains.

Whether the present inhabitants surrounding the Borno plains are indigenous or stem from such refugee movements is at present impossible to say. What one can say with confidence is that the Kanuri language is intrusive in Borno. There are today records of Chadic-speakers giving up their language and replacing it with Kanuri as they became absorbed into the Borno polity.

Leaving aside the problem of specific historical events, it is valid to say that in general the emerging power of Borno stimulated a response on the part of its neighbours. Many groups simply ran away, generally in a southerly direction toward the hills and forests of the Benue-Chad divide. Round the southern fringes of Borno power, those who settled there or who elected to stay, or mixtures of both, were forced to develop some form of protective response. It is clear from the writings of a sixteenth-century Borno writer that villages to the south of Borno villages along the southern rim of the empire were constantly raided for booty, slaves, plunder, and failure to pay annual tributes.[22] In the general area of Biu only a few miles to the northwest people are described as coming out of their 'gate' toward the Borno army.[23] Towns were beseiged and then pillaged for slaves and other wealth. Sometimes local 'Sultans' of Yamta (an early term for the Pabir area) are referred to as allies against hostile pagans.[24] How well organized the area was at this time is unknown. The fact that there was some central leader, and some degree of fortified settlement seems clearly established in the literature.

The founding of the Borno state is therefore associated with a period of great conflict and change among those peoples who were forced to adjust to this development. And the result was a ring of more highly organized petty chieftaincies that ran along the southern edges of the Borno state. In Buraland these Pabir chieftaincies pose an historic problem. Who are they? Were they migrants into the area from somewhere else who brought with them concepts of chieftaincy and fortification? Or were they simply northerly Bura-speaking groups who stood their ground and developed adequate responses to the emergence of powerful and aggressive neighbours?

Oral accounts in the area attribute these developments to a small group of migrants under Yamta-ra-walla, the hero founder of the royal clan who came from the Borno capital where he had failed in his succession to the throne. These adventurers subdued many of the locals, married Bura women, and settled down. They are said to have learned the local language and customs, but retained their own methods of warfare, the concept of political centralism, and a sense of superiority to the local population. These then according to legend were the original Pabir, and from them stems that peculiar variant that resembles the more complex cultures to the north.

On the other hand, the legends also mention chieftaincies or at least local chiefs at Mirnga, Gur, and elsewhere that were already partially developed. Furthermore, the Pabir chieftaincy is strikingly similar to others at the southern perimeters of the Borno emirate. Unfortunately such data support several interpretations. We can say that Pabir chiefship is similar to earlier more northerly institutions. Therefore, the Pabir founder, Yamta-ra-walla may very well have brought it. Or peoples running away from Borno could have brought such ideas with them. Conversely, Bura who were evolving chiefship could simply have copied concepts of chiefship from their northerly neighbours. I suspect that not one but all these possibilities is to some extent true. The founders of the present royal lineage certainly copied ideas, titles, court procedures, and pre-Islamic religious ideas from Borno. Other groups in the area were also picking up such ideas *as they needed them.* Only detailed historical and archaeological work on town sites and chiefly burials will help solve these questions.

For the present, explanations must be socio-political and evo-lutionary, disregarding arguments about diffusion and/or independent development. I suggest instead, that no matter who moved, who mi-grated, or who remained to resist northern raids and encroachments, the Pabir chiefly variant of Bura society would have developed anyway, just as it has among ethnic groups both to the east and west of this area.

For the Bura, hostility has always been a small-scale affair. Feuding may make life dangerous, but the weaker or those who do not wish to be involved need only move further away to be free of it. The idea of full-scale warfare, of attacking and demolishing entire villages, is foreign to them. Hostility against Buraland from the northern emirates was of a completely different order. Rubin notes that this was a new kind of warfare, one in which the enemy 'played for keeps' in terms of different 'objectives, particularly the capturing of large numbers of slaves and a wholly focussed, highly mobile elite military organization'.[25] Where Bura peoples were primarily interested in revenge or wife-stealing or other personal kinds of objectives, these northerners had foreign policy objectives which involved vanquishing, killing, and weakening the non-Muslims, who would then either be absorbed into the Borno state or stop any harassment or non-payment of tribute they may have practised. For those Bura on the frontier, indeed for Mandara, Marghi, Tera, Ngala, and many others, the only answer was to flee, or make peace, or adopt workable defensive measures.

All of these possibilities occurred. Some form of cooperation between border peoples and Borno did actually occur. Records are better on this point for Mandara and Marghi, but as we have already noted the rulers of Borno recognized and worked with 'Sultans' of Yamta as early as the sixteenth century. Under such conditions of cooperation Kanuri titles, dress styles, the use of Kanuri by leaders, house styles (at least for chiefs) and a host of other cultural items flowed into the southern area through the leadership who were in constant, enforced, contact with Borno. It is this leadership class with its close interaction to the Borno government that came to be called 'Pabir' and who have been influenced by these local and foreign cultural contacts for the last three centuries.

The literature and the oral tradition clearly record, however, that times of cooperation were constantly interspersed with times of intense hostility. Under such conditions, traditional Bura warfare and defence proved useless. The answer was to move into more densely populated towns, often on hills or more easily defended promontories. Traditions have it that at first walls were made of stones, sometimes crossing valleys to stop cavalry charges and to afford cover for archers and their poisoned arrows. Ruins of such walls can be seen today near major Pabir towns.

In organizational terms founding lineages of towns or the most appropriate leaders of these lineages were now not simply heads of small scattered lineages. People were living close together within the walls — and many more of them than previously. This had serious results on the relations within and between local groups. In traditional

Bura society, disputes often led to segmentation – the group simply split up. However, with the constant threat of external raiding the northern towns became in effect sanctuaries, forts for defence against northern hostility. Major towns such as Mirnga, Kogu, Biu, Mandaragirau, Gulani, and Wuyo ranged from 500 to 2,000 inhabitants,[26] with a number of smaller outliers whose occupants could come into the walled town for protection. This should be seen in comparison with 50 to 300 for more traditional Bura settlements.

If we use present-day distributions that cross-check with oral history material, we can make some rough estimates of population density. Bura villages, even with wide-spread wards, usually cover about one to two square miles including the exploited farm lands, surrounding the village. On the other hand Pabir towns including related settlements can range from about four to six square miles including all exploited farmlands. In order to keep the figures conservative I am using a slightly larger set of area figures for Pabir than are warranted. Even so, putting this together with the fairly accurate population data and using medians for calculation, we get an estimated 250 persons per utilized square mile for Pabir and about 120 for Bura. If I exclude related settlements among Pabir and cut the exploited area down to two to five square miles, the estimated Pabir density rises to 350 per square mile. In other words, Pabir population density is demonstrably greater than that of the Bura.

Under such circumstances there is strong pressure for the usual adjudication role of the village head to grow in power, enhancing the authority of his office. The advantage of remaining in the town (obviously many did move away) meant that relations between contending factions or lineages had to be settled by the elders and the town chief. Making large-scale foritifications, organizing defensive measures, or making temporary peace meant again that the leadership must have enhanced authority. Greater density of population in more compact settlements and greater need for coordinated activities required an enhanced and expanding role for the leadership of the traditional Bura village autonomies.

Under such circumstances the office of the Bura village head differentiated. Traditionally he was the chosen heir of the founding lineage. He settled village disputes, discussed policy with the other lineage elders, allocated rights to village lands, decided on dates of first planting, and served as a town crier by announcing public events. As the 'shadow' or soul of the village he sacrificed at the village shrine, consulted with supernatural forces and protected the village against evil doers and their malevolent 'medicine'. Lineage elders who were often heads of dispersed wards, the male and female heads of youth, and household heads in general felt him to be the most senior authority in their political system.

To say that such a system is egalitarian and non-hierarchical is misleading. Respect for authority, deferential behaviour, and a clear-cut hierarchy from compound membership through lineage elders and ward heads to the village was clearly recognized. Those who were the descendants of the founding lineage felt themselves to be the original owners of the village, and certainly the owners of the office of village head. Offices of ward head, heads of youth organization, hunt heads, and earned respect and leadership resulting from experience and personal skills were open to all adult men. In this sense the society was and is more open and more competitive than that of the Pabir.

The Pabir royal leader carried out many of the same duties as the Bura village head, while dropping some as well. He was still the last court of appeal in the judicial hierarchy, although first and last court in capital cases. He still organized local work forces and still had much say in the distribution of land rights. The short war horn used by the Bura was now a long brass horn kept in the royal compound and sounded for purposes of rallying people for offense and defence. His compound was not at the edge of town like that of the Bura leader, but in the very centre and much larger than everyone else's containing within it possibly ten to twenty times more people. The royal council composed now of titled nobles who were heads of noble lineages sat in a special seating arrangement in the royal court. Conversation and discussion in the court was guided by rules of order not found among the Bura. The Pabir ruler not only distributed land-use rights, but was the protector of all property and the inheritor of all wealth for which there were no heirs. He was also a major source for salt which he redistributed to his people and traded for with long-distance traders who brought it in from the desert and possibly other areas to the west. In this regard he exchanged annual formalized gifts with surrounding states as the representative of the kingdom. He sacrificed at the royal tombs for the welfare of his people and performed other rituals to assure rain, good crops and the welfare of his people. His identification with dead kings, his power over life and death, and his responsibility for the general well-being of the people made him a 'lion' rather than a 'shadow' even though his 'shadow' (soul) was very powerful.

Bura succession to village headship was comparatively ascriptive. To allow competition would be to invite fission by the losing faction. Pabir were held together by the needs for common defence. However there were no limits on numbers of royal wives in the traditional system working therefore for dozens of possible contenders. Given these conditions the Pabir developed a system of limiting the succession to the oldest one or two sons of the monarch plus the oldest living brother of the king. This produced competition between two to four factions which was enough for such a system to cope with while ensuring against incompetence by a new recruit to office.

Leading lineages and groups closely related to the chief emerged as a titled nobility in each of the Pabir towns. The titles came from Borno but the offices were primarily that of a court who helped the chief to adjudicate cases and decide on matters of public policy. There is no evidence that such officials were given fiefs or any other means of raising revenues. Possibly the Chief Councillor *(Birma)* received tributes since it was through him that cases were presented to the Kuthli (Chief).

Close relatives and heads of leading lineages therefore began to emerge in each chieftaincy as an upper class with close connections to the chief. Their compounds were close to his and they gave each other daughters in marriage to cement their association. This created a problem in traditional Bura kinship rules which do not allow for such unions to be reciprocated because of stringent exogamy. In order to carry out such unions Pabir chiefs and titled nobles ultimately dropped or avoided the Bura exogamy rule and used the Kanuri cross-cousin terms as well as Kanuri terms for parents of cross-cousins. Today the closer one comes to the upper reaches of Pabir society, the more likely they are to use Kanuri kin terms for cross-cousins and the parents of such cousins.

Cultural diffusion, however, is no accident. The reason why this particular kinship practice was adopted by the Pabir stems primarily from the emergence of chieftaincy and a titled nobility who wished to marry amongst themselves. This does not mean they did not marry outside among the ordinary Bura. They did so, and often, but unlike the Bura they were also able to marry close cross-cousins as well using such unions to consolidate an emergent solidarity among the governing class.

But how powerful were these Pabir towns? Accounts by informants tell of kidnappings for ransom just outside the Biu town walls within human memory. Although various towns did accept some adjudication by the Biu Kuthli in the nineteenth century, relations between towns were always semi-hostile. Songs from one town satirized and denigrated people and leaders from other towns. Any person walking alone outside his own town was a potential captive and if such a person had no kin to ransom them he or she became a slave and ultimately an incorporated member of the captor's group.

On the other hand, local traditions speak of some form of inter-village organization in which local Pabir leaders around Biu were all referred to by a similar title and were viewed as subordinate to the ruler in Biu. Early legends never mention such organization. This supra-local system seems to have developed in the nineteenth century. Disputes could be be sent to Biu for settlement and each town aided the other in war and defence. Thlerima (Yerima in Kanuri), as the local leaders were called, appeared periodically in Biu with gifts for the central chief or king, especially at times of royal enthronements and burials. However, there was no regular taxation or tribute, no authority at the centre to depose local chiefs although the King of Biu could influence the choice of local leaders albeit within a set group of eligible heirs to those local chieftaincies.

Oral data indicate that these Pabir Thlerimas or subordinate chiefs can trace their ancestry back about six to ten generations (Davies claims 7 to 15,[27] but I have been unable to replicate his results). This suggests a time depth of approximately two centuries, or a range of about 150 to 250 years ago that this system began to operate. In other words I hypothesize that centralized chiefship in which some form of inter-village subordination and hierarchy was initiated goes back to the late eighteenth and early nineteenth centuries.

It is at this time that the Biu Plateau was increasingly threatened not only by traditional enemies, the Nvwa (Kanuri), but by Fulani forces from the west (Gombe) and north west (Misau). Local traditions generally lump most of these incursions together associating them with

the name Buba Yero the founder of Gombe emirate. The Biu king lists
tell of leaders who were killed in wars against the Fulani some time in
the mid-eighteenth century. Certainly these people made many incursions into Biu during this period, raiding, pillaging, and looking for
new lands in which they could settle. Davies spoke to informants who
told of successful attempts by these conquerors to set up permanent
settlements over the entire Biu Plateau. Villages that previously recognized Kogu-Biu were subordinated to the Muslim Fulani within a much
more hierarchized organization.

In response, traditions state that on several occasions Pabir rulers
tried to unite and drive out the invaders. Finally, this was done, or it
was done several times (accounts differ), under the leadership of the
chiefs of Biu. In order to accomplish this, previously autonomous
towns had to unite and produce sufficient manpower to repulse a
numerous and determined enemy. It was these attempts at defence,
plus Fulani emirate organization which had actually penetrated the
Plateau, that finally produced a Pabir centralism in which several towns
emerged as capitals while others were more or less subordinate.

Along with these changes in organization came fundamental changes
in political culture. The hero-founder of the Pabir kingdom embodies a
number of these ideas as well as indicating continuities with the wider
Bura values. He was a superb hunter and warrior, wily, brave, and a
successful leader. These qualities are valued by both Bura and Pabir.
However, he was also a giant – much larger than ordinary men, much
stronger, and thus singular in appearance and qualities. In this sense he
represents a leader who is different from all other men. His story, his
relics, his burial place, and his top-knot of hair (sewed into the hair of
the living monarch) creates impressive continuity of sacred leadership
that separates this lineage from all others. A Bura headman founded a
village; Yampta-ra-walla did that but he symbolizes as well the founding
of extraordinary leadership in which Bura headmanship is transformed
into a permanent stable monarchy that sees fission as evil.

Many of the symbols of Pabir monarchy emphasize this anti-fission
quality while at the same time pointing out the superior strength,
status, and supernatural powers of the leader. Let me summarize two of
these very briefly. First, there is the legend of the death of the royal
founder. The story is complex but basically refers to rivalry between
the founder's two sons, the younger of whom flaunts his father's

authority and causes him to sink into the ground whereupon a wife seizes and detaches his top-knot of hair in an attempt to save her spouse. Afterwards the sons found two rival kingdoms. The tale shows that lack of respect for authority and fraternal jealousy lead to conflict, fission, and the weakening of the polity.

Secondly, there is the curious and widespread institution of the 'queen mother'.[28] The queen mother lived in a separate unwalled town a mile or two from the capital. She ran her own administration and visited the king twice a year to discuss affairs of state and to admonish him about good government. She was also the keeper of the sacred royal objects used to enthrone a king. She represents unity and integration. Dissidents may go to her and she will protect them.

More importantly she must never be a real mother to the king. Instead she is a wife to the previous king chosen from a segment of the royal family whose male members are losing their claim to the throne. She uses such male heirs, plus officials of her dead husband's court who are now not in office, as the basis of her own court in the queen's village. This is the group most likely to split if the society were not a centralized one. Instead they form a separate 'woman's' segment of the centralized society. Thus, the queen concept is used to symbolize wholeness, integration, continuity, and to organize opposition but keep it within the system rather than using it as a reason for cleavage and break-up.

Although the point is complex, it is important to note that among the less hierarchized Bura lineage splitting that tends to break polities is reckoned as occurring among half-brothers once the common father is dead. The point of union and origin of lineages is the 'door' or women whose co-wife statuses produced the half-brother. 'Door' is also the word for lineage. Thus, unity and possible splitting occurs in the less hierarchized system because co-wives or 'doors' produce separate lines of half-brothers. The half-brothers are linked to one another by a woman.

The queen mother is an elaboration of this original idea in which gender is used to symbolize unity and the possibility of splitting. She keeps the royal objects because she is a woman. If a man has them he would make himself king. Finally her town is unwalled because she houses the political opposition and this rule keeps her vulnerable and dependent upon the royal capital.

Finally, Islam was entering the area. I raise this point to show that along with indigenous ideas of centralized authority outside ideas were becoming acceptable as well. Islamic concepts of jurisprudence, of state-craft, and administration were becoming available in the persons of 'ulema' or Muslim teacher-priest-jurists. With or without colonialism, the Pabir were moving toward the evolution of a Muslim emirate. The British did not create the Pabir state, they merely hastened and forced its development along lines being tried elsewhere in northern Nigeria.

CONCLUSIONS

Substantive

Buraland is an African melting pot. Into it have flowed cultural influences from pre-Islamic Sudan, from its surrounding peoples, and from the emergence of states to the north and the west. Its original social and political organization involved a dynamic equilibrium in which excess population flowed in a generally westwards direction, and some form of local unity was maintained through marriage, religion and inter-settlement cooperation in farming and periodic communal hunts. Cultural and social change sifted gently through this localization so that new cults, new clans, and new trading contacts could be created with very few basic changes as long as local settlements were permitted to maintain their small-scale and independent way of life.

In the northern part of the area, Buraland witnessed the evolution of the Pabir variant — a Bura culture and society adapted to the development of more centralized political institutions. This radical change was triggered by raiding and other forms of hostility from the newly-founded northern kingdoms. Aided by a migrant warrior-hero and by other contacts to the east, west, and north, these northern Bura-speakers reacted by creating more defensible, more stable, and more densely-populated towns. As towns grew in size and stability, the forces of segmentation which maintain small-scaled locally autonomous governments were constrained from operating. Local leaders grew more powerful and their roles differentiated toward monarchical styled offices. Many aspects of Bura culture remained, but great numbers and degrees of hierarchy were recognized and strong values developed surrounding the kingship along with the unity, continuity, and integration of the polity.as a whole.

Incursions into the area by Fulani who were bent on setting up their own centralized government (related ultimately to the Sokoto caliphate) produced a second more recent surge toward centralized hierarchy. The effect of these later events was the unification of small chiefly towns under a chief of chiefs. It also produced more intimate contacts with Islam, and set the stage for the founding of the present-day Biu emirate. The process was then completed, rather violently and brutally by the British, creating thereby a legacy of bitterness over conquest that has become worse rather than better as time has elapsed.

These historical incidents and the reaction to them were accompanied by socio-cultural and political changes that supported the move to greater hierarchy and made the bifurcation into two types of polity a systemic process rather than an isolated event. Rank differences are not unknown in Bura culture, albeit the society has many egalitarian ideals. However, Pabir society is much more highly stratified and more permanently so. The founder-lineage and clan is now a royal dynasty surrounded by noble lineages all of whom inter-marry to maintain class interaction and solidarity. This meant dropping an exogamy rule that interrelated large-scaled descent groups, and adopting instead cross-cousin marriage with concomitant shifts in kinship terminology. It meant adopting diffused titles for heads of noble lineages, the idea of a royal court, and the concepts of royal burials, installations, a queen mother and many other items of upper class culture that are widely dispersed throughout the pre-Islamic Sudan.[29]

Possibly the most important point is the conclusion that within Bura society itself there are already well-developed institutions out of which greater hierarchy and more centralized government can and did develop. Traditionally Bura society is small-scaled and locally autonomous with low levels of stratification and some well-developed concepts of local leadership based on descent from the founding lineage. This leadership, although never absolute, was recognized across the entire community. Youth organization, hunting, cooperative work groups, and on rare occasions of offense or defence, organizations were also organized loosely on a community-wide basis. Settlements varied within these overall patterns and adapted to local conditions. Although Bura culture, polity and social system fit the classic model of the 'acephalous' society it is in no way pledged by tradition to be anti-hierarchical. The Bura were adapted to conditions which supported a comparatively low level of hierarchy and centralized control. Once such conditions were removed or changed then local variability enabled the development of greater centralization as normally as segmentation had produced a lack of it. Those institutions that could be used for greater centralization shifted toward newer institutions that could be used to sustain and elaborate a more stratified and complex polity. At the same time institutions that helped in this development and were useful to it such as titles, royal burial practices, and the utility of integration ideology embodied in the queen mother concept were borrowed from neighbours who already had such practices.

System-Theoretical

The development of Pabir centralism is an example of secondary state formation. Borno witnessed the founding of a highly centralized and expansionist state centred at Birni Gazargamu at the end of the fifteenth century. This development of a primary state led to the secondary developments described in this paper.

In systemic and evolutionary terms we can say that once a new state appears in an area of non-state societies the peoples of the more poorly organized groups can react in three ways. They may remain and be incorporated into the rising expansionist state; they may run away and preserve their former way of life; or they may, along with others already there, organize themselves more thoroughly to withstand the power of the new state.

All of these reactions do in fact occur. The expansionist state provides a strong selective pressure which upsets previous inter-societal and intra-societal relations within locally autonomous polities in its region. The essence of non-centralized political organization is a constant tendency for segmentation as population and land pressure, along with internal disputes, force lineages to hive off from the wider descent group which produced them. A dynamic equilibrium is reached in which greater organizational hierarchy and complexity (negentropy) is kept within limits by cultural, political, and economic variables that unite groups, and interlock them in a highly adaptive system of ordered, yet autonomous localized settlements. Inter-group hostility is mostly a personal, or lineage, affair to be settled by revenge killing, seeking compensation, or using 'medicine'. There is no concept of conquest, of plunder, of raiding for slaves, or demanding tributes. These are the policies of states. Once practised, they produce the selection pressure already referred to; absorption and running away occur. The surrounding acephalous societies are forced into denser, larger population centres. Segmentation can no longer operate as an equilibrating process.

The values of the other variables contributing to the maintenance of such a system must then all shift toward greater centralization. Political disputes cannot so easily be settled by breaking up. Security requires town life which in turn means that the authority of leaders is enhanced sufficiently to adjudicate and enforce decisions. Heads of lineages, especially the older ones, form a council of titled courtiers and this emerging upper class disregard any restriction placed on close marriages that ally them to one another.

Continued threats of outside hostility provide grounds for unification of these separate town chieftaincies into a loose federation under a recognized *primus inter pares* — and negentropy takes another step when each town head becomes in some sense a follower and subordinate of the central chief of chiefs. This latter takes a title depicting his superior position and there is a tendency for some generic title to develop to express the next lower set of positions in the hierarchy.

This is one way for centralized hierarchies to develop. There are undoubtedly others. The end-product, however, wherever it is found in human history, is remarkably similar. Hierarchy is a constraining structural feature that makes narrowing demands upon the variety of structures that precede it in social evolution. Thus, no matter which factor sets the process off — the outcome is always predictable because increased hierarchy demands centralized control, a line of subordinate officers connecting outlying areas to the centre, and a means of maintaining the structure against fissionable forces. This latter requires integrative mechanisms, i.e. ideology, bureaucracy, and a monopoly over the use of force. Such constraints leave history little room for variety.

From a comparative theoretical point of view, it is clear that the stress on population pressure in the contemporary literature is well-founded. However, population pressure can be stimulated by political as well as technological factors. Pabir food production is in no way different from that of its Bura precursor culture. Instead population pressure increased as a direct function of the need for defence and the means available to accomplish it. Population pressure led in turn, or more accurately it is associated with, other developments all of which, again, point the direction of change toward the same narrow set of outcomes.

In terms of more controversial issues these data lead us to agree with Horton rather than Fried.[30] Warfare does help to create the centralized state. However, whether stratification precedes or follows centralizing tendencies is really something of a non-question. There was some stratification in Bura society and much more in Pabir after it centralized. What is much more important is the necessity to revise our view of small-scaled locally autonomous societies not just as non-states but as almost anti-state, anti-hierarchical and dedicated egalitarian systems. The Tiv and Nuer segmentary systems from which much theorizing about locally autonomous societies has proceeded are in fact quite unusual in their nature. Much more common, especially in Africa, are societies of the Bura type, composed of flexible and heterogeneous clans united under the variable authority of a local head whose descent group founded the settlement.

Horton sees such groups becoming more stratified once they become more compact, giving rise to community-wide organizations such as central offices, age grades and secret societies. It is now possible to say that community-wide organizations can be present under dispersed non-compact conditions. The state, greater centralized control of society, and more hierarchical organization are the result of selective factors such as warfare (but this is certainly not the only one). These selectors utilize variants in kin-based systems, such as community-wide organizations and offices, in order to build a system adapted to the new pressures. The result is a society that not only contains heterogeneous clans but one that unites them into a centralized polity.

NOTES AND REFERENCES

1. Research for this paper was carried out with the cooperation of the North-eastern State Government, Borno Provincial, and Biu Divisional authorities. Funds were generously supplied by the National Science Foundation, the National Endowment for Humanities, and the Rockefeller Foundation. The author is grateful to all these agencies but takes full responsibility for the information contained herein. The author is grateful to his colleagues and students for their many comments and criticisms especially Professors Paul Newman and Robin Horton from whose comments the paper has gained immeasurably. A previous version of this paper appears in Savana.

2. See, for example the following: D. E. Dumond, 'Swidden agriculture and the rise of Maya civilization', *Southwestern Journal of Anthropology*, 17: 301-16, 1961; 'Population growth and culture change', *Southwestern Journal of Anthropology*, 21: 304-24, 1965; E. Boserup, *The Conditions of Agricultural Growth* (Chicago: Aldine, 1965); R. Carneiro, 'On the relationship between size of population and complexity of social organization', *Southwestern Journal of Anthropology*, 23: 234-43, 1967; M. H. Fried, *The Evolution of Political Society* (New York: Random House, 1967); M. J. Harner, 'Population pressure and the social evolution of agriculturalists', *Southwestern Journal of Anthropology*, 26: 67-86, 1970; R. Horton, 'Stateless societies in west Africa', in: J. F. Ade Ajayi and M. Crowder (eds.), *History of West Africa*, Vol. I (Oxford: Longmans, 1971), pp. 73-119; A. Alland Jr, 'Cultural evolution: the Darwinian model', *Social Biology*, 19(3): 227-37, 1972.

3. M. H. Fried, op. cit., 196-204.

4. R. Carneiro, op. cit., 239.

5. M. J. Harner, op. cit.

6. A. Alland Jr, op. cit., 236.

7. M. Harris, cited as personal communication in A. Alland Jr, op. cit., 234.

8. H. Spenser (1896), *The Principles of Sociology*, Vol. 2 (New York: Appleton), 520-24.

9. M. H. Fried, op. cit., 215.

10. R. Horton, op. cit.

11. Ibid.

12. R. Carneiro, op. cit.

13. R. Horton, op. cit.

14. Ibid.

15. R. Cohen (1967), *The Kanuri of Bornu* (New York: Holt Rinehart and Winston); (1971), 'From empire to colony: Bornu in the nineteenth and twentieth centuries', in: V. W. Turner (ed.), *Colonialism in Africa 1870-1960* (Cambridge: Cambridge University Press), 74-126.

16. P. Newman, 'Study Kanakuru, understand Hausa', *Harsunan Nijeriya*, 2: 1-13.

17. R. Cohen (1975), 'The pull of opposites: autonomy and incorporation in

Nigeria', in: Ibrahim Abu-Lughod (ed.), *African Themes: Northwestern Studies in Honor of Gwendolen M. Carter* (Northwestern University: Program of African Studies).

18. Nigerian National Archives, Kadura [NNAK], BIUDIST J. 1.

19. P. Newman (1969-70), 'Linguistic relationships, language shifting and historical inference', *Afrika und Ubersee*, 35 (3/4): 217-23.

20. *Quarterly and Annual Reports of Biu Division 1924*, BIUDIST H. 19 NNAK.

21. For a more detailed description of the concept of incorporation and its application to Borno, see R. Cohen and J. Middleton (eds.), (1971), *From Tribe to Nation in Africa* (Intext (London) Scranton, Pa.).

22. Ahmed Ibn Fartua (1926), *History of the First Twelve Years of the Reign of Mai Id is Plooma of Bornu 1571-1583* (trans. H. R. Palmer) (Lagos: Government Printer), 39-41.

23. Ibid., 29.

24. Ibid., 25.

25. A. G. Rubin (1970), 'The arts of the Jukun-speaking peoples of northern Nigeria', PhD thesis, Indiana University, 189-190.

26. Cf. R. A. Talbot, in: Boyd Alexander, *From the Niger to the Nile*, 1907, 23; J. D. Falconer, *On Horseback Through Nigeria*, 1911, 170.

27. G. A. Davies, *The Biu Book* (Zaria: Norla, 1956 (mimeo)), 34.

28. R. Cohen, 'The feminine principle in African political thought', Paper delivered to Canadian Africanist Association, York University, Toronto, March 1975, to appear as 'Oedipus, rex and regina', in *Africa* (in press, 1976).

29. R. Cohen, 'Multi-ethnicity in Nigeria', Paper delivered at American Anthropoligical Meetings, Mexico, November 1974.

30. R. Horton, op. cit.; M. H. Fried, op. cit.

10

META-POWER AND THE STRUCTURING OF SOCIAL HIERARCHIES

Tom Baumgartner
University of Quebec at Montreal

Walter Buckley
University of New Hampshire

Tom R. Burns
University of New Hampshire

Peter Schuster
University of New Hampshire

Part One: Introduction

Some social scientists emphasize social system stability: once institutionalized, the system is predominantly 'morphostatic' — i.e. tending to maintain its characteristic structures. Others assume that 'morphogenic' processes prevail, that is, structures tend to change or to be reorganized. In the latter case, structural stability is problematic and to be explained in the face of ever-present tendencies for structures to reform, change, or evolve. What we try to suggest here is a framework that allows social systems both morphostatic and morphogenic processes which are often working at odds with one another. Thus, attempts to strengthen a given

---

For Deena and Valerie who made the impossible possible this time as well as on many other occasions.

institutional structure may unleash forces that lead rather to its change; and the opposite may happen as well. Analysis requires that we examine the particular historical and structural conditions to identify and model the morphostatic forces and the potential morphogenic processes. Equally important, these forces and processes will be related to events in the external environment and internal milieu of the system.

Morphostatic and morphogenic processes may be conceptualized in terms of the mutual interaction of four analytically distinguishable sets of variables:

(i) environmental, technological, and other material forces;

(ii) social structural factors (political-legal, economic and social class relationships and structures, in particular);

(iii) cultural or ideational factors (e.g. ideology, socialization, education, and related information and evaluation processes); and

(iv) social action and interaction.

The latter are partially constrained and changed by the former three sets of factors, but they also constitute the fluid and dynamic factor supporting or undermining the given institutional structure. That is, while the collective actions of individuals and sub-groups are partially shaped and regulated by material, social structural, and cultural factors, they in turn constitute the driving force for the preservation or change of social structural and cultural conditions as well as of the material conditions of life. Societal stresses and strains generated from social system-environment and intra-system dynamics continually build up or dissipate and consequently form or deform social structures, idea sets, action and interaction potentials, and material conditions as they do so.

This paper investigates processes and conditions which structure (and restructure) social relationships and social structures. *Such structuring constitutes, in part, the 'historical forces' underlying the given institutional structure of societies at a given time, and also the dynamics of new institutional forms continually struggling to emerge.* The main objective of the paper is to model and analyze morphostatic and morphogenic processes related to the development of stratification systems and of social control hierarchies. Such structures are characterized by chains of domination (under elite control). The development, maintenance, and change of hierarchical systems (e.g. in state formation or the development of industrial organization) depend both on material conditions and on the social-cultural context; ecological constraints and the distribution of physical resources, on the one hand, and ideological and institutional support structures, on the other, structure the patterned ways actors orient to and interact with one another.

This paper examines the multiple structuring processes and conditions — ecological and technological, social structural, and cultural — operating either at cross purposes or in more or less compatible ways on interaction systems to structure them. They structure in particular, the complex of action possibilities, their outcomes of payoffs, and the ideological and cultural orientations of actors in relation to one another. Also, actors through their own efforts make up a part of these forces.

In the second and third parts of the paper, we identify and examine several of the important structuring processes and their structural products. Among the structuring processes and conditions examined are: geographical and ecological factors shaping human action possibilities; the conscious efforts of different individuals and groups to structure interaction systems; productive and distributional factors underlying structuring potentialities and activities of individuals and groups; and structural outcomes which represent secondary or unintended consequences of human action and interaction. The main objective of this investigation is to explore and model complex combinations of structuring processes and conditions which contribute to or limit stratification and hierarchical development.

Of special interest in this investigation are the multiple feedback relationships between structuring processes and conditions and social structures. The social structures which result from structuring forces operate themselves as structuring forces through their effect on human activities and the flow of human and material resources. In the second part of the paper we relate structuring processes — and in particular the exercise of structural control by actors in the development of hierarchical relationships — to differential control of resources. Differential resource control entails a difference in action opportunities among actors. The resources enable an actor to engage in structuring activities by manipulating the payoff structures and ultimately the action possibilities of other actors.

Because the establishment and maintenance of relationships and control processes that connect parts into a network or structure require resources, this paper pays special attention to the relationships between, on the one hand, the expansion, contraction, and distribution of populations and strategic resources and, on the other, the development of stratification systems and hierarchical control structures. Several relationships of particular concern in the paper are:

(i) processes of power amplification, e.g. the processes whereby initial power differences of a minor nature enable, under certain conditions, those in an advantageous position to gain or attract yet additional strategic resources and to carry out restructuring activities to develop and maintain a more highly differentiated power system;

(ii) the relationship between constraints on mobility or emigration and the development of stratification systems and hierarchical control structures; that is, the relationship between demographic flows and structural stability and change;

(iii) the relationship between structural stability and change and strategic resource distribution – and changes in such distributions – among actors committed to different structural arrangements;

(iv) the relationship between morphostatic processes and the flow of resources to those committed to the existing structure, enabling them to overcome or counteract restructuring forces, including efforts on the part of other actors to restructure it; and

(v) the relationship between morphogenesis and the lack on the part of those committed to the existing structures of sufficient power over, or effective counter-measures against, restructuring processes.

One of the complex structuring patterns which we investigate in the second part of the paper links productive and distributional factors underlying structuring potentialities and activities of actors to ecological constraints. Specifically, we examine the hypothesis that unequal distribution of power resources (as a result of exchange, conflict, demographic, or productive processes) *in conjunction with* geographical and/or social constraints which limit emigration or withdrawal from the social system of those in less favorable positions, generally facilitates the development of highly stratified systems. We find that this occurs in part because a *positive feedback loop* between initial power differences and differential accumulation of power resources *makes the social system structurally unstable.* The power differences enable *relational control,* i.e. influence over the existing matrix of action possibilities, action outcomes, and orientations within which social interaction occurs. Superordinate or advantaged groups are able to gain societal resources disproportionately and to use these in further structuring activities to maintain and develop the system of inequality. At the same time, constraints on emigration from the social system compel subordinate or disadvantage groups to accept their inferior positions. In general, initial power differences, even quite small ones, in positional advantage and power accumulation can be amplified under such conditions into major institutional class structures. Such developments, combined with inter-societal competition and conflict, reinforce internal social stratification as well as stratification among societies. These processes underlie the emergence and development of state and empire, as we hope to demonstrate in Part Three.

Part Two: General Concepts and Principles:
The Structuring of Social Relationships and Social Structures

The object of a dynamic structural theory of society is to specify and explain the historical processes and conditions under which social structures emerge and develop, are maintained, decay, or are replaced. Furthermore, it is to model and analyze the conditions under which these events occur. In most actual historical processes, several structuring processes go on simultaneously. What is of interest here are the ways in which these various processes operate, interact with one another, change, and so forth. This part of the paper outlines certain general concepts and principles relating to structuring processes and their outcomes: ecological constraints, meta-power and relational control, exogenous controls and social ecological constraints, and structuring processes as secondary or unintended consequences of social action. We then explore certain of the productive and distributional processes underlying structural stability and change, in particular the relation of the availability and distribution of resources to the structuring of social structures.

SYSTEMS OF INTERACTION

For the purposes of conceptualizing and analyzing the structuring processes and conditions pertaining to the maintenance and change of social structures, we treat any ongoing social system as a *system of interaction* within a *social structural context* (encompassing economic, political, and other bases of power differences).

An interaction system, involving actors *A, B, C, . . .*, can be conceptualized as consisting of at least three system components: the action and interaction possibilities of the actors, the likely outcomes or payoffs of their interaction in specific situations, and a culture of normatively defined as well as emergent values and orientations among the actors which, among other things, define qualities of their established or potential social relationships. In our general model, the *behavioral outcomes* of the interaction system are a function of the states of its three system components.

(1) The interaction *situation* — the *complex of possible actions* available to the actors in a particular situation, both those implicit in a given structure as well as available alternatives. Possible actions are constrained by the physical and social environment, the availability of resources, and the actors' perceptions of available actions. Of particular importance for the analysis of the development, maintenance, and change of structures is the way conditions and processes produce differing degrees of assymetry of action opportunities within a given institutional framework; that is, the degree to which actors have more or less unequal rights, perquisites or, in general, access to societal resources. Specifically, one actor's control of a scarce resource represents action opportunities with respect to that resource which other actors do not have. Structuring conditions and processes may also facilitate or inhibit the possibilities for actors to communicate, combine, and cooperate or to segregate and compete or conflict.

(2) The interaction *payoffs* — or outcome structure — is the aggregate of outcomes associated with particular actions or combinations of actions. The structure of gains and losses associated with actions may promote certain actions and discourage others. For instance, it may promote competitive private interests or cooperative interests.

(3) The actors' attitudes and *orientations* toward one another — i.e.

their predisposition to act in particular ways toward particular (classes of) actors based on a culture of normatively defined as well as emergent values and orientations among the actors. Such orientations may promote vertical orientation and loyalty to 'superior' persons or groups as opposed to horizontal cooperation with other actors in co-equal situations. They may also promote a general distrust and an individualistic self-interest ideology or trust and social cooperative ideology.

SOCIAL STRUCTURES AND STRUCTURING PROCESSES

In addition to the concept of interaction system, we make use of two other basic concepts: *social structure* and *structuring process*. Structuring processes are those mechanisms or processes through which social relationships between and among actors are formed and transformed. The resulting social structure refers to the set of characteristic relationships among actors in a social system. These relationships entail on the one hand, the mutual orientations of the actors and, on the other, patterns of action which are intermittently enacted in the physical world.[1]

Structuring processes operate on the three components of interaction systems to structure mutual orientations and interaction patterns and, therefore, play a role in the building up and the maintenance or change of social relationships and structures. (In this paper we focus on the first two components.)[2] There are a variety of such processes and conditions. Below we discuss several which play a major part in the building up and the maintenance or change of social relationships and structures. As suggested above, these processes operate by shaping the action and interaction possibilities and payoffs (as well as orientations) of actors in a social system. A given institutional or socio-cultural structure may be viewed as the macroscopic resultant of such structuring processes, including the application of power to determine permissable or acceptable activities and relationships of individuals and groups to one another and to forms of property or resources. This system also defines the distribution of benefits and costs for categories of persons and groups.

Of ultimate concern in this paper is the structuring of hierarchical relationships, that is, relationships in which there is differential control over resources and differential action possibilities and payoffs between actors or classes of actors in a social system.

Ecological Constraints on Human Action and its Products

Human action takes place in a physical world which constrains or shapes action and interaction possibilities. The physical environment of actors makes certain actions possible and excludes others. It also determines, to some extent, the outcomes, benefits and costs, associated with particular actions. As a result, the ecological setting of action and interaction has played and continues to play an important part in the structuring of social relationships and social structure.

(i) Geography may have a significant impact on human affairs through its effects on the productivity of human effort and the differential availability of resources which may be used for purposes of production, consumption, or the structuring of social relationships. It may also affect inter-societal communication and diffusion of knowledge and technology. Such conditions have been key factors in uneven development and the socio-cultural evolution of societies.

(ii) Control activities, and structuring activities generally, require communication and transportation of resources. Geography and environment — mountains, rough terrain, jungles — constrain or may make terribly costly communication and transportation. In this way, they can delimit the centralizing (control) potentialities of social systems, other things being equal. Of course, the level of technological development, particularly in the areas of communication and transportation, may offset or overcome the limitations imposed by geography and climate.

Social Ecological Constraints

Social constraints arising in the social environment may contribute, like those of a geographic nature, to the structuring of social relationships and social structures, in spite of possible efforts of control agents to exercise 'relational control' over the relationships and structures. For example, an elite group *A*, pursuing a divide and rule strategy to assure dominance over subordinate groups, may be unable to isolate effectively such groups from one another, so as to prevent their association or organization, and thereby their challenge to *A*'s power over them. This may be the result, for example, of the high density of a subordinate population under conditions of frequent interaction, at the same time that the dominant group lacks sufficient personnel or resources to prevent the emergence and development of such association.

Structuring Processes as Secondary or Unintended Consequences of Social Action

Structuring processes and conditions may entail secondary outcomes (by-products) or unintended consequences of action.

(i) Action takes place in a social world. *A* in pursuit of his objectives, for instance domination and exploitation of *B* and *C*, may set in motion counter-processes in the *B/C* sub-system or in other related systems which ultimately undermine or erode an hierarchical structure of *A* over *B* and *C*. Subordinate actors may react to the unequal distribution of power, and to its (possibly) exploitative exercise, by coalescing and mobilizing either openly or covertly to oppose *A*'s efforts or to make them most costly. In general, structures of institutionalized power and hierarchical control systems generate opposing forces which often undermine the institutionalized assymetrical relationships and structures.

(ii) The goals and interests of a dominant actor *A* may lead him to structure conditions with respect to *B* and *C* which lead to the emergence and development of (unforeseen) social relationships and social structures not directly under *A*'s control. Thus, rulers or leaders, in order to exploit their subordinates more effectively for productive or defence purposes, often intentionally bring them together in larger numbers and organize them. But this density of population and organization can be used for purposes of opposition to their rulers.[3] The genesis of working class consciousness and organization hinged on the heightened density and interaction of workers brought together in the factory context.

(iii) The unintended outcomes of action may reflect the aggregated effect of the more or less independent decisions of a multitude of actors pursued for purposes not necessarily reflected in the structural outcomes. There is no deliberate social control, at least in any collective or organized sense, within the particular social system affected. These unintended consequences may structure and restructure the conditions of action and interaction, i.e. radically altering the complex of action and interaction opportunities for different groups of actors and substantially redistributing payoffs. Examples are numerous: the commercialization of social life, economic and technological development, and group or state formation. Also, competition between groups and in general, pressures to adapt or survive, bring about changes in human activities which are inconsistent with the existing social structure and, therefore, lead to pressures to change established social relationships and social structures (Burns, 1976; Burns and Mattin, 1976). A radical change in the mode of production and conditions of social interaction such as that which occurred through industrialization and urbanization affected every aspect of social life. In particular, extended family ties were significantly modified or in some cases eroded (i.e. the emergence of the modified extended family or in some cases the nuclearized family under conditions of urbanization and high rates of geographic and social mobility); relationships between parents and children, parent and parent were similarly radically altered, and authority relationships in general and community relations were transformed.

*Meta-power and Relational Control: The Human
Structuring of Social Relationships*

We view the exercise of power as oriented substantially toward the shaping of social relationships and social structures through the manipulation of the components of the interaction system.[4] Human actors deliberately try to alter the existing matrix of action possibilities, outcomes, and orientations within which social action occurs. We refer to the exercise of such 'meta-power' as *relational control*, that is, control over social relationships and structures, which we distinguish from power within a given structure: clearly, although an actor may have social power within an interaction framework or 'game' (e.g.

greater ability than others to select a preferred outcome or to realize his will over the opposition of others within that social structural context) he may or may not have power to structure social relationships, to alter the 'type of game' the actors play, or to manipulate or change the distribution of resources or the conditions governing interaction or exchanges among the actors involved (these conditions institutionally define the power and control possibilities for the exercise of behavioral control).

We are especially concerned with situations where an elite *A*, a power group in a social structure, may be in a position to manipulate one or more of the components of an interaction system involving *B*, *C*, *D*, . . ., so as to structure social relationships and their action outputs; in a word to exercise meta-power. Relational control of the interaction situation consists of exercising power to shape the aggregate action and interaction possibilities of those involved in the situation, i.e. to remove certain actions from their repertoires and to create or facilitate others. This may be done, for example, by limiting their ability to communicate or to associate with one another (Baumgartner et al., 1975c). Structuring the gains and losses associated with particular actions and interactions so as to promote or to discourage certain interaction patterns represents relational control with respect to interaction payoffs; for example, the creation of payoff structures such as 'zero-sum' or 'prisoner's dilemma' to promote conflictive or competitive interests. Relational control carried out with respect to orientation might entail promoting distrust or an individualistic self-interest ideology or trust and a social cooperative ideology.

Actors other than an elite *A* may exercise relational control with respect to the social relationships and social structures involving *A*, *B*, *C*, . . . Such power agents may consist of actors outside the social system consisting of *A*, *B*, *C*, . . ., or may consist of *B*, *C*, . . . In the latter instance, the power agents may be members of an organization or social movement (such as a national liberation front, trade union or work group) having ideological or sanctioning power over fellow members to counteract *A*'s divisive structuring attempts. They use their collective power in relation to their own relationships. Through selective sanctions, group normative influence, and other structuring means, they may be able to maintain and develop solidary relationships or particular forms of group relationships and structures in opposition to *A*'s wishes or efforts.

Although an elite may have dominant power in a social system, it none the less may lack complete or unambiguous control over social relationships and structures. Both the discussion on ecological constraints and on unintended consequences of structuring activities point to factors and processes which can limit the elite's meta-powers. (Also, as pointed out in note 3, *A* may be faced with the dilemma between developing social relationships and structures compatible with *A's* domination over subordinate groups and developing social relationships and structures conducive to other goals, e.g. the improvement of production or defence.)

RESOURCE DISTRIBUTION AND SOCIAL DIFFERENTIATION

Social differentiation is understood here in terms of the emergence and maintenance of differences among actors in their action capabilities and control over valuables or resources potentially or actually useful in structuring activities in a particular structural context. Such differences in power result from processes and conditions which operate to *distribute* action capabilities and control over valuables (resources in the broadest sense) unequally among actors in a society as well as between societies.

There are at least four major general sources of such differentiation:[5]

(i) natural capabilities (physical, mental, and levels of energy) are distributed unequally through biological (as well as social structural and cultural) mechanisms among members of a society;

(ii) natural resources are distributed unequally over human populations because of their differential availability in a non-uniform environment;

(iii) the distribution of property rights among actors in social systems and the positions of actors in a social structure provide differential control possibilities with respect to the disposition and use of material and non-material resources; and

(iv) social exchange and conflict, as well as population movements typically result in differences in resource control and action possibilities or in processes relating to resource control among actors in a society as well as between societies.

Several of the specific, historically important distributional processes underlying social differentiation and ultimately the development of stratification and hierarchical control are discussed briefly below.

Defeat in War or Political Struggles

The victors gain control of resources, booty, slaves, land, etc. as a result of the use of force. The unequal payoffs associated with warfare lead to social differentiation between victors and vanquished as well as *within* each of these groups. The victorious group may simply take booty from defeated groups or it may establish itself over them in lord/serf or master/slave relationships or other more or less permanent forms of domination and subordination (e.g. tributary status).[6] (Of course, conquerors may simply push indigenous populations out of the way, as in the settlement of the North American continent.)

The distribution of resources acquired in warfare (booty, conquered territories, captives who will be made slaves) among the members of a victorious group tends to be unequal, going more to the chiefs and their lieutenants. Because it contributes to hierarchical structuring of relationships between societies as well as to stratification within societies, warfare is closely associated with state formation and empire development.[7]

Allocation of Meta-power to Superordinates by Subordinates

Members of a collectivity may allocate structuring power to the leadership A in response to an internal crisis or a threat from outside. The internal crisis may be the need to mediate strife, to deal with major problems of production or distribution or to coordinate large public works. The group may also allocate power to its leadership to deal with an external threat (e.g. war) or simply to interact with agents in the external environment. In the latter case, A becomes an agent for the group in dealing with other actors in the external environment. In general, internal crisis or external threat induce subordinates to provide 'social capital' to the central leadership or to elites (e.g. religious leaders) already controlling community-wide institutions, with which to create or change existing structures and societal processes.

Migration into Dependence

Population pressures or fissionary tendencies in a community may result in groups migrating to areas where they enter into dependent relationships to the original settlers or dominant lineage in an area.[8] In this context, they are allocated inferior land and enter into a wife-taking relationship to the dominant group, thereby tending to reinforce the domination relationship (see section on 'Unequal Exchange', below).

Gorlin (1972 a, b), Burns et al. (1973) and Ruyle (1974), have suggested that population pressure, fluctuating man/land ratios, and fissionary tendencies among horticulturists where all the land is owned or controlled by patrilineal descent groups may cause some individuals to affiliate with maternal or affinal kin, rather than their own agnatic kin group. In such cases, especially if land is in short supply, non-agnates are likely to be given less land and/or poorer land than are agnatic members of the group. Furthermore, they may be asked to pay rent or provide labor services to the agnates for use of land (Ruyle, 1974).

Unequal Exchange (Baumgartner and Burns, 1974; Baumgartner et al., 1975b)

The allocation of resources through exchange and through the system of distribution of economic and other goods may be unequal, favoring some individuals or groups over others.[9] Because of variation in the capabilities and in action opportunities among the actors involved (e.g. their different positions in the social system), some may gain more from exchange than others. There also may be biases built into an exchange system, particularly one with any degree of complexity, which favor one or more actors or classes of actors over others, by providing them with more resources or greater capabilities in the course of exchange activity. Examples of unequal exchange processes are numerous:

(i) Friedman (1974), drawing on Levi-Strauss, suggests how in generalized exchange in simpler societies, increased production or increased accumulation of resources through clever tactics, kinship support, etc. can be turned into prestige through feasting, that is, by distributing surplus. When differential production and ability to distribute, and resultant differentiation of prestige are linked to wife-giver/wife-taker exchange relationship (which favors the former over the latter), *status differences may be accentuated and stabilized.* Cattle is the main item of bride-price, and is returned to wife-takers in the form of feasts. Prestige moves in the opposite direction. As a result there is a tendency toward *differential accumulation of prestige and ability to attract resources, distribute them, and alter their relative value.*

(ii) The products of productive activity in employer/employee exchange in capitalist society are not distributed equally in a structural sense, for the employer is provided with action opportunities and powers both within the productive system and in the larger social system which are not made available to the employee. In particular, the employer gains the meta-power to structure relationships in the productive system as well as in the larger social system (for example, in the latter case by trading economic concessions and favors for political advantages). The employer also gains opportunities to acquire control over goods, resources or conditions which enhance his long-term action capabilities and social position, for instance, to maintain and stabilize the domination relationships of employer over employee. On the other hand, workers gain little or no power leverage from the income they receive, since this generally provides only *short-term* individualistic consumptive benefits. The exchange is asymmetrical not only because the employer retains exclusive control over the physical means of production, but because he gains control over the actions of employees and the economic and non-economic products, spin-offs and spill-overs of such action applied to the means of production.[10/11]

In general, the horizontal and vertical division of labor and social differentiation has had other than economic consequences such as increases in productivity. It has entailed substantial shifts in the distribution of power and control, the formation of new groups, etc.

CHANGING CONTEXT OF RESOURCE
CONTROL

Differential control over certain resources may be unimportant in a particular context in that control over them does not provide a basis to build and maintain structure (see related discussion on p. 234). However, circumstances may develop which make the resource valuable and control over it a major basis of social power in the society. Thus, persons or groups B, lacking the resource, enter into relation with A to obtain it, although initially it may not be essential for them to do so. However, other sociological, ideological, or material developments occur, altering the relative importance of the resource and making the Bs greatly dependent on A. These changes may be gradual and imperceptible. Several examples of such developments are provided below:

(i) Population increases lead to changes in the value of land. This contributes to a process of power differentiation among those having differential control over the resource.

(ii) External threat or even internal crisis may lead to conditions or processes which enhance the relative importance of leadership positions and community-wide institutions, and thereby enhance the power and status of those associated with them (see Cohen, this volume).

(iii) Differential control over money may not be of major significance until society shifts to a money economy with private banking and other monetary institutions in which control over money flows and money creation is critical to economic and eventually political power.

(iv) Control over land and agricultural production becomes a particularly strategic resource relative to manufacturing resources when the large-scale export of agricultural produce brings in money and provides tax revenue and other benefits to important sectors of society. The absence of such opportunities or possibilities for other economic sectors makes for a power amplification process within society, favoring and reinforcing the power of those controlling land and agricultural production (see related discussion on p. 253). In this way, the power of those controlling such resources and associated activities develops, and the hegemony of agricultural, or in other instances of commercial and manufacturing interests is established in societies which have come to depend (for their income and acquisition of resources) primarily on agricultural or commercial activity and manufacturing, respectively.

AMPLIFICATION AND LIMITATION
OF SOCIAL DIFFERENTIATION

Here we explore several conditions under which the development of inequality, in particular stratification systems and hierarchical control structures, is enhanced or limited. In other words, differences in action capability, resource control, and structuring capabilities, are amplified or restricted by positive or negative feedback loops linking current differences in action possibilities and payoffs among actors to future differences.

Limitations on Social Differentiation

Most social systems exhibit the differentiation tendencies discussed above. But the development of stratification may be inhibited or prevented by ecological and social ecological factors mentioned earlier. Geographical constraints on communication and transportation can limit A's possibilities of building up or maintaining a centralized structure of control. Subordinated groups may have opportunities to emigrate. Institutional and social structural factors may permit the diffusion of knowledge, technology, and generally, resources so as to maintain a more homogeneous society. Normative and ideological views, when backed up by social organization and resource control, can enforce resource redistribution and inhibit extreme social differentiation. It may also be that the hierarchical development itself sets in motion, at least over the long run, social and economic processes which limit its development.[12] Groups unite in response to exploitation and subordination and use collective effort and struggle to counteract or countervail an elite's attempt to amass further power or to abuse its power; they may possibly institute a more egalitarian system. Below we illustrate in more detail two processes which constrain the concentration of power. We focus attention on the role of emigration and on the

role of institutionalized opportunities for opposition — or to use the
metaphors of Hirschman (1970), 'exit' and 'voice' — as factors constraining the development of hierarchical structures.

Emigration possibilities. In general, under conditions where the
productive activity and products of subordinate productive groups are
not readily replaceable, there is an inverse relationship between emigration opportunities for subordinate actors in a social system and the
hierarchical development of society. To the extent that *A* depends on *B*
for the production of resources which *A* then appropriates, for
example, through a structured unequal exchange system, emigration of
B effectively limits hierarchical development to a level which *B* finds
acceptable or tolerates; this limits not only differential but absolute
accumulation (by *A*) of resources through unequal exchange between
A and *B*.

The availability of emigration possibilities means that the total
supply of basic resources such as hunting and gathering grounds or
agricultural lands are not and cannot be monopolized by powerful or
influential figures in the society and denied to weaker or more subordinate actors.[13] It means that one of the action opportunities open
to subordinates who are subjected to efforts to create a more stratified
or exploitative system is simply to leave the system.

The inverse relationship between emigration possibilities and limited
political integration and hierarchical development have been pointed
out by a number of studies. We summarize a few of these briefly.

(i) *Ndembu of Zambia* (Epstein, 1968; Turner, 1967). Village conflicts generate fissionary tendencies. The availability of land permits the
secession of conflicting groups, generally along lines of lineage segmentation. Subordination is avoided by emigration, thus limiting the
extent of political integration and hierarchical development.

(ii) *Africa in general.* Goody (1971) emphasizes that migration to
acephalous systems at the peripheries of centralized kingdoms, facilitated by the low intensity of agriculture and low concentration of
resources, has made it impossible to build up despotic regimes of the
oriental type.

(iii) *Toradja of Sulawesi, Indonesia* (Burns et al., 1973). Among the
Bare'e-speaking Toradja people, the area was sparsely populated, and
there was no shortage of land and ample opportunity for mobility. If a
chief became overbearing, people tended to shift their allegiance to

another chief or leave their villages and join others. In general, there were few opportunities for an individual, group, or village to establish stable hegemony over others — either by force or by the accumulation of property or other resources.[14]

(iv) *Majanjir, Southwest Ethiopia* (Stauder, 1972). The expansion of the Majanjir, slash and burn horticulturists, has been a process of pioneering forested areas not exploited by any other groups. The domestic group among the Majanjir is not attached over time to any particular property, but depends for its continuing existence on the working relationships among its members. The domestic group dissolves when these relationships break down for any reason. The absence of stratification and significant hierarchical structuring depends not only on the availability of abundant and widespread natural resources but on minimal economic and social disadvantages to residential mobility, in short minimal costs and social ties. These conditions have, as Stauder argues, inhibited the formation of organized or coherent local groups, the development of organized corporate pan-tribal sodalities, or the emergence of institutionalized political leadership (Stauder, 1972, p. 167).

(v) *Amazon Basin* (Caneiro, 1970). The Amazon Basin provided almost unlimited agricultural land to simple horticulturists. 'Warfare' was frequent but occurred only for revenge, the taking of women, or the gaining of prestige and similar motives. Defeated villages often chose to flee to a distant part of the forest, not to avoid subjugation, but simply to avoid attack. A defeated group was not as a rule driven from its land. Nor did the victor make any real effort to subject the vanquished or to exact tribute from him. It would have been difficult to accomplish in any case, since there was no effective way to prevent the losers from fleeing to a distant part of the free forest (Caneiro, 1970, p. 735):

> With settlement so sparse in Amazonia, a new area of forest could be found and occupied with relative ease, and without trespassing on the territory of another village. Moreover, since virtually any area of forest is suitable for cultivation, subsistence agriculture could be carried on in the new habitat just about as well as in the old.
> It was apparently by this process of fight and flight that horticultural tribes gradually spread out until they came to cover thinly but extensively, almost the entire Amazon Basin. Thus, under the conditions of unlimited agricultural land and low population density that prevailed in Amazonia, the effect of

warfare was to disperse villages over a wide area and to keep them autonomous. With only a very few exceptions ... there was no tendency in
Amazonia for villages to be held in place and to combine into larger political
units.

In sum, conflict and substantial subordination — in the case of
communities with unclaimed frontier areas which is of the same general
character as settled areas and which cannot be policed effectively by
superordinate groups — will typically lead to emigration and fissionary
processes. These prevent amplification of power differentiation and
therefore limit the development of stratification and hierarchical structures. In general, one can hypothesize that the more readily subordinate
actors have access to basic resources outside of an *A/B* superordinate-
subordinate system of relationships, the less *A* will be able to dominate
B, exploit his labor or the products of his labor, and to build up
hierarchical control structures. And if extreme subordination does
develop, the system is unlikely to remain stable, especially under
conditions where the emigrating subordinates (or their products) are
not readily replaceable.

If subordinate actors are able to exit, then an elite is limited to
manipulating payoff structures and making normative appeals in order
to establish and maintain hierarchical structures and to accomplish its
ends. Of course, hierarchical control structures may be built up using
available resources to structure payoffs and therefore social relationships. However, such power is dependent upon the availability and
continuity of a flow of resources and upon the maintenance of the
structure of control over resource flows and distribution by those
committed to the hierarchical control structure. But power based on
the manipulation of payoffs does not provide opportunities to establish
absolute domination.

If, in a particular context, *A* has access to valuable resources which
other actors do not have, at least to the same degree, e.g. trade, mines,
slaves, or land, then he can establish social relationships in which
subordinate actors are to some extent dependent on those resources.
But as long as there are alternative sources of the resources ultimately
available — frontier land, other social systems of collectivities to mi-
grate to or participate in, then it is impossible for *A* to *absolutize* the
relationships since the use of the resources is still limited to the
manipulation of payoffs.[15] For subordinate actors in this case, sub-

mission to *A's* power is marginally better than attempting to obtain the necessary goods from another source. There is still an element of choice involved: if *A* pushes the *B's* too far, they simply leave. Hence, hierarchical structures will tend to be limited in degree and stability.

This suggests that differential control over resources, in and of itself, is not a sufficient condition to create lasting structures. In the absence of scarcity, it is difficult, if not impossible, to structure systems of extreme social domination or hierarchy in any permanent way through using resources for inducements. An absolute abundance of resources makes long-term subjugation and obvious, extreme exploitation most difficult to achieve.

Institutionalized Decentralization. A major source of constraint on centralization, and in some instances hierarchical development generally, is institutionalized decentralization. Owing to the distribution of property rights, positions of authority in the society, fighting skills and weapons, or institutionalized 'civil rights', actors other than the central leadership *A* control strategic resources. This gives them the possibility of mobilizing these resources to carry out structuring activities and to counteract *A's* attempts to amass further power. Independent organized power is found in institutionalized structures not under *A's* control. The consequence is that the central leadership enjoys only limited social power.

Lloyd (1965), for example, finds the power of the royal lineage in competition with the king as a major variable in explaining the structure and degree of centralization in African kingdoms. Or, among the Kpelle of Liberia, the largest of the secret religious societies, the Poro had its own society-wide organization cutting across all segments. Consequently, the king, although the 'supreme ruler' in name, owner of the soil and controller of men's fate, depended on prominent members of the Poro for support in all great questions (Krader, 1968; Burns et al., 1973).[16]

Corporate groups such as the military and police with their considerable control over the means of coercion may play similar countervailing roles. Shifts in the relative scarcity of resources has often allowed their owners to redistribute political power and economic benefits in their favor. This was true even for labor in the wake of the great plagues of Western Europe: serfdom disappeared in many parts of France and England and real incomes of the peasantry increased. Possession of supernatural, administrative, and judicial functions in the form of titled offices with authority and policy-making powers, or possession of the means to activate or call upon constraining normativy rules and procedures of due process,[17] also contributes to checking the central or maximal leader's power. At best, he shares control over these resources with other groups.[18]

Thus, although the distribution of control over resources in several major power domains may be unequal, the distributions are incongruent.[19] In such 'pluralistic' power systems, there may be competion and political struggle among the various actors controlling power resources in the partial systems as they use such resources to influence decisions, policies, and social action.[20] In contrast to the fully centralized system, the maximal leader can exercise independent control over fewer areas of social life. There are more pressures or incentives for leaders to distribute resources, in their competition with one another for followers, especially loyal ones, thus tending toward greater equality in the control over resources. A leader in one sphere will find difficulty in carrying out his will against the opposition of those controlling other power domains, whether the others are a few or many. Yet, if those controlling major power resources concur about an issue, then they are in a position to make binding decisions. Of special interest are the alignments and conflicts among the various actors controlling power resources with respect to specific issues or decisions and the unequal control over the means of coercion under such circumstances.[21]

What we have here are sub-systems in a larger system which are sufficiently developed and in command of resources to be able to resist subordination to *A*, the maximal leader or dominant group in the larger system. They can make the establishment of complete dominance very costly, if not altogether prevent it. The inability of any one of the Western European powers to establish its phyical domination over any of the others for an extended period of time is an illustration. Also, non-Western colonized peoples, who developed group consciousness, learned to organize and use modern military weapons, made the maintenance of direct imperial structures prohibitively costly, leading to at least formal decolonization.[22]

Amplification of Social Differentiation

Initial social differentiation may provide a power advantage which in a particular social structural context can be translated into meta-power. This in turn offers further opportunities to gain and exercise meta-power.[23] Such a positive feedback loop between initial power differences and differential accumulation (over time) of resources *amplifies* social differentiation: certain actors or groups enjoy increasingly greater control and others decreasing control over strategic resources. The process entails uneven development among the actors and creates conditions for the establishment of domination and dependence relationships.

An *amplification process* may occur whenever power differences, even small ones, enable relational control, that is, changing the matrix of action possibilities, action and interaction outcomes, and the orientations within which interactions occur. The process may take the following characteristic forms:

(i) Initial differences in action possibilities or in resource control lead to unequal payoffs (e.g. through conflict or exchange processes) between or among actors with different capabilities and resources. The unequal payoffs make for further differentials in action capabilities and resource control both within the system to which they belong as well as with respect to other systems (and their actors).

(ii) These differences in action capabilities and resource control translate into differential probabilities for further gains. Above all, the power of those in advantageous positions give them opportunities to produce, maintain, or change social structures and in general to structure the social system to a greater or lesser extent to their advantage, for instance by transgressing or overcoming institutionalized constraints on power accumulation. In particular, they can use resources they control to affect interaction systems, specifically to shape action possibilities and payoffs. In this way, they can attract supporters or weaken opponents. Supporters in turn can be used to engage in relational control on a larger scale. Ultimately, an actor *A* in such a position may use the power gained to construct and maintain under his control, hierarchical control structures and networks with compliant participants and supporters. These would be available to carry out *A's* desires and policies with respect to the larger society, for instance encouraging or discouraging cooperative or conflictive links among different individuals and groups. Thus, A may be enabled (for example through divide and rule strategies) to erode or weaken competing segments of society and the structures they control so as to prevent the development or maintenance of structures or processes which might countervail and limit A's power or power development. A's supporters and dependents may also engage in activities of persuasion and culture formation to form the attitudes and orientations of actors to one another.

(iii) As a result of the developments described in (i) and (ii), a positive feedback loop is generated and a new, highly differentiated, structure and system under A's hegemony emerges and develops. Thus, in the particular socio-structural context, A gains comparative ad-¡ vantage in systemic power compared to competing or potentially competing groups.

The establishment of a positive feedback loop between initial power differences and differential power accumulation may arise in several different ways:

(i) Those with initial power advantages attract followers and additional resources away from those with fewer advantages, and they use these to restructure social relationships, rules and institutions, thereby amplifying their power advantages.

(ii) The development of ownership and inheritance rules and rights (as opposed to generalized generosity and egalitarian rules of distribution of resources, etc.) sustains differential control over strategic resources. An elite A may use what might be an initial power advantage to strengthen ownership and inheritance concepts and practices which in turn structure distributional processes assuring maintenance and reproduction of the stratification system benefiting A.

(iii) Those in subordinate positions lack group consciousness and organization, or control over strategic resources and, therefore, are not in a position to oppose A and his domination, exploitation, or division of them. Processes tending to fragment or weaken opposition groups that have previously played a critical role in limiting A's power would contribute to stratification development. And, of course, such developments may have been initiated by A through divide-and-rule strategies (Baumgartner et al., 1975c).

(iv) Demographic movements across societal boundaries may serve to amplify the power of a group or elite A: on the one hand, by the import of persons or groups who become dependent on A and contribute to A's power of collective action within the society, and on the other, by the export of opposition groups (see note 28). Slaves and aliens are particularly useful for structuring activities since they have few social ties in the society and are relatively free from normative and social counter-pressures to the exercise of power and, in addition, have minimal possibilities of organized resistance within the society. Possession of slaves makes for a more *independent social power* (Adams, 1975).

On the other hand, A's position would also be reinforced and stabilized by the emigration or exile of opposition persons or groups.[24] Such emigration may not only open up opportunities for the promotion of those remaining behind into the vacated positions but permit the more selective recruitment of loyal persons and groups into political and economic roles — manipulations which can serve to gain and stabilize commitment to the regime (Hardin, this volume).

Emigration may have a detrimental economic impact with long-term political ramifications, if those emigrating are persons or groups with valuable skills and knowledge, etc. (for example the expulsion of the Moriscos from Spain). Also, the emigrant population may be made up of persons who would support and reinforce the regime and, therefore, this movement operates to undermine the existing socio-political structure. Such pressures to emigrate might arise because of economic difficulties or because of social conflict, e.g. ethnic conflicts.

(v) Ecological or social constraints on emigration or on other withdrawal actions of those in subordinate positions — who contribute resources (labor and the products of labor) to their superiors — typically reinforces social differentiation and hierarchical development (see p. 232).[25] The establishment of national frontiers has been historically a chief instrument of structuralization. (Schumacher, 1973). Boundary control to prevent or inhibit migratory movements is established using the administrative and police power of a more or less well developed state. This may also entail limitations on internal movement.[26] In this respect it is interesting to consider the initial economic and political development of Eastern Europe.

In the early twelfth century, Eastern Europe was very sparsely settled. There was such a great abundance of land that it was viewed as being nearly valueless. Under these frontier conditions and the intense competition for immigrations among lords, obligations for holding land were minimal (Trethewey, 1974). They remained minimal even after villages were established, because the possibility of migration remained.

Famine combined with epidemics, particularly the plague, during the fourteenth and fifteenth centuries reduced immigration from the West and depopulated Eastern Europe. This confronted the nobility with serious losses in income, given the existing rules of distribution of products which had been established to attract and keep immigrants from the West.

But during the earlier settlement and economic development of Eastern Europe, centralized authority had not only developed but had come increasingly under the influence of the nobles. Eventually, the latter used their political power to establish and enforce laws that were directly beneficial to landholding aristocracy.[27] In particular, they imposed increased obligations on the peasantry and restricted their freedom of migration. The end result was the establishment of a manorial system where the right of the peasant to emigrate was eliminated and disputes between peasants and lords were handled in manorial courts on the village level under the control of the local lords. Typically, means were developed to tie the peasants to their manors and to standardize obligations for tenants in order to prevent competition among lords for peasants who had or might abscond from an estate (Trethewey, 1974, p. 37). In sum, boundary control to prevent or inhibit effectively migratory movements can be established using the administrative and police power of a more or less strongly developed state. Such structuring activities reinforce as well as stabilize the stratification system.

As argued in Part Three of this paper, the development of the territorial, fully centralized state is significantly facilitated in a more or less extensive, but (geographically or socially) circumscribed, fertile area which constrains emigration.

THE AVAILABILITY AND DISTRIBUTION
OF RESOURCES RELATING TO THE
STRUCTURING OF SOCIAL STRUCTURES

Differential control over resources, or generally valuables, is the basis of
social power, and in particular of meta-power. The social structuring of
a society structures in large part the action and interaction possibilities
of actors (their 'opportunity structures'). Persons or groups lacking
control over essential material and social resources are unable generally
to initiate and carry out many types of collective actions (either of an
exchange or conflict nature), in particular, the ability to engage in
structuring activities. On the other hand, those with high social status
and power (and therefore greater access to or control over resources
essential for structuring purposes) have greater action possibilities,
including the opportunities to generate new action alternatives and to
engage in structuring activity. Clearly, control over a resource provides
action possibilities and payoff gains based on that particular resource
which those lacking the resource do not have.

Several types of resources for political action can be distinguished:
material, human, and socio-cultural (Nicholas, 1968). Material resources
are the instruments, weapons, tools, machines, goods, land, money, etc.
which an individual or group may use in social action to bring about a
desired outcome. Human resources are actors, either individuals or
groups, whose behavior is under the control of a resource holder. Like
material resources, human resources may be committed to various kinds
of social action with the object of gaining a desirable outcome. Unlike
material resources, however, human ones have goals and values of their
own and may choose to submit to control or not or to aid one's
opponents as well as one's self.

Non-material resources — which are not investigated to any substantial degree in this paper — are represented by social orientations and
relationships and by social norms and values. These are political resources because members of a social system orient to and are guided by
(or respond to) them in their actions. They are factors shaping action
and the structures which generate activities, constraining or facilitating
certain patterns.

Political activity entails the struggle over, and use of, such resources, as individuals and groups attempt to gain or to expand their relative control over them. Typically, actors invest resources and effort to expand their control. That is, they try to establish and maintain for themselves the type of amplification processes described earlier. In the following sub-sections we discuss the relationships between the availability of resources, changes in control over them, their distribution as mediated by social structure, and the morphostatic and morphogenic consequences of resource acquisition and distribution.

Productive and Distributional Processes Underlying
Structuring Capabilities

Extensive structuring activity, particularly as would be involved in producing, maintaining, or transforming a complex social structure, requires resources at a minimum subsistance for those engaged in such activities. Beyond that, resources are used to motivate and to gain the compliance (as well as the long-term commitment and loyalties) of those persons involved in such activities. And, of course, resources are essential to produce or obtain technical means for conducting structuring activities — means of communication, transportation, resources for administration, distribution of valuables, etc.[28]

Of fundamental importance in a structural analysis are the processes of production and distribution of resources potentially available or actually utilized in structuring activities. Climatic, technological, as well as ideological and institutional factors which affect the production and distribution of such resources will influence the structuring and re-structuring of social structures. Of particular interest in this paper are conditions and processes which permit or faciliate such structural developments as centralization or decentralization, structural reversals or cyles in a system. These matters are taken up below and in Part Three.

Resource Availability

Clearly, a certain level of societal productivity, or access of one society or segment of society to the products of another society or segment which has high productivity, is required to provide surplus resources in order to carry out structuring activities. The resources available to establish and maintain elaborate hierarchical structures may be strictly limited, due to the limited productivity of the society and/or limited access to the resources of more productive systems.

For example, the hierarchical development of Kachin society from the egalitarian *gumlao* to the stratified *gumsa* form is normally reversed by a gumlao rebellion which reinstates the egalitarian form (Leach, 1954; Friedman, 1974). Gumlao rebellions occur when Kachin chiefs try to increase the socio-economic distance between themselves and their people by refusing to fulfil kinship obligations and by attempting to transform the wife-giver/wife-taker relation into a lord/peasant relation. However, the limited productivity of the system of production fails to provide sufficient resources for relational control which could effectively change the rules and social relationships in a direction of greater inequality.[29]

However, in other Kachin groups which have direct or indirect access to additional resources, for example jade mines or trade routes, non-egalitarian structures have generally developed and been maintained wherever access to such resources is exercised differentially by chiefs and commoners and, therefore, where the former can appropriate more of the gains to themselves (Friedman, 1974).

Irrigation agriculture permits permanent settlement and high population density. As a result, the absolute surplus available for structuring activities (including the construction of large public works) is usually substantial (Friedman, 1974). In addition, resultant specialization, better organization and, above all, diffusion of technological discoveries may lead to improvements in agriculture and also to an increase in the relative surplus, thus providing additional resources with which to support structuring activities.

Distributional Processes and Structural Stability and Change

The distribution of resources depends to a considerable degree on the existing social structure, since that structure mediates the distributional processes. To the extent that resource distribution, including that of new resources, depends on and therefore reflects the existing social structure, the structure will be reproduced. Although those enjoying hegemony in a social system typically try to use their meta-power to maintain the existing social structure, they lack control over all of the structuring processes which act on the social structure. Social systems interact with their environment, especially other social systems, and are subject to both internal and external forces of change. Hence, regardless of the intentions of those in a dominant position, there tend to be morphogenic developments over the long run.

Consequently, the differential allocation of power resources and action possibilities through distributional processes may either maintain or modify the existing or established pattern of control over power resources and the action capabilities and positions of actors in the structure of social relationships. Three types of structural outcomes of distributional processes may be distinguished in terms of the beneficiaries of the allocation of power resources.

(i) The outcome maintains the original distribution of power resources. The social structure is maintained and reproduced (morphostasis).

(ii) The distribution of power resources may be unequal and reinforce the original distribution of power resources including position in the structure of social relationships, thereby solidifying and elaborating the existing structure.

In cases (i) and (ii), the process favors those actors (or systems) already occupying positions of power advantage.

(iii) Important changes in resource distribution and related transformations of the structure of relationships may work in the direction of a substantially different social structure, possibly one of increased power equality. Also, social structures based on a particular distribution of control over certain strategic resources and action capabilities may undergo a significant transformation due to a shift in the relative importance of resources and capabilities, *thereby altering the basis of social structure.*

Morphostasis and Resource Distribution

Morphostasis obtains whenever the structuring processes and conditions operate in their complex pattern so as to maintain existing character-istic structures: either the structuring processes do not change or any changes occurring in them offset one another. Morphostasis requires that resource flows lead to a structure of meta-power compatible with the existing characteristic structures. In short, the established order is maintained or reproduced. This means that *the resources essential in that historical and socio-political context to the structuring activities* are distributed to those *(As)* committed to maintaining the structure and that these are sufficient to counteract or overcome restructuring processes. If other members or groups of the society (or actors outside of the society) are opposed to the prevailing structures and intent on restructuring the social system, either the *As* must be in a position to counter these efforts and/or there must be constraints (possibly im-posed by the *As* themselves) operating to prevent them from carrying out restructuring activities which could alter the existing structure.[30]

Certain conditions and processes, e.g. social fragmentation among opposition or potential opposition groups, may reduce the resources necessary to develop or maintain a hierarchical control system, and correspondingly, may permit considerable exploitation by dominant groups of their subordinates and mismanagement at the top.[31] As suggested earlier, this may be all well and good for internal control processes, but may prevent societal developments, e.g. the development of capabilities for competition with other societies (Alker et al., 1977).

Morphogenesis and Resource Redistribution

Morphogenesis occurs whenever the complex pattern of positive and negative feedbacks associated with a particular institutionalized struc-ture is significantly altered. In particular, this might entail changes in productive, distributive, and demographic flows that underlie the exer-cise of relational control and maintenance of established structures.

The transformation of social structure may come about because actors previously in a more or less disadvantageous position gain re-sources or develop capabilities which enhance their power — relative to those who have been in a dominant position — to exercise relational control. Such changes occur typically whenever an actor exogenous to the system provides some actors but not others within the system with additional power resources or opportunities for new relationships with power advantages.[32] Also, new valuables (or sources of valuables) may emerge, or be created or discovered within the system or new relationships may emerge, particularly in connection with the various changes just described. The resultant redistribution, or production and distribution of new resources and action opportunities, are *incompatible* with the previous distribution of resources and the established social relationships and structures associated with it. This usually leads, whether intentionally or unintentionally, to morphogenesis and may come about through exogenous (e.g. war, trade) or endogenous (e.g. economic expansion, political realignments) processes.

Certain groups within a system may try to maintain a particular structure, not infrequently with the support of outside groups. But typically, a redistribution of control over resources or distribution of control over new or emergent valuables, which does not correspond to the established social structure, will generate pressures for the development of a different social structure compatible with the current resource distribution.[33]

The long-term effects of the new valuables or new social relationships on the distribution of power and the social structure in the system may be unknown, misjudged, or disregarded. Reasons for this are:

(i) Those in a dominant position are distracted by wars, internal crises, and other problems. Those not affected adversely by these affairs gain opportunities to develop themselves.

(ii) As a result of previous commitments and the institutionalized system with which their position is identified, those in a dominant position allocate fewer resources to newer, developing areas than competitors.

(iii) Cultural and social constraints, e.g. concern with matters of 'status', may inhibit those in a dominant position from involving themselves in areas having development potential, even though they have the possibility to do so.

(iv) Those in a dominant position may be more conservative in outlook and, therefore, less disposed than those in more marginal social positions to take advantage of new power resources or action opportunities that avail themselves as a result of technological innovations, differential diffusion of education and skills, rise in the level of consciousness and self-organization of previously less organized groups, emergence of new political conditions, and other socio-structural changes.

In general, structural change can be linked to:

(i) an increase or decrease in resources available for structuring activities.[34/35]

(ii) an imbalance between the resources available and the resources necessary to maintain or reproduce a structure (such an imbalance may arise from a decline in available resources or an increase in those necessary — e.g. as a result of restructuring pressures, including the opposition of groups internal or external to the society — or a combination of both); and

(iii) resource redistribution (resulting from conflict, exchange, or demographic processes) or the emergence of new, important resources or social relationships under the control of more marginal actors.

In the following discussion, we treat centralization and decentralization as morphogenesis, and examine a few of the factors that play a role in these structural developments.

One of the recurrent themes in all societies is the struggle for power and influence between central leadership and local or peripheral leadership. The latter may be locally selected, or they may be members of the governing class or bureaucratic officials appointed to local office by the centre. Some combination of these may also occur.

In the development of political centralization, structuring factors, as found in ecological conditions, and demographic and strategic resource flows, favored those committed — the rulers (emperors, kings or other members of a ruling elite) and their dependents and allies — to a more centralized structure. The centralization process is characterized initially by power amplification, whereby resource flows and the structuring activities (e.g. bureaucratic expansion) of the centre increase resources accruing to it, thereby enabling the centre to develop its power further.

The gains in power of the centre A in relation to other more peripheral actors B, C, . . . depend on a redistribution of strategic resources or differential influx to, or loss by, the society of such resources, in a way favorable to A. The development of centralized control structures and centre/periphery relationships of domination[36] may come about through participants allocating meta-power to leaders under conditions where there is a positive feedback loop linking the granting of initial power to continued differential power accumulation. On the other hand, the central leadership may gain from religious, economic, military or demographic developments providing it with advantages relative to rivals or more peripheral groups.

In general, what is crucial is the capability of the centre to attract and to keep a following (see p. 237). The basis for this may be economic, political or religious. However, such a following can often be used to exercise coercive power in relation to others, to produce or to acquire (e.g. through taxation and tribute) economic goods and to attract yet other followers, and to mould public opinion. Given an initial power advantage, a central leader may be in a position to gain additional resources, to change rules, relationships, and institutions in the society favorable to his position; for example, dividing his opponents. But, as pointed out earlier, there may be ecological, technological, and social constraints preventing or limiting such an amplification process and resultant morphogenesis. In any case, such factors will limit the size of the centralized polity.

In a system with expanding resources (which may come through imperialistic activity, trade abroad, or economic expansion), those enjoying greater control over resource flows have greater opportunities to increase structural support committed to or dependent on them. They accomplish this through creating new structures (bureaucracies as well as more informal social networks) and maintaining effective con- trol over existing ones. They may also dilute or fragment opposition within previously established structures.

The capability to create or establish new linkages, networks, and structures and to generate social structural developments is referred to as *generative structural power*. The exercise of such power by definition entails morphogenesis, at least at certain societal levels.

System expansion which increases resources coming under *A*'s control provide him with the wherewithal to build up social networks and control structures under his hegemony, that is, enable him to play a generative role. He may expand structures under his control, selecting persons loyal to him and capable of effectively managing his interests and providing career opportunities in order to gain additional supporters and allies. The dominant actor *A* may also take steps to erode social networks and structures of opposition groups through strategies of divide and rule, cooptation, or forcing or encouraging opposition groups to secede or emigrate. West European kings played just such a generative role in the rise of Absolutism, both in terms of creating a bureaucratic class and a structure which depended on them at the same time that in the West they fostered the development of the bourgeoisie (and relied on them in their administration of the state).

The ability of the central leadership to alter the payoff structures of subordinates is dependent on the rate of growth of revenues. As they expand the bureaucratic hierarchy, superiors have considerable power since they are capable of altering the payoff structures of subordinates (by promotion and increase in perquisites). When hierarchical development stabilizes, they can no longer offer rapid promotion and the attendant increase in perquisites. For the average member of the hierarchy, swift promotion is highly unlikely, hence the average commitment to the leadership is likely to be reduced. The sanctions available to the leadership are no longer positive (increased and increasing payoffs) but negative (ability to block promotion or to dismiss). *The structure becomes difficult to change:* obviously, individuals or groups will attempt to block any reallocation of resources which they consider harmful. Under the conditions of non-expansion, reallocation translates into a zero-sum game among those likely to be affected by the reallocation. Also, although an individual may know more members in an expanding structure than in a static structure, he will know them less well, generally speaking: the ability to make agreements which are dubious to the leadership is impaired since there is the possibility that others might expose him or her for their own benefit. A stable hierarchy implies increased organization both for and against the leadership, that is, both for the purposes for which the structure has been institutionalized as well as against the leadership in so far as it may wish to make structural changes.

When expansion stops, the central leadership loses, at least relatively speaking, relational control and generative power to deal with opposition or countervailing structures as well as emergent structures which are generated by others (above all subordinate groups within the administration), and which typically lead to de facto changes in organizational goals and policies (see related discussion on p. 266).

Political decentralization is likely to occur when the resources (such as bureaucratic expenditures in kind or in money) *required* to maintain the existing centralized structure becomes imbalanced with respect to

resources *available* (e.g. from imperial ventures, tribute, taxation) to
those committed to maintain the structure. Such imbalances arise either
from a decline in available resources or from increased requirements for
resources to maintain the centralized structure (without any corresponding increase in resource availability to those committed to the
structure). The increased demands may arise from the need to expand
the bureaucracy to deal with social or economic problems (e.g. state
welfare functions designed to maintain civil order) or to expand the
armed forces to meet increased internal or external threat. Political
disintegration would occur, for example, if the costs of the best
military techniques required to maintain secure borders and internal
order increase with time, and an empire has static revenues or revenues
rising more slowly than the costs of military preparedness and warfare
dictate (Elvin, 1973, pp. 20-21).[37] In general, maintenance of a structure (empire, centralized state, or class domination) subject to restructuring pressures from hostile forces from within or outside the
social system requires that those committed to it be continually improving their technologies of control, above all military and organizational technologies, at a pace sufficient to counter-balance improvements made by external powers or by subjected but still hostile populations (cf. Elvin, 1973, p. 18) (see further discussion of this in the fourth
section in Part Three).

Of particular interest in the study of morphogenesis are devolution
processes whereby the policies and actions of a regime set in motion or
accelerate processes which erode ultimately the economic and political
base of the regime and lead to structural transformation.[38] Historically
important examples of such actions are:

(i) attempts to compensate for declining production and revenue
through increased taxation, confiscation, or imperial ventures,

(ii) efforts to expand the bureaucracy or military forces; or

(iii) attempts to extend the territory of the state or empire.

Thus, increased taxation in the case of the Roman and early Chinese
empires undermined the fiscal soundness of the state. Elvin (1973, pp.
19-20) writes:

Typically, the peasant cultivator is impoverished and forced to sell his land.
The need to find a haven from the tax-collector leads him to seek for
patronage or protection from the powerful evading public exactions at what is
often the cost of his personal independence. As wealth, especially landed

wealth, accumulates in the hands of a few persons, the government's revenues fall.[39]

When the central government no longer has the resources to maintain military, bureaucratic, and social network structures supporting it — much less to exercise generative structural power — in the face of restructuring forces, the stage is set for ultimate political disintegration or dynastic collapse. We expand on these ideas and provide further illustrations in Part Three.

Drawing on principles of morphostasis and morphogenesis outlined above, one may specify and model in a suggestive manner certain processes and conditions which underlie cycles of centralization and decentralization in social systems, and dynastic cycles in particular.

Imbalances between pressures for increased structure-maintaining activities (and related resource expenditures) and the limited resource availability or productive capacity of a system may set in motion economic and political processes which reduce further the resources actually available to the centre. The end result of this vicious spiral is a restructuring in the direction of a more decentralized system. The system may even disintegrate into separate states or polities.

Processes of competition or struggle ('warring states') are likely to take place in the resultant decentralized system, for reasons discussed at greater length in Part Three. If conditions for empire formation obtain (see Part Three, second section), then integration of the separate or loosely governed polities or states into a centralized system is likely to reoccur. However, certain key external and internal factors determine the likelihood of a re-emergence of a centralized system: the geopolitical context of the larger system; ecological conditions; the state of transportation and communication; the internal cohesion of the separate states and their capability of resisting domination; the administrative and military costs of such a system in relation to the total resources available; economic productivity; and demographic conditions.

It is worth noting that China was reconstructed on numerous occasions whereas the Roman Empire collapsed and was resurrected only in Western mythology (Elvin, 1973). But then Rome never achieved the cultural unity of China which was maintained to a considerable degree through the Confucian literati and bureaucracy.[40] The Roman empire embraced a heterogeneous population with a variety of religious and cultural groups, some of which were capable of effective resistance to Roman domination, raising substantially the administrative costs of the empire. Moreover, Rome had extended boundaries, and lacked a communication and transportation system (which more advanced naval technology would have provided) to effectively guard those borders, even if it had had the economic base to support the army required.[41] Above all, the Romans failed to develop transportation, military, and productive technologies at a rate sufficient to deal with the ever more effective enemies on the outside as well as inside the Empire, not to speak of problems of soil erosion, floods and droughts, climatic changes,[42] and epidemics. Elvin (1973) argues convincingly that the Chinese Empire remained essentially immune to disruptive forces because the Chinese did manage to innovate in the relevant technical skills, military, economic, and organizational, especially in comparison to their neighbors. Apparently, the Chinese agrarian empire had an inherent dynamism.

Part Three:
Applications and Illustrations

In this part of the paper, we apply our framework to the analysis of morphostatic and morphogenic processes relating to stratification systems and hierarchical control structures. Of ultimate interest are the development of the generative powers of capitalism (first section), state formation (second and third sections), the development and decline of empires (second and fourth sections), and processes of decentralization (fourth section). Our effort is no more than a preliminary one, a progress report, in which we specify a few of the factors and processes underlying such phenomena. In the application of our theoretical framework here, we do not claim to add to the sum of historical or ethnographic knowledge. Rather, our purpose is to introduce a series of interlocking themes as a basis on which to apply and elaborate the theoretical framework. In doing this, we do not limit our illustrations and analysis to particular geographical boundaries or periods of time.

GENERATIVE STRUCTURAL POWER:
THE RISE OF CAPITALISM

Those actors who control or gain disproportionately from resource flow in a system with expanding resources are in a position to exercise generative structural power. The resource gains, as indicated earlier, may come about through imperialistic activity, trade abroad, or economic expansion within the society. The maintenance or amplification of generative structural power depends on the context in which meta-power resources are obtained and used.[43] In certain settings the structural development generated leads to further gains in resources and continued structural development. Thus, statist or communist regimes may take control of the economy and bring about rapid economic development and expansion of public services, particularly in the context of relative under-development, an available labor supply, and favorable demographic conditions (Hardin, this volume). By establishing an expanding system under their control, they are able to exercise generative structural power over an extended period of time, in particular, building up and expanding hierarchical control structures and social networks.[44] These developments contribute, as Hardin argues, to regime institutionalization.

Similarly, a group such as the bourgeoisie during the economic expansion of Western Europe prior to and during industrialization may be closely associated with the economic growth or development and enjoy special access to or control over expanding economic resources (as well as important spin-off and spill-over resources). These enable it to encourage further development of favorable expansionary processes and to institutionalize itself. We discuss below the context and certain critical aspects of this development in Europe.

The Rise of Capitalism. Merchants and small manufacturers were to be found in all agrarian states and empires. What is of ultimate interest from the perspective developed here are the processes and conditions which enabled them as a group to take off in a spiral of power development during the fifteenth and sixteenth centuries, eventually leading to their hegemony in Western Europe.

In agrarian societies merchants and small manufacturers had been subject, to a greater or lesser degree, to controls of either the local aristocracy or bureaucratic officials.[45] But above all they had been subject to the constraint of distance, of the high costs of transportation. This restricted or discouraged large-scale export production. In general, trade — particularly international trade — was not a trade in essentials but a trade in precious stones, precious metals, luxury goods, spices and slaves. The basic requirements of life were (had to be) indigenously produced, either by the consumers themselves or by small artisans at competitive prices and quality for local markets (Muller, 1952).

The development of naval technology in the fourteenth and fifteenth centuries led to the substantial reduction of transportation costs and the great opening of new sea routes connecting all parts of the world (see related discussion, pp. 259-260).[46] This set the stage for the key role that merchants and small manufacturers were to play in Western expansion (of course, they played a role in these initial breakthroughs as well). The developments in transportation permitted the establishment of larger, and eventually, global markets for a great variety of commodities, which could be transported cheaply in bulk. Merchants and producers were provided with almost unlimited opportunities to reach new markets, to forge links, networks, and trade flows on a global scale. These opportunities and the sustained stimulus it provided encouraged expansion and innovation in production. For each merchant or country which failed to seize the opportunity there were others ready to do so. Merchants from England and Holland would produce for and distribute to the world. This amplified the development of their social power at home, above all, by providing a growing fund of resources for the mercantile elite and groups associated with it to generate structural developments which increased their power and furthered their interests. In particular, much of the resource gain associated with the expansion of trade and production ended up in the hands of merchants and entrepreneurs,[47] who used it for further expansion in response to still more opportunities to produce for and sell to new markets. This amplification process associated with capital accumulation — which in a money economy translates into accumulation over material and human resources — lies at the basis of capital formation and development.

The incentive to exploit expanding markets led to efforts to expand production, and therefore, to recruit labor and to innovate technologically (of course, this presupposes the availability of labor), for instance, a pool of workers free to sell their labor in a market. Their own actions and processes also generated additional markets and set the stage for further development. They contributed to the monetization of the economy, the development of wage labor, and to greater government interest in and capability of regulating and managing the economy (and continued economic growth).

The different locations of European countries in relation to the new world system as well as internal economic and political differences among them affected their possibilities of taking advantage of the initial opportunities in the emergent world system and developing economically (Baumgartner and Burns, 1974, 1975; Baumgartner et al., 1975a). Those Western European countries with ocean coastline and ship-building capabilities and an enterprising merchant class would be stimulated and developed *initially* by the commercial and manufacturing opportunities that opened up.

On the other hand, Eastern and Southern Europe were stimulated in a different direction: agricultural and raw material production was emphasized. *This meant that different groups obtained the means to play a dominant generative role within each society. But these specialized groups did not gain to the same degree generative powers and opportunities to gain further through amplification processes associated with their activities and resource control.* In the European maritime states the power of commercial and manufacturing interests (the bourgeoisie) were strengthened by the influx of resources and their further expansion in an increasingly monetized economy. On the other hand, societies in Eastern and Southern Europe remained agrarian or specialized in the export of primary products as a result of their geographical location as well as internal structure (see Baumgartner and Burns (1975) for a discussion of the structuring efforts by external powers, for example England in relation to Portugal). This specialization reinforced the power of those groups controlling agrarian production and distribution at the same time that it led to the relative under-development of their countries (Wallerstein, 1974; Baumgartner et al., 1975a; Alker et al., 1977).

In sum, looking at nations or regions in the international system of conflict and exchange, we see that their particular role in the international division of labor has had implications for internal stratification and hierarchical development. This affects the possibilities (or potentialities) of society to develop economically or politically. For instance, the role of Eastern Europe as grain exporter reinforced the position of the nobility which controlled the agricultural lands. As exports expanded, their generative structural power increased. Similarly, the development of wine exports to England strengthened the position of the agrarian aristocracy in Portugal in the seventeenth century. Western European economic expansion and development taking place at the same time but with an emphasis on manufacturing and shipping reinforced the position of commercial and manufacturing interests. The two developments had vastly different structural consequences: economically, politically, and socially, which are still apparent today.

THE EMERGENCE AND DEVELOPMENT OF EMPIRES[48]

In this and the following section we take up two related topics: centralization across societies, in terms of empire formation, and centralization within societies in terms of state formation.[49]

The structuring of an action complex facilitates or prevents certain interaction patterns, and therefore favors the development of particular social structures. Unequal control over strategic resources in a society, in conjunction with geographical and/or social constraints limiting emigration from the system of those in disadvantaged positions, generally facilitates power amplification and the development of highly stratified systems. On the basis of this proposition, one can formulate a model of the emergence of agrarian empires from warring communities or pristine states and their subsequent development.

Broad fertile flood plains, and resource-rich areas generally, could support not only a dense but also a sizeable population. Where the plains were circumscribed by mountains, deserts, or oceans, the expansion (or emigration) into surrounding areas was limited. As long as lands were available, however, fissionary processes and minimal hierarchization would prevail (see p. 232). But once the readily available land in the area was being farmed, then population pressures in the face of ecological constraints typically intensified competition for and conflict over strategic resources such as land (Caneiro, 1970).[50] Warfare became oriented increasingly to the acquisition of land or the products of land (in contrast, for example, to warfare in Amazonia (see p. 233)). Defeated or weaker groups in these competitive processes were compelled to accept subordination in a political unity dominated by the victors or stronger groups, since mountains, desert, sea or neighboring villages blocked escape or made the costs and risks of leaving unacceptably high. Dominant groups were paid homage and obtained tribute as well as slaves. These contributed to their internal stratification and gave them the possibilities of mobilizing resources both internally and externally to stabilize as well as extend their dominance.[51]

In this way, a power amplification process occurred, underlying the development of social hierarchies, broader political integration, and state and empire formation. Large chiefdoms emerged from autonomous neolithic villages. As demographic pressures continued and recurrent warfare and expansion became institutionalized, chiefdoms were succeeded by kingdoms and kingdoms by empires. Caneiro writes (1970, p. 736).[52/53]

> The last stage of this development was, of course, the most impressive. The scale and magnificence attained by the early empires over-shadowed everything that had gone before. But, in a sense, empires were the logical culmination of the process. The really fundamental step, the one that had triggered the entire train of events that led to empires, was the change from village autonomy to supravillage integration.

In the valleys of the Nile, Tigris-Euphrates and Indus Valleys, and the Valley of Mexico and the mountain and coastal valleys of Peru all the conditions indicated above were present, above all the environmental circumscription (Caneiro, 1970, p. 734):

> These areas differ from one another in many ways – in altitude, temperature, rainfall, soil type, drainage pattern, and many other features. They do, however, have one thing in common; they are all areas of circumscribed agricultural land. Each of them is set off by mountains, seas, or deserts, and these environmental features sharply delimit the area that simple farming peoples could occupy and cultivate.

Ecological constraints, by limiting the options of those in less favorable positions, reduced considerably the resources required and the costs born by the dominant group to develop and maintain a hierarchical structure. A broad flood plain itself made communication and transportation easier. This, together with technological developments, such as the domestication of the horse and construction of roads and canals, faciliated further development of centralized control structures. The extensive fertile plain enabled those in a dominant, central position to mobilize and exploit resources from a wide area, increasing in an absolute sense the resources available to the centre, for both consumption and structuring activities. In turn, construction projects could be carried out on a greater scale. The administrative apparatus with domination/dependence relationships to peripheral systems helped to construct and maintain communication and transportation systems and obtain resources as well as to stabilize their procurement.

Stratification developments were both *internal and external.* Internally, there was the formation of a hierarchy of nobility or rulers, soldiers, and religious elite. But the expansion of one community at the expense of its neighbors, the forging of hegemony in the form of an annual tribute payment or incorporation into an integrated empire, represented social differentiation *between societies.* The pressure upon the agriculturalists at the base of the economy and society to produce more led not only to production developments but also set in motion processes which altered substantially the social structure (see pp. 268-271).

Agrarian empires emerged where intensive agriculture, capable of supporting a dense population, was spread over a more or less extensive, 'controllable' area. Various factors constrained the expansion of intensive agriculture or an irrigation system, thereby restricting its demographic ceiling: geographic (e.g. northern areas above China),[54] technological (problems of accessibility), or social (e.g. powerful hostile neighbors).[55] Also, geographical and economic conditions may limit (or make very difficult) the possibility of merging several smaller systems into a single larger and more highly centralized one.[56] In general, the size of empires was determined by a variety of internal and external factors (see p. 251). Geographical factors, as pointed out earlier in regard to communication and transportation conditions, play a major part in defining system limits, particularly in pre-industrial agrarian societies. Economic productivity and the security and distribution of resource flows are essential factors in the development and maintenance of an administrative and military apparatus, so important to system integration and management. Finally, internal and international structures of social relationships and interactions play a major role in defining the limits of system size as well as the centralizing and decentralizing tendencies within the system (see the fourth section, below).

Successful conquest or expansion faced leaders and 'organizers' with problems of control and management of large societies extended over vast areas, which more traditional modes of social organization based on an extended family or simple patron/client relationships could not handle. Although rulers continued to rely on relatives and loyal friends to help them perform essential tasks of government, they turned increasingly to others, in the process creating new categories or classes of persons and new types of organizational structures (not based on ties of kinship or kinship principles) that went beyond patron/client or patrimonial relationships. This process led to the emergence of professionalized military and civil bureaucracies. Another strategy in trying to maintain control over and manage vast territories was to incorporate conquered groups as subdivisions of the state, often leaving former rulers or leaders in charge, but in a subordinate capacity.

The incorporation of diverse peoples into a single political system created the need to clarify and standardize judicial practice, leading ultimately to the promulgation of formal codes of law. During the Ch'in Dynasty (256-207 *B.C.*) of China, difficulties in communication resulting from dialect differences in script motivated its standardization. In addition, there was standardization of weights and measures as well as the gauge of the tracks for wagons, so that roads could be used effectively (especially for the purpose of bringing grain to the capital).

The discussion above has focused entirely on the great territorial empires of history, which were highly dependent on particular ecological conditions and systems of roads and canals. More global empires could not develop stable forms until transportation costs had been reduced considerably, initially through the development of naval technology. Cipolla (1966) and Braudel (1972) link the development of such technology by Atlantic Europe in the fourteenth and fifteenth centuries to their imperialistic successes and long-term economic and political development. The technological breakthroughs encompassed sail and ship design permitting the unparalleled exploitation of non-human energy; light, more accurate naval cannon; and navigational techniques. These developments changed the balance of power, or contributed initially to economic and military developments which ultimately changed the balance of power between Atlantic Europe (Portugal, Spain, Holland, and England) and Eastern countries (Arabia, India, and China) as well as enabled the establishment of global empires.[57/58] This opened the first global epoch in human history: the 450 years of European colonialism and imperialism. This period saw at the beginning the increased wealth of European societies, the development of the absolutist state, and in England and Holland and to some extent in France, improvements in the power and status of the merchants who were in a position to tap the resources of new global empires and to initiate processes of expansion, thereby not only contributing to their own economic and political power but enhancing the wealth of their nations and setting the stage for industrialization.

STATE FORMATION

Elias (1969), in analyzing the formation of the state, emphasizes the importance of new resources coming under the more or less independent control of the central leadership (the king or lord) and his agents. This development enhanced the meta-powers of the central leadership relative to other segments of society and permitted the building of a central control apparatus — the state — which it could use to further structure conditions to its advantage.

In the early Middle Ages, given poor means of communication and the undeveloped monetization of commercial life, the king or lord had to recompense his knights for their services with land from his own domain or from newly conquered territory. This assured the allegiance of vassals, at least in the short run. However, once the knights had obtained control over the land, which at that time constituted an independent means of production, the power of the king waned.[59] The state of war technology, the subsistence nature of the economy, and the poor state of communication and transportation did not permit centralized control and administration. Clearly, the larger a state and the poorer its transportation and communication facilities, the greater the opportunities for members of the governing class (*Bs*) to infringe on the prerogatives of the central leadership (Lenski, 1966, p. 235). Of course, rulers used various strategies to overcome this problem: moving the capital around, insisting that family members of local top administrators remain in the capital, etc.

Only so long as the king succeeded in defending the borders of the territory against invading enemies, and thus proved to be invaluable to the vassals in his position as successful military leader and political ruler, or so long as he was able to conquer new territories for replenishment of his domain and for future distribution, again obliging vassals, could the lord maintain his central power (Elias, 1969, pp. 11-37).[60]

In later periods, population pressure against land resources, improved communication, developments in trade and production, and urbanization led to significant changes in the power distribution. In particular, the king's (or in the case of Germany, the regional lord's) power increased initially relative to the feudal classes because often he was a protector of the emergent towns. The king participated in the increased monetization of life and the growing economy in two ways. In the first place, the king appropriated the rights to levy taxes and to mint money (and to claim seignorage). Incidentally, the exploitation of this right through monetary debasement was often part of the reason for inflationary pressures which in many instances impoverished the feudal classes. Secondly, the king benefited from his taxing power through economic growth in both real and monetary terms. Real economic growth increased his real base and the inflationary increase in values and incomes protected his tax revenue from inflationary erosion (in contrast to the situation of the feudal classes). An increasing part of the national income thus accrued to the central power, providing the king with an independent, renewable fund of resources that grew with increased monetization of life and expanding economy. In the process, the king reduced his dependence on the feudal knights and acquired at the same time the ability to structure a more permanent or institutionalized hierarchical control system, the royal bureaucracy and mercenary armies, than that possible under feudal conditions.

The process of monetization permitted the substitution of payment in money for payment in kind and allowed the king or the more powerful lords to avoid giving away land for recompense of services (see p. 266ff.). Strayer (1971, p. 81ff.) points out how the increased monetization of feudal dues in the twelfth century brought about a shift in power away from local lords. The latter were dependent on highly *personal relationships with their vassals* for their power. Monetization of feudal dues decreased the strength of such relationships. At the same time, regional lords were largely able to monopolize aids and scutage (a tax in lieu of military service), leaving the local lords with little if any compensation for the loss of followers. Regional lords were also able to use the revenues from feudal dues for the hiring of mercenaries. The fixing of the monetary rates of land rents was to have further implications for the loss of local power in the gradual inflation of the late Middle Ages.

This process coincided with the movement of impoverished knights to the cities where they eagerly sought employment in the services of the king or lord controlling money revenues. Employment in administration and mercenary armies made the formerly quasi-independent knights dependent on the king or lord as their employer.

The development of new war techniques reduced the military importance of the knight on horseback and increased the effectiveness of the mass of foot-soldiers which could be readily recruited and cheaply paid out of the king's treasury. This process increased the relative power of the large lords and of the king, who were the only ones able to afford such armies. The development in the fifteenth and sixteenth centuries of effective cannon which could reduce feudal castles shifted power away from local lords, who could not afford cannon, to regional lords and kings who could. The effects of centrally-produced firearms were similar.[61]

The increasing inequality in control of power resources enabled the king to enforce his will and decisions, to administer and control ever larger territories and populations, and to develop administrative, judicial, and communication systems that facilitated economic development, providing a larger revenue basis for centralized power (Elias, 1969, pp. 90-91, 9-12). In this process of state formation, we find several critical factors affecting the relative power and the outcomes of power struggles between central leadership and more local or peripheral actors (see pp. 237-239).

Change in Resource Availability
and Distribution

War and confiscations may provide A with land and booty to distribute among his followers. The threat from without is also conducive to the delegation of meta-powers from Bs to A. When the centre possesses a standing army, war opens the possibility of increased taxation and, potentially, taxation with the consent of the Bs.[62] The character of the external threat bears a relation to A's gain of meta-power: if the threat is one of major invasion by a large army, A clearly has advantages over pripheral leaders; if, however, the threat is one of localized border raids, the peripheral leaders may gain increased control.

Increased trade and its taxation generally offers strategic advantages to regional lords (kings) rather than to local lords. The merchant has some choice in the route he will take; thus, the local lord lacks sufficient control to benefit from increased long-distance trade. In the growth of states in Western Europe, regional lords and kings protected the growing towns and were able to tap the increased flow of money and production. Local lords were unable to do so to the same extent.

Technological innovation, especially in military and transportation matters, can also affect significantly the relative power of the centre.

Amplification Processes

The increases of power which accrued to regional lords and kings were used to increase control of other strategic resources. The gains in power often attracted, or were the basis on which to attract, followers who could be used in structuring activities, as previously noted.

The extent of the amplification process (and the size of the realm) depended on geo-political considerations as well as on the level of development of transportation. Rugged and mountenous terrain as well as jungle are serious obstacles to communication networks, administrative or other control activities, movements of armies, etc. This was especially true prior to industrialization. In general, geographical conditions may make very costly or obstruct, for a given technological and economic level of society, communication and transportation from 'centre' to 'periphery'. Structuring activities beyond a localized area is

increasingly difficult and, typically, exceeds the resources available to
those pursuing the objective of structuring an extensive centralized
control system.[63]

During much of the medieval period, Europe's feudal lords were
virtually autonomous. The rulers of the far-flung Chinese and Indian
Empires had considerable difficulty in maintaining effective control
over the governors of the more remote provinces. Such officials often
usurped many of the prerogatives of the emperor and, in some instances, went on to challenge his right to the throne (Lenski, 1966, pp.
235-36). However, as a result of advances in the methods of transportation and communication, autocratic rule tended over the long run
to be favored over oligarchical rule (not without significant short-term
reversals and dynastic cycles as discussed later).

Generative Structural Power and
Structuring Activities

The meta-powers that *A* gains were used to structure relationships and
to create hierarchical control structures which could insure *A*'s continued domination.

Often, *A* created relationships between *A* and *C* (e.g. lower nobility)
where previously only *A/B* and *B/C* relationships (or none at all) had
existed. During the twelfth century in Western Europe there was an
increasing tendency to reduce alodial lands (i.e. lands not held as fiefs
but as the absolute property of the possessor) and to place everyone
under homage to someone. Characteristically, kings used their increased
power to create *A/C* and *A/D* relationships where none had existed
before, especially in the creation of 'the King's justice' (Strayer, 1971,
pp. 83-84).

But of greater importance was the creation of hierarchical control
structures. Using resources gained initially through several processes as
described earlier, the central leadership *A* was able to attract and
support followers and dependents, usually non-kinsmen (or at least
non-agnate kinsmen), commoners, and clients (such as immigrating
exiles). Followers were recruited generally from subordinated groups
(*Cs* and *Ds*) rather than from *As*'s competitors (the *Bs*).[64] They were
used to create a new class (of bureaucratic officials and military

personnel) and a new social structure (the bureaucracy and a military hierarchy). These new structures, bureaucratic organizations, were counter-poised to the structures of more aristocratic forms of governance. *A* used them to carry out social actions of different types, administrative, judicial, information gathering, as well as military, and was thus freed from a reliance on the cooperation and goodwill of local leaders. In this way, and also through further structuring activities, *A* extended his power over society.

The use of such bureaucratic structures for the exercise of relational control by *A* was accomplished, as suggested above, through the recruitment of persons willing to accept subordinate positions and through gaining their commitment to the system and its leadership, as opposed to commitments and loyalties to other segments (and structures) of the society, at least in the context of state action. The persons and groups recruited lacked (ideally) diffuse relationships across the boundaries of the system or they were socialized to develop detached professional orientations and commitments. The recruitment of members of alien groups, slaves, commoners or persons especially socialized for the system and its status group made it easier to segregate them from the social environment of the hierarchical control system. Moreover, they were likely to accept a subordinate status and to appreciate opportunities to gain status and leadership opportunities.[65]

Equally important to the development of stable hierarchical control structures is the structuring of the system's social rewards, particularly in terms of status, access to and promotion in opportunity chains, and other advantages which are more or less controlled by the leadership and through which participants develop organizational commitments and compliant orientations.

There is a significant difference between a hierarchical control system which is temporary or unpredictable, one based for example on the tentative allegiance of a vassal to his lord, and one which is institutionalized, providing a stable system of social domination that can be used for social action and the exercise of social power: hence, the significance of the shift from payment for services rendered with land allocation or with possession of office to payment in money and the provision of career opportunities under centralized control. As suggested earlier, the former assures only temporary domination whereas the latter provides a more continuous and dependable means of social domination (see p. 266).

PROCESSES OF DECENTRALIZATION
AND DISINTEGRATION

Centralization processes such as those described in state and empire formations do not progress unimpeded. Morphogenic pressures for decentralization may arise in several ways. Such pressures can come about when an absolute decline in resources available to the society (and especially to A) inhibit the central leadership in its structure-maintaining activities. The same result obtains when resource require-ments for morphostasis increase without A being able to mobilize the necessary *additional* resources. Decentralization tendencies may also come about because redistributional processes favor peripheral actors over the centre in strategic resources, thereby contributing ultimately to the erosion of centralized power.

We shall first discuss how specific redistributional processes may contribute to decentralization before going on to examine ways in which resource contraction may lead to the erosion of centralized power.

Redistribution Processes

A originates exchange with B for structuring purposes: to establish or maintain a centralized control structure. But such exchange may entail long-term structural implications not apparent in an analysis focused on short-term consequences and calculations. (In any case, A may not have alternative means of structuring available.) Initially, the exchange activity establishes A's domination over B accompanied by appropriate expressions and symbols (tribute, deference, etc.). However, A may be unable to prevent B from using his control over the resources received to appropriate various spin-off and spill-over resource gains. We have already seen how the kings and lords reigning over the undeveloped economies of the Dark and early Middle Ages had to exchange land (and the population on it) for the services and loyalty of their vassals.[66] But the lords were unable to assert continuous control over these resources due to the poor means of communication. Moreover, there was no administrative or military apparatus which could have outweighted clearly the resources controlled by the *Bs*. The vassals not only gained independent economic resources and manpower for military purposes, due to the need for the lord to delegate decision-making powers to the vassals (since decisions could not wait for the long periods that it took for communication), they also became middlemen between the king and his 'subjects', a situation the king was unable to circumvent given the infrastructural limitations.

Initially, of course, *B* may have been selected entirely at *A's* discretion.[67] *A* had organizing or structurally generative power. But once the *Bs* were placed or located, the processes of alliance and group formation, competition and cooperation begin to take place, outside of *A's* (complete) control. This is especially likely when the *Bs* as a class have concepts and orientations toward private property ownership and inheritance of resources over which they exercise control. *A* will generally be unable to prevent these processes as long as he is required to redistribute sources of power (i.e. capital-type goods) for structuring purposes without at the same time enjoying a continued inflow of similar resources, which he can distribute.[68] Consequently, *A* cannot reinforce or maintain the original centralized control structure, and to establish and maintain secondary structures (to ensure that the first operates according to *A's* will). *B* comes to consolidate power in local areas, leading to decentralization.[69] This process may in turn be associated with greater exploitation of peasants or of peasants coming into dependency relationships to the *Bs*, resulting in a loss of taxes to the central government and social unrest. Such processes can lead to serious challenges to the central government and eventually to its collapse, especially as they are likely to actually increase the resource requirements for morphostasis.

The end result of such processes is 'feudalization', with a set of more or less autonomous regions or areas. However, one such area may be better situated or developed than others, so that it becomes an 'emergent power centre' on the periphery, acquiring sufficient resources not only to oppose the 'original centre' but to take over the role of centre (see pp. 251-252).

Relationship between Morphostatic Resource
Requirements and Resource Availability

A steady flow of resources coming in, as in an expanding empire or an expanding economy, gives *A* the capability to expand, alter, substitute, and outflank existing structures *through structuring activities made possible by the resources available to him or his government.* Thus, we have seen that *A* may gain resources through taxation, seignorage, or other sources of steady revenue to create an enduring dependent class and structure of bureaucrats.

Clearly, events impeding or significantly reducing the production and flow of resources would be likely to lead to the erosion or disintegration of the administrative and military apparatus established by *A*, other things being equal.[70] Resource contraction can be the result of changes in the physical environment or 'historical forces' associated with conflicts, exchange, and demographic developments both within and between societies:

(i) climatic changes, soil erosion[71] or natural disasters may reduce the productive capacity of the system (Dale and Carter, 1955);

(ii) population decreases due to epidemics,[72] civil strife, reduction in natality, and emigration deplete the productive man-power pool and therefore output;

(iii) economic recessions and depressions;

(iv) warfare may entail high resource costs without producing compensatory gains which would allow for the customary level of resource use (Eberhard, 1966); and

(v) social and economic policies of the government may have unintended consequences such as in the case where increased taxation leads to changes in social and productive relations that undermine the productive or tax base.

We are particularly interested here in resource contraction that results from internal and external developments. For example, the process of sea routes replacing overland routes or vice versa. Thus, Middle East countries which had previously profited from trade flows between East and West suffered significant resource deprivation when Atlantic European countries discovered sea routes to the East (Cipolla, 1970). Or the Kiev state, initially the governing authority of Russia, secured its resources primarily by taxing the rather considerable volume of trade that flowed through the Russian trade routes. In the twelfth century, the trade routes shifted away from Russia toward the Mediterranean in favor of the Italians. As a result, the resource base of the Kiev state weakened significantly. Ultimately, Kiev was unable to resist the Mongols who conquered it and established their dominance over Kiev.

Or the state may experience a reduction of external (colonial) contributions to national wealth, e.g. looted treasures and additional slaves (both of which boosted Roman economic activity during the wars of conquest (Cipolla, 1970)). At the same time, there may be pressures to expand public expenditures due to increased social unrest, and to maintain extensive communication and transportation systems, and an elaborate hierarchical control apparatus. The response of the centre may be to rely more heavily on taxation to maintain, or even to provide increased, revenue. Increased taxation, at the point where productive capabilities of the peasantry are already taxed to the maximum, typically generates socio-economic processes altering relations of production and social organization at the village level. In a word, the centre's response to its problems leads to erosion of the basis of its power structure, bringing 'feudalization' in its wake.

Taxation typically falls heavier on those who are weaker, at least in hierarchical agrarian societies. Pressures of taxes tend to drive the poorer peasants into debt or alienation of their holdings. In this process, some enter into subordination/domination (client/patron) relationships with the powerful landlords who have greater resources to meet or to resist the pressures of taxation.[73] Some poorer peasants may simply be driven off the land into local banditry or into the city. The increased power of local lords tends to reduce tax revenues even further, weakening *A* and strengthening the *Bs* correspondingly. If, because of the weakness of the state, gangs of peasant bandits and marauding 'barbarians' create social disorder, agricultural estates become fortified and isolated. Whenever the state or central forces are unable to provide protection at the local level, peasants, even wealthy ones, are driven to seek protection of the great landlords and warriors who provide military and police protection. Dependent free men may take an oath or fealty to their local lord. All of this contributes to the process of decentralization.

In sum, increased taxation at the point where the productive capabilities of the peasantry are already taxed to the maximum, in conjunction with the concentration of wealth and power in the countryside, results in increased stratification in the countryside and a shift in power favoring local landlords and power agents over the central leadership.

It was exactly processes such as these described here abstractly, which contributed to the disintegration of the Roman Empire after the 4th century *A.D.* (Bernardi, 1970). A decline in war booty (slaves and precious metals)[74] in the wake of the end of the expansion of the Empire forced increases in open and hidden taxation. These were attempts to maintain an already large administrative and military apparatus. At the same time that tax revenues began to fall, the demands on the system increased. Economic stagnation increased the need for welfare payments, and the threat of barbarian invasions demanded an enlarged military effort. But these costs soon turned out to be well beyond the tax-yielding possibilities of an economy that was essentially (and precariously) agrarian.

The bureaucratic organization, advantageous in the beginning, developed structures and patterns of action that were not up to their tasks and beyond the carrying capacity of the system. To procure the means to keep it going, fiscal pressure had to grow beyond reasonable limits. Immediate victims of its pressure were the medium and the small property owners, little by little absorbed by the large ones. The large proprietors, in turn, when the pressure grew unbearable, defended themselves with evasion and immunity which became ever more frequent. The result was a redistribution of wealth and power distinctly in favor of those classes that in one way or another were able to avoid paying tribute to the state. This vicious circle could lead to only one result (Bernardi, 1970, pp. 82-83):

> The bankruptcy of the enormous state at the same time as small privileged groups, while they evade taxation, heap up riches and create around their villas economic and social microcosms,[75] completely cut off from the central authority. It was the end of the Roman world. It was the beginning of the Middle Ages.

As the example of the Roman Empire suggests, processes of decentralization and disintegration may be initiated not only by a decline in available resources. Actions, which require increased governmental resources, may be called for in order to 'save' a regime or society from an external threat or competitive challenge. For example, China's competition with northern 'barbarian' societies drove Chinese emperors time and time again to deal with them by locating armies on the northern frontier, building walls, paying tribute, etc. This set in motion processes undermining political and economic power of the centre and Chinese society as a whole.[76] Impoverishment of peasants, increased power of local landlords over peasants, and decline in taxation and manpower available to the centre were the usual results, reducing the total resources available and/or redistributing available resources to the disadvantage of the centre.

Clearly, external or internal enemies (for example, in the latter case subject peoples), may increase military and administrative expenses substantially.[77] Indeed, these costs are likely to increase as a result of improvement in skills, military weaponry, and organization of opposition forces, for example, in the case of neighboring countries. And the diffusion of techniques across frontiers is, in the long run, virtually impossible to prevent (Elvin, 1973, p. 18). Drawing on Charles Oman, Elvin refers to the fact that 300 years of close contact with the Roman Empire had taught the Germans much about military techniques, with the consequence that the 'ascendancy of the Roman infantry . . . was no longer so marked as in earlier ages'.[78] There may also be increased group consciousness and organization as well as the spread of advanced military technology among subjects, as opposed to soldiers of the empire. For example, the diffusion of muskets among the Chinese population after about 1700 lowered the relative effectiveness of soldiers vis-à-vis civilians and led to increased social and economic strains, either in the form of reduced internal control or heavier taxes to pay for more soldiers.[79] In a similar vein, Elvin (1973, p. 18) points out:

> Recent European empires in Africa and Asia have found it virtually impossible to resist quite modest improvements in the political and organizational skills of their native subjects, in spite of retaining a clear economic and military superiority on a man-for-man basis.

CONCLUSION

The point of view toward the study of power and social structure presented in this paper is a developmental one — with the focus on the system-environment dynamics of morphogenesis. Groups of varying sizes and degrees of cohesiveness interact with one another in economic, political, and other terms. They struggle in their physical environment, at times for survival itself, as well as in their interrelationships, some trying to rise and to better themselves in the face of strong opposition, some who have risen trying to hold what they have and some going down (Elias, 1969). Exchange, competition or conflict occur, depending on environmental, social structural, and ideological conditions. The result is the genesis of wider cohesion, group formation and the domination or subordination of groups in relation to one another.

NOTES

1. Since such relationships are often expected to exist even between the times when the patterns of action are performed, 'social structure' is not a simple synchronic generalization of empirical reality. It represents a more complex abstraction from an intermittent diachronic reality. Thus, empirically, the existence of any relationship at a given time may be problematic. Relationships and structures entail *probable* patterns of mutual orientation and interaction (in Weber's phrase 'the probability that certain kinds of meaningfully oriented social action will take place').

2. We are minimally concerned in this paper with the phenomenology of power, and cognitive lag or discrepancy between conceptions of power relationships and of social structures and the underlying reality shaped by dynamic forces.

3. Hence, there is often a contradiction or a dilemma facing rulers between, on the one hand, maximizing system power or the social product by bringing about or maintaining social organization among subordinates, and on the other, maximizing domination by alienating *B* and *C* through divide-and-rule strategies.

Rulers concerned only with domination are not faced with this dilemma. However, if the system they control comes into competition or threatening conflict with other systems or groups, they are likely to be motivated to try to increase their system's output, thus causing the dilemma. There may also be internal reasons for improving the social organization of production. For instance, the goals or needs of the ruling elite may be unrealizable under a more fragmented system of productive relations; in order to increase production, they reduce or transform the alienative relationships among producers or producer groups.

In response to the dilemma and to the power implications of greater integration, rulers or leaders frequently develop or evolve new control strategies, techniques and institutions enabling them to increase the level of cooperation in society while remaining firmly in control (Baumgartner et al., 1975c).

4. Analyses of power typically focus on differences in resources, skills, strategies, etc. among actors who interact *within* a matrix of rules, resource distribution, and structural constraints. The institutional structure and cultural framework remain in the background or are taken for granted. Power relationships are analyzed in terms of interpersonal or intergroup relationships in which one actor tries to get another to do something, usually against the latter's will. Actors maneuver their resource strengths and weaknesses in an effort to maximize their returns and minimize their costs. However, such assumptions about power relations capture only a part of the power activities of groups, organizations, and states. They are inherently morphostatic, since they take for granted the existing structure.

5. These sources are not necessarily of equal importance for processes of social differentiation, nor does the listed sequence imply a scale of importance.

6. Patterson (1975) reports on the basis of his comparative study of slavery that where *As* conquer Bs and Bs remain 'hosts', then the domination relationship established is unlikely to be one of master/slave. The victors in this case attempt to utilize existing structures of production, community organization and politics, legitimation, socialization, etc. for their own purposes. On the other hand, persons captured in war who are brought forcibly to areas where their conquerors serve as hosts are typically 'owned' and brought into master/slave relationships. Their original structures are more or less dissolved, and they are incorporated as individuals or small groups into the social structures of the conquerors.

7. Ruyle (1974) suggests that the population concentration, level of affluence, relative sedentary life, and opportunities for warfare among the Northwest Coast Indians was associated with the taking of captives in warfare and their enslavement. The nobles, particularly chiefs had slaves, or at least more of them. This contributed to their social power and, in Ruyle's words, to 'pristine state formation'. The slaves also contributed to the status of noblemen, since they could be used to carry out 'impure' or 'lowly' tasks, freeing the nobility from having to engage in such activities. The latter could 'specialize' in political, military, hunting and other high value, prestigious activities, while commoners were compelled to do menial tasks themselves.

8. The process of social differentiation associated with migration can be contrasted to the differentiation process referred to in the section on 'Defeat in

war', above, where a migratory group establishes its domination through force (leading to lord/serf relationships). 'Immigration' and 'conquest' are similar, except in the first case new-comers enter at the bottom of the existing structure and in the other they enter at the top.

9. Unequal exchange may be realized through 'coercion' and the establishment of lord/serf or master/slave relationships. However, expropriation as a basis for social differentiation is only one type of distributional and redistributional process.

10. Obviously, the particular valuables or resources which are unequally distributed in the exchange system should be distinguished in terms of the power and meta-power they provide to their controllers. A valuable may be viewed and manipulated in terms of the prestige it confers (as in the first example above) rather than in terms of some material advantages.

11. Although the example here has focused on meta-power entailed in the ownership of the means of production, such power can also be acquired by virtue of relational control in other spheres. It was control of imported raw materials and through this, control of access to markets, which enabled medieval cloth merchants to gain considerable control over the means of production. The merchants of Bruges, who in the thirteenth century, became strictly middlemen, assured their position in relation to foreign importers and exporters by the simple expedient of prohibiting foreign merchants from dealing directly with one another (Roerig, 1967, p. 76).

12. In the third part of the paper we discuss how the exploitation or taxation of subordinate groups may alter the productive and distributive infrastructure in such a way as to undermine the economic and political basis of a hierarchical structure, which enabled the exploitation or taxation in the first place.

13. Exit constraints imply an absolute resource scarcity, and facilitate resource monopolization within a social system. Conversely, absolute resource abundance, as for example in the case of the availability of frontier land, gives subordinate actors in the system access to resources and therefore prevents, or makes costly any efforts at resource monopolization.

14. The ease of changing or leaving a 'dominance' relationship (such as chief/non-chief) is due to the fact that such superiority as is achieved or granted is not based on any scarce resource of which the chief has exclusive control.

15. When alternative sources are unavailable, then monopoly over the distribution of resources constrains the action possibilities of those lacking such resource control; they lack the alternative of going outside the system to realize their goals or to maintain themselves. Of course, dominant actors also try to make subordinates believe that there is no viable alternative source of the necessary resources, that is, that they hold a monopoly.

16. While the Poro did not possess the highest political power, niether did the king. There was a balance of forces between the two and decisive power shifted from one to the other (Krader, 1968). Southall writes (1965, p. 243):

The secular hierarchy of chiefs exercised control and authority over much of the ordinary day-to-day life of society *but only within the limits* of obedience and subordination to the ultimate rules and sanctions of Poro, between whose official hierarchy and that of the secular chiefs there was an important but unknown degree of overlap in incumbency. Political power in day to day life and Poro power tended to be lodged in the hands of the same persons, and it is not unlikely that chiefs utilized Poro mechanisms to underscore their political decisions.

The organized power of the Poro society, which did not totally depend on secular chiefs, served as a *constraint* on their power and, in particular, on that of the king.

17. The membership has internalized due process norms and has sufficient control over strategic resources in relation to the central leadership to institutionalize due process procedures. Such norms regulate conflicts, including conflicts between the centre and the periphery with a semblance of fairness, which in turn promotes loyalty and internal cohesion of the organized system (Evan, 1975).

18. Shared control should be distinguished from delegated control. The latter, which is characteristic of highly centralized systems, is subject to recall by the maximal leader.

19. In other words, we are speaking of the distribution in a society of control or 'property rights' in the most general sense.

20. Note that this was central to the Investiture Controversy of the Middle Ages: who was to have the power to invest clerical lords with their symbols of office, the Crown or the Pope.

21. In the case of fully centralized power, the maximal leader monopolizes through 'his' administrative apparatus control over specialized warriors and police, controls directly or indirectly the most land and its allocation (or other strategic economic resources such as access to trade routes or to irrigation systems), controls access to public office, and can promote or remove individuals or groups from local administrative or leadership positions.

22. Even *within* more or less homogeneous nations, we find this may be a factor. The French crown was unable to extend control over peripheral territories until long after each of them had established their distinctive dynasties, laws, and institutions. Thereafter, France was obsessed by the 'demon of secession' (Finer, 1975).

23. Clearly, the conditions and processes which elaborate social differences in resource control and action possibilities may differ from those which initiate the process. Thus, social differentiation in control over resources or resource accumulation may arise because of the distributional rules associated with exchange or warfare. Such differentiation *combined with* constraints on the emigration or protest possibilities of subordinates contributes to further development or at least to the stabilization of relationships of inequality. The resulting accumulation of resources (produce, labor, etc.) by *A* may make possible yet further elaboration of the unequal relationships as well as the subordination of others previously independent of or co-equal with *A*.

24. For example, the export of warriors such as in the early Norman states (twelfth and thirteenth centuries) may contribute to stable internal structures. Also, emigration to the US probably reduced internal turbulence in nineteenth century Europe and facilitated the trend to stable 'representative democracies'. In

this regard MacDonald reports that the socialist vote and labor militancy was high in those Italian provinces that showed low rates of emigration and vice versa (see Rokkan (1974)).

25. As suggested earlier, social constraints may derive from loyalties or social ties which commit actors to a locale and make the opportunity costs of withdrawal or emigration especially high. Such commitments to locale may arise for political and military reasons, for instance when an expanding system offers the promise of career, power and wealth. Religious and cultural factors as well as entanglement in a web of social relationships can also lead to such a commitment. Similarly, small businessmen are constrained from leaving a local area in which they have invested in time, local information-gathering and the development of goodwill, because these investments are not readily *transferable* to a new environment (Margolis, reported in Rokkan, 1974).

26. Note that resources are required to carry out such constraining operations and hence represent costs not borne by societies which have naturally occurring environmental constraints or social constraints arising exogenously.

Of course, groups within the society may oppose the socially imposed constraints on the freedom of movement of one group or another, since such conditions affect the distribution of power in society, strengthening stratification in some domains and possibly weakening it in others (see note 27).

27. In Russia prior to the twelfth century, the Kiev state had been unwilling to lend support to the lords' efforts to restrict the freedom of the peasantry and to develop manoralism, since it secured its resources primarily by taxing the considerable volume of trade that flowed through Russian trade routes and recognized the landed nobility as a threat to its power. On the other hand, the Muscovite state emerging after the decline of the Mongols, was much more dependent than that of Kiev on the nobility for its resources. For this reason, the state supported the nobility in their efforts to tax the peasantry and eventually to tie the peasants to the land (Blum, 1966; Trethewey, 1974).

28. For example, a common pattern in the historical emergence of the state is the availability and acquisition of resources which can be used for structuring purposes by the central leadership. Typically, the latter is enabled to attract and support a body of followers and dependents, using resources gained through warfare, trade and other economic activity, political alliance and various legitimation activities. These followers and dependents are the lord's or the king's men supporting him and executing his will. Through them he has the possibility of extending his capability to gain additional resources and to carry out structuring activities – to develop and maintain a hierarchical control structure under his hegemony – even over the opposition of rivals or of subordinates.

29. The resources produced (at least those available to group leadership) are sufficient to support only individuals and small groups. Resources are not available to support large numbers of specialists engaged in large-scale governmental and structuring activities. Of course, temporary accumulation of resources may permit some expansion of organization, but the system is always precarious, since it may be subject to erosive forces for which it lacks the surplus resources to counteract or overcome. Obviously, systems vary in the extent to which they are

able to make maximum use of such surplus resources.

30. But any structure represents a 'negotiated order' (Buckley, 1967; Strauss et al., 1963).

31. At each level of a bureaucratic hierarchy, subordinates are typically divided with respect to their superior. Thus, the principle of divide and rule is built into the very form of the hierarchy.

32. Bailey (1969) describes a process whereby the distillers of Bisipara in Western Orissa in India were given a monopoly in the drink trade by the British Administration. As a result they became exceedingly rich and were able to use their wealth within the village subsystem to caste-climb, that is, to improve their power and status position in relation to less polluted castes.

In the case of the Tonga of Africa, Van Velsen (1964) points out that the arrival of the British made direct access to exogenous power resources (from a larger system) possible. One chief in particular, became a firm supporter of the local mission and was in turn supported by the mission, providing him and his followers with goods and services. This gave him distinct advantage over other, neighboring chiefs, including his kinsmen in the same 'house'.

33. Established social relationships entail certain conceptions or models of social relationships, and procedures of calculation and decision-making based on a conception of what is valuable in the context and what are the likely outcomes of various patterns of action. The emergence of new valuables and new control and power relationships alters all of this, forcing not only new patterns of interaction but new perceptions and conceptions of social relationships and social structures (Burns, 1976).

34. Deprivation of resources may ramify in a social system by undermining certain social relationships and structures. Aberle (1962, pp. 210-11) describes how in the case of the Navahos the loss of livestock in the 1930s reduced the power and status of the large herd-owners. The man who had had followers to herd for him, had gained gratitude for generosity, and had improved his standing because of his wealth, became almost as badly off as any other Navaho. Society was reduced to far more egalitarian relationships.

35. Although the emphasis here is on 'material' and social structural conditions and processes relevant to structuring, ideological and cultural forces obviously play a significant role (Burns, 1976; Burns and Mattin, 1976).

36. Fully developed systems of domination are those in which there are at least two categories of actors: dominant and subordinate. They are differentiated in terms of their resource control and action possibilities and their action and interaction payoffs (as well as ultimately their ideological and cultural orientations in relation to one another). Members of class *A*, either individually or collectively, have the power to issue commands or to exercise control over members of the subordinate class *B*, and to make decisions about conditions or processes affecting subordinate actors, whatever the basis of this power. The subordinate actors are excluded from such power and must obey the authoritative commands of dominant actors and accept their strategic decisions. Such differences in action opportunities along with characteristic unequal distributive mechanisms and rules result in unequal benefits and costs to participants in a

system of domination. In sum, the pattern of control and accumulation systematically favor the dominant actors.

37. Elvin (p. 21) refers to the case of the Ottoman Empire after the late sixteenth century:

> In order to keep up with the Europeans, it was necessary to increase the use of firearms and artillary. This meant that the cavalry, accustomed to a campaigning season and rewarded with fiefs, had to be progressively replaced with full-time paid professionals. The resulting pressures, at a time of financial crisis brought about by the inflow of New World silver, were disastrous.

38. As pointed out earlier, social action may have unexpected and unintended, yet structurally significant consequences.

39. Elvin goes on to point out (p. 20):

> Against this, statesmen employ such policies as confiscating the possessions of the rich, imposing limitations on land-holdings (both the acquisition of land and the sale of land), and distributing public land to small farmers, soldiers and veterans. On the relative success or failure of these attempts, well-exemplified in the seventh century A.D. by the Byzantine Themes and the T'ang 'equitable fields' and divisional militia, the political cohesion of empires and even their survival often depend.

40. The successful administration of the Chinese Empire depended on gentry-bureaucrats who maintained their political and administrative powers in administrative centres as well as their economic power in local landholdings – all of this through large kinship groups. Because of this, they were also able to block effectively *restructuring attempts, either from above or below*. Restructuring efforts from below were overcome either by cooptation or by allying themselves with external forces. Efforts from above could be effectively opposed because the gentry-bureaucrats *as a class* could not be replaced (except possibly by military commanders, a strategy which had special dangers of its own). In sum, their strategic administrative/political and economic powers enabled them to maintain the system in the face of reform movements from above or below. A challenger could only extend and stabilize his position by using the existing administrative system to extend and exercise effective control over such a vast area. Only the gentry-bureaucrats had the 'intelligence' and training to carry out this necessary task. Thus, although there were possibilities of effective peasant revolts (because China did not have a military aristocracy), even peasant revolutionary movements depended on the writing and professional administrative skills controlled by the literati as a class.

41. Elvin suggests (1973, p. 19) that it was not only a matter of the high cost of maintaining troops on longer frontier lines, but the fact that they were far removed from the main sources of *trustworthy* manpower and supplies.

42. The agricultural base was extremely fragile and could not support in any stable way an elaborate bureaucracy, the luxury of urban civilization, and an ever-growing population (Braudel, 1972).

43. Many empire building efforts start out with activities which provide a high

return on these efforts, but which also, and more importantly, lead to control over resources and generate loyalties of persons and groups which contribute to the maintenance and development of empire structures: its army, internal security apparatus, administration, system of taxation, etc.

44. This is not to say that in recruiting personnel and in the processes a regime sets in motion there will be no morphogenic processes outside the regime's control, or unanticipated by them. Further, a regime faces dilemmas, for example between promoting loyal persons who support those at the top versus promoting highly competent persons (whose loyalty may be somewhat weaker than the former) who can manage the system effectively, and keep it expanding.

45. In contrast to the oceans, roads and inland waterways can be supervised rather easily. But, it is also important to keep in mind that there was generally less such supervision in Europe, witness the emergence of more or less autonomous towns and cities.

46. The global system of trade existed earlier, but could not stimulate economic development or develop a powerful merchant class to the degree it later did until the breakthroughs in naval technology linked the world into a single global system (Wallerstein, 1974).

47. The central governments also gained from these developments. It was more difficult for purely local lords to tap these resource flows. Local attempts to exploit or regulate them, especially once the oceans were opened up, would drive commerce out of the territory into more favorable surroundings.

48. Empire refers here to a relatively highly centralized political system encompassing a wide territory. It is a system of domination with a centre (as embodied in the person of the emperor and in the central political institutions) and subordinate peripheries (with their own centres and peripheries) which have been integrated into the larger system, typically through conquest and subjugation. The core structure is used to manipulate and exercise relational control over other structures and networks, including well-established ones such as previously independent or autonomous states (Eisenstadt, 1963; Mason, 1971).

49. In studying centralization/decentralization problems, it is essential to keep in mind the levels under consideration. Centralization is typically taken to mean centralization at a higher, more suprasystem level in relation to the peripheral or regional systems, but it may also occur at the 'regional' level in relation to yet lower levels.

50. Fried suggests (1973, p. 22) that the violation of rules under conditions of abundance presents few problems, but competition for scarce resources generates pressures for enforcement of rules relating to resource use or control, including rules of descent and inheritance. Of course, these pressures also contribute to changes in agricultural techniques: the tilling of land under cultivation is intensified; new, previously unusable land is brought under cultivation by means of terracing and irrigation. Also, the requirements to pay tribute or taxes in kind probably encouraged increased food production.

51. In the development of empires, as in state formation, one typically finds booty, land, slaves, money, opportunities for careers and leadership being used as resources to gain and maintain loyalties and commitment of individuals and

groups willing to serve the empire. Through the use of such resources, networks and structures are tied to the leadership of the empire, permitting yet additional structural expansion and the effective outflanking or erosion of opposition structures. Special efforts may be devoted to trying to control structures which oppose the leadership or could be a potential threat as well. These attempts may be directed at fragmenting or eroding particular social structures.

52. Fried (1967), Sahlins (1968), Service (1966) and other evolutionary theorists argue, as Stauder (1972) has pointed out, that the population increases associated with neolithic domestication of food supplies ultimately led societies into competition for land and other resources. But such population increases and competition may not take the form of 'zero-sum' games. It is only when competition takes place in circumscribed conditions (which limit emigration), that the processes of domination/subordination described above and external offense-defence requirements serve to stimulate political consolidation, higher population densities, and the emergence of more regularized and formal leadership.

53. While Caneiro emphasizes a process of social differentiation and subordination based on warfare, these developments may come about through other social processes (see p. 226 ff). Also, warfare may bring about such differentiation in at least two ways: subordination of conquered peoples, and the internal allocation of meta-power to leadership (Cohen, this volume).

54. Price (1973, p. 232) suggests that in the case of Mexico, the multiplicity of individually limited water sources and their *localized* distribution effectively barred the development of a unified and centralized basin-wide *single* system.

55. The general picture must have been quite complex, since there is evidence that population flows took place and, indeed, were encouraged among warring groups and states prior to the emergence of the great empires (e.g. see Eberhard, 1966, p. 53).

56. The local irrigation systems of Sumer were coalesced into the unified pan-Mesopatamian system only much later (Price, 1973).

There is increasing evidence, contrary to the Wittfogel hypothesis, that the distribution of water and regulation of irrigation in China and other parts of Asia did not require large-scale government direction but were handled by local group action. Intensive hydro-agriculture occurs without state forms. Our theoretical formulation of structure creation and maintenance would argue that the productive basis for a large-scale state apparatus must precede the development of that state (Friedman, 1974, p. 462). Of course, a positive feedback process may obtain where development of intensive farming and expansion of agricultural productivity provide an expanded resource base on which to expand the state apparatus (into the 'oriental despotic state'). Friedman points out (1974, p. 463):

> In this sense, hydraulic agriculture allows for an unprecedented development of stratification and control to the extent to which surplus, absolute and relative, can be increased and appropriated by non-producers. Formerly ranked or minimally stratified societies can increase the degree of stratification by enlarging the productive base of the economy.

57. The shift in the balance of power was a complex process. Although the Portuguese had completely destroyed the naval power of the Arabs within 15 years of their first arrival in the Indian waters, the Europeans continued to be vulnerable on land until the Industrial Revolution.

58. In contrasting the powers and motives of the Romans and modern Europeans, White (1969, p. 6) points out:

> Romans were as predatory as were early modern Europeans but the Romans were not equipped to spread their dominance far beyond the basin of the Mediterranean. They lacked (1) the agricultural productivity; (2) the industrial skills; (3) the superiority of weapons; and (4) the nautical arts available in Europe by 1500.

A major weakness in the Roman Empire, just as in the Greek, derived from its failure to make any notable improvements in naval technology, on which their empire so largely depended (Muller, 1952, p. 231): 'Transportation by sea remained slow, uncertain, and expensive and in stormy seasons almost impossible'.

59. Although the lands of feudal lords were typically royal grants given in exchange for pledges of service, rulers in fact lacked power to enforce these pledges because of the difficulties of communication and transportation and the ability of local lords to develop independent local power bases, and because rulers lacked the administrative apparatus to deal with and to overcome such problems (Lenski, 1966, p. 233).

Strayer (1971) makes the point that the pledge was a *form* the king sought to promote, although in the early Middle Ages it was not validated strictly in practice. From 1100 *A.D.* on, the concept bore social structural fruit.

60. The early weakening of the external threat in the case of the 'West-frankische Reich' compared to the 'Ostfrankische Reich' accounts for much faster and more radical decay of the central authority of the king in the West. He was deprived of a major opportunity to assert his control and to prove the need for his central role. As a result, the process of decentralization and fragmentation set in earlier and more rapidly (Elias, 1969, p. 28). Also, given the absence of new territories to conquer, the barter character of the economy, and the lack of developed means of communication and transportation, the central authority was in no position to accumulate and distribute resources, or to build up a bureaucratic apparatus which could be centrally controlled and which could give the king continued control over his vassals.

61. In a word, the critical factor is control (or distribution of control) over the means of force (Andreski, 1968; Goody, 1971).

62. In the development of absolutism in Western Europe, war permitted the monarchy to keep large standing armies and to levy many taxes without soliciting the consent of subjects. This decisive step was taken in France under Charles IV when monarchs ceased calling the States General; in Franderberg after 1631 at the height of the 30 years war and especially after 1665 when taxes began to be collected at the will of the sovereign, and a military-bureaucratic system was created. Foreign danger in all its forms played a great part in the appearance of

this system and its development. The necessity of defending national sovereignty permitted consolidation of royal sovereignty (Lublinskaya, 1972).

63. On the other hand, the availability of substantial resources enabled the centre to build roads, canals, and generally to alter the environment in order to faciliate structural growth and conditions favoring the centralized system, for example Roman roads, Chinese canals, and English ships in their respective empires.

64. This may go hand-in-hand with fostering or exploiting dissension within the governing class. One of the most important causes of divisions within that class has been unequal wealth. Thus, Russian Czars recruited bureaucrats from the lower nobility, a common pattern in state formation and development. Other differences which may be exploited are: ethnicity, family prestige, rank, place of residence (court versus province), military skill (Lenski, 1966, p. 239; Baumgartner et al., 1975c).

65. One problem that has always challenged leaders of centralized systems is how to prevent local officials from using their local associations as a power base. Traditionally, this problem has been dealt with through such means as rotation of officials so that tenure in any one position is too short to permit the establishment of secure power. Another method is the continual inspection by other officials whose sole allegiance is to the central power, e.g. the *intendants* of the French Monarchy.

66. In the absence of a continual inflow of new resources to A, this process in itself shifts relative power. In an undeveloped economy, A has to give B *capital resources* (land, monopoly over trade, minting of money, etc.) in order to establish the patron/client relationship to B. The latter not only gains a certain independence from A in the process but can use his power to carry on relational control at the local level. Thus, one problem with payment in slaves or in land distributed as fiefs, as opposed to consumable resources such as grain or even the income from specific estates, is that these are not simple consumables utilized by A to alter a payoff structure, which will then *remain* restructured since the recipient is dependent on a constant flow of the resource. Rather, they are themselves potential sources of future resources and hence may be used by the recipient to alter his action possibilities and payoffs and to exercise generative structural power. *It is only when* A *is in a position to give* B *resources which are limited mainly to consumptive use that the morphogenic forces tending toward decentralization are likely to be overcome on a more or less stable basis.*

67. For example, A distributes territories obtained through conquest to his best military leaders and loyal servants.

68. In early state formation in Western Europe, particularly England, the structuring activities of the centre were financed by the granting of sources of power instead of distributing fruits of power. (This was because the king had been generally unable to support the bureaucracy and army from normal revenues: and the power of the central hierarchy was dependent on the ability to pay for the expenses of administration without recourse to unusual subsidies (that is, taxes), since unusual grants had to be negotiated with the people to be taxed (or

at least the various estates): in England, Parliament; in France, separate districts at a time.)

For a while, under the Tudors, the English crown was able to support its bureaucracy and army without recourse to funds from Parliament — hence the growth of absolutism. The costs of government were paid by the sale of confiscated Church lands during the Reformation (and under Elizabeth, by the alienation of crown lands). The Crown in effect shifted substantial power from the clerical big landowners to the lesser gentry.

The Reformation land settlement was part of a power shift within the landed ruling class, from the great feudal families, with their centrifugal traditions, to the aspiring gentry and new men who were coming up into their places through royal favor; yet, it was these very 'new men' who would eventually challenge the king.

Under the Stuarts, the windfall revenues of the Reformation ran out. The Stuarts were forced to seek other sources of revenue, always attempting to do so without recourse to Parliament. Their sources included forced loans, sale of monopolies both within and outside of the country (in time the monopolies came to overlap one another, thereby alienating those who already had monopolies), sale of patents of nobility (and the fining of those who, although they had sufficient estates, had failed to obtain such patents — Cromwell was so fined in the 1630s) and stricter (and corrupt) enforcement of laws against enclosure and recusancy to obtain revenues through fines.

69. The agricultural base and generally low level of technology (particularly in transportation) of earlier empires and states tended to the consolidation of power and control at the local/regional level favoring an aristocratic world (which was typically resistant to innovations) (Braudel, 1972).

70. The size of the working population and its productivity in the particular ecological niche define the productivite capacity of society and, therefore, the size limit of the administrative structure, its form, and range of activities.

71. For example, in the case of Mesopotamia, over-irrigation caused a gradual salting effect in the soils of the delta, which resulted in greater dependence on salt-resistant crops such as barley. Agricultural economies became more dependent on a single crop, thus reducing the self-sufficiency of peasant villages and increasing their vulnerability to famine. Heavy taxation and increasing state control of farmlands were symptoms of increasing bureaucratic interference in agriculture. In times of political instability or warfare, the administrative structure fell apart, causing chaos and starvation among both rural and urban populations (Price, 1973).

72. Plagues and epidemics have been shown to be strongly linked to a decline in nutrition and adverse changes in diet, which in turn can result from climatic changes, economic recession, and increased exploitation of the population.

73. Apparently, a related process can occur when cities are taxed, driving the population to the countryside where landlords have obtained an exemption from taxation.

74. Factors other than a decline in the inflow of war booty may also provide the impetus for the process of system disintegration (see pages 268-269).

75. This developed in part because the small landowners, pressed for taxes

they were unable to evade, put themselves under the protection of the wealthy and large landowners who had the power to evade their taxes and to accord their protection to the people under their control. This accumulation of people and resources helped in turn the defiance of the demands of the tax collector and the bureaucratic state in general and at the same time made the local clus more and more self-sufficient. Similar developments occurred periodically in China.

Lewis (1970), in writing about the deline of the Arabs, suggests that one of the primary causes of the economic decline in the tenth century was undoubtedly the extravagance and lack of organization at the centre in the absence of any great technological progress or greater development of resources.

76. Interestingly enough, 'barbarian pressures' were often enough the result of initial Chinese action. For example, Eberhard (1966, pp. 57-58) points out that the Ch'in Dynasty in their imperialistic move to push their frontier to the north, set in motion (secondary) state formation among the nomadic peoples, the result of which was a powerful state, Hsiung-nu, which raised substantially the costs of supporting a border army and of fortification.

77. While an imperialistic nation gains resources during its period of expansion in the form of booty, lands to distribute, slaves, etc. these gains may be substantially short-term from the viewpoint of maintaining the structure of the empire. Similarly, the immediate costs of maintaining control may be minimal whereas the long-term costs for underwriting a vast bureaucracy and army are likely to be substantial indeed, and very often will not be justified by the returns over the long run. Elvin (1973, p. 20) emphasizes that both the Roman and the Chinese empires were initially conquered by citizen-soldiers. In both, these were eventually replaced by professionals as the empire grew too large for a citizen-soldiery:

> The cost of this army led to dangerous and ultimately fatal expedients. Barbarian troops were increasingly relied upon as auxiliaries, or even as the main fighting force. An active defence policy was too frequently rejected on the grounds of its expense; and attempts were made to subdue hostile barbarians by diplomacy, bribery and settlement on imperial lands. The outcome was a weakened internal structure . . . finally a total or partial collapse.

78. Lattimore (1951) and Aswad (1970) emphasize the continuing interaction between neighboring societies occupying different ecological niches, for example sedentary agricultural societies and normadic societies. One of the principal themes in Lattimore's work is that when China was strong as an empire, it dominated the steppe regions, yet could never fully integrate them because of the 'cellular' structure, the distance of communication, and 'above all . . . the intervals of arid un-Chinese terrain' (Lattimore, 1951, pp. 169-70, 205; Aswad, 1970, p. 56). When the empire weakened, the steppe would encroach upon the empire's borders, frequently enough defeating its armies, collecting tribute, and even assuming the position of dominant group.

79. In order to prevent such developments, the central leadership may have to invest substantial sums in police and in welfare payments, which again can set in

motion one or another of the processes discussed here. Also, the costs of maintaining a system of domination in opposition to peripheral forces will depend on the relative efficiency or effectiveness of the army and weaponry of the centre and on the conditions of transport and communication. These costs increase greatly if the terrain favors guerrilla warfare, if the sense of nationalism and cohesion among subjugated peoples are strong, or liberation groups have access either to strategic resources locally or to supplies from a foreign power or empire interested in their cause.

REFERENCES

O. F. Aberle (1962), 'A note on relative deprivation theory as applied to Millenarian and other cult movements', in: S. L. Trupp (ed.), *Millennial Dreams in Action* (The Hague: Mouton).

R. N. Adams (1975), *Energy and Power* (Austin (Texas): University of Texas Press).

H. R. Alker, Jr., T. Baumgartner, and T. R. Burns (1977) 'The Structuring of Dependence', *International Organization,* **31,** forthcoming.

S. Andreski (1968), *Military Organization and Society* (New York: Pantheon).

B. Aswad (1970), 'Social and ecological aspects in the formation of Islam', in: L. Sweet (ed.), *Peoples and Cultures of the Middle East* (Garden City, N.Y.: The Natural History Press).

H. Aubin (1966), 'The lands east of the Elbe and German colonization eastwards', *Cambridge Economic History,* **6.**

F. G. Bailey (1969), *Stratagems and Spoils* (New York: Schocken Books).

T. Baumgartner and T. Burns (1974), 'A structural theory of unequal exchange', Paper read at *Annual Convention of the Eastern Economic Association* (Albany, N.Y.).

T. Baumgartner and T. Burns (1975), 'The structuring of international economic relations', *International Studies Quarterly,* **19** (June).

T. Baumgartner, W. Buckley and T. Burns (1975a), 'Toward a systems theory of unequal exchange, uneven development and dependency relationships', *Studies in Comparative International Development,* **11,** in press.

T. Baumgartner, W. Buckley and T. Burns (1975b), 'Meta-power and relational control in social life', *Social Science Information,* **14:** 49-78.

T. Baumgartner, W. Buckley and T. Burns (1975c), 'Divide et Impera', *Theory and Society* (in press).

T. Baumgartner, T. Burns and P. DeVille (1975d), 'Middle East scenarios and international restructuring: conflict and challenge', *Bulletin of Peace Proposals* (in press).

A. Bernardi (1970), 'The economic problems of the Roman Empire at the time of its decline', in: C. M. Cipolla (ed.), *The Economic Decline of Empires* (London: Methuen).

M. Bloch (1973), *French Rural History* (Berkeley: University of California Press).

J. Blum (1966), *Lord and Peasant in Russia from the Ninth to the Nineteenth Century* (Princeton: Princeton University Press).

F. Braudel (1972), *The Mediterranean* (New York: Harper & Row).

W. Buckley (1967), *Sociology and Modern Systems Theory* (Englewood Cliffs: Prentice-Hall).

T. Burns (1976), 'Dialectics of Social Behavior', Manuscript.

T. Burns and W. Buckley (1974), 'The prisoners' dilemma game as a system of social domination', *Journal of Peace Research*.

T. Burns and M. Cooper (1971), *Value, Social Power and Economic Exchange* (Stockholm: Samhaellsvetarefoerlaget).

T. Burns and M. Mattin (1976), 'Societal reactions to disaster', in: I. Brady et al. (eds.), *Disaster and Survival* (in preparation).

T. Burns, R. Downs and C. D. Laughlin (1973), 'Political structure and political process', Manuscript.

R. L. Caneiro (1970), 'A theory of the origin of the state', *Science,* **169**: 733-38.

C. M. Cipolla (1966), *Guns, Sails and Empires* (New York: Pantheon).

C. M. Cipolla (ed.), (1970), *The Economic Decline of Empires* (London: Methuen).

R. Cohen (1976), 'The natural history of hierarchy: a case study', this volume, ch. 9.

T. Dale and V. G. Carter (1955), *Topsoil and Civilisation* (Norman: University of Oklahoma Press).

D. Dumond (1975), 'The limitation of human population: a natural history', *Science,* **187**: 713-19.

W. Eberhard (1966), *A History of China* (Berkeley: University of California Press).

S. N. Eisenstadt (1963), *The Political System of Empires* (New York: Free Press).

P. Ekeh (1974), *Social Exchange Theory* (Cambridge, Mass.: Harvard University Press).

N. Elias (1969), *Ueber den Prozess der Zivilisation* (Bern: Francke Verlag).

M. Elvin (1973), *The Pattern of the Chinese Past* (Stanford: Stanford University Press).

A. L. Epstein (1968), 'Power, politics and leadership: some Central African and Melanesian contrasts', in: M. J. Swartz (ed.), *Local-Level Politics* (Chicago: Aldine).

W. M. Evan (1975), 'Power, conflict and constitutionalism in organizations', *Social Science Information,* **14**: 53-80.

B. M. Fagan (1974), *Men of the Earth* (Boston: Little, Brown and Company).

S. Finer (1975), 'State building, state boundaries, and border control', *Social Science Information* **13**: 79-126.

M. Fried (1967), *The Evolution of Political Society* (New York: Random House).

M. Fried (ed.) (1973), *Explorations in Anthropology* (New York: Crowell).

J. Friedman (1974), 'Marxism, structuralism and vulgar materialism', *Man,* 9: 444-69.

R. E. Frykenberg (1968), 'Traditional processes of power in South India: a historical analysis of local influence', in: R. Bendix (ed.), *State and Society* (Boston: Little, Brown and Company).

J. Goody (1971), *Technology, Tradition and the State in Africa* (London: Oxford University Press).

P. Gorlin (1972a), 'Health, wealth and agnation among the Abelam: the beginnings of social stratification in New Guinea', Unpublished PhD Dissertation, Columbia University.

P. Gorlin (1972b), 'Medical variation and the origins of social stratification: a New Guinea case', Paper read at *71st Annual Meeting of the American Anthropological Association,* Toronto.

R. Hardin (1971), 'Emigration, occupational mobility, and institutionalization: the German Democratic Republic', Unpublished PhD Dissertation, M.I.T.

R. Hardin (1976), 'Stability of statist regimes: industrialization and institutionalization', this volume, ch. 7.

C. Hill (1967), *Puritanism and Revolution* (New York: Schocken Books).

A. O. Hirschman (1970), *Exit, Voice and Loyalty* (Cambridge, Mass.: Harvard University Press).

L. Krader (1968), *Formation of the State* (Englewood Cliffs (N.J.): Prentice-Hall).

O. Lattimore (1951), *Inner Asian Frontiers of China* (New York: American Geographical Society Research Series, No. 21).

E. Leach (1954), *Political Systems of Highland Burma* (Boston: Beacon Press).

G. Lenski (1966), *Power and Privilege* (New York: McGraw-Hill).

G. Lenski and J. Lenski (1974), *Human Societies,* 2nd edn (New York: McGraw-Hill).

B. Lewis (1970), 'The Arabs of eclipse', in: C. M. Cipolla (ed.), *The Economic Decline of Empires* (London: Methuen).

P. Lloyd (1965), 'The political structure of African kingdoms: an exploratory model', in: M. Banton (ed.), *Political Systems and the Distribution of Power* (London: Tavistock).

A. D. Lublinskaya (1972), 'The contemporary bourgeois conception of absolute monarchy', *Economy and Society,* 1: 65-92.

L. Mair (1962), *Primitive Government* (London: Pelican).

P. Mason (1971), *Patterns of Dominance* (London: Oxford University Press).

H. J. Muller (1952), *The Uses of the Past* (New York: Mentor).

R. W. Nicholas (1968), 'Rules, resources and political activity', in: M. J. Swartz (ed.), *Local-Level Politics* (Chicago: Aldine).

C. Parkinson (1963), *East and West* (New York: Mentor).

O. Patterson (1975), 'Lecture', *Sociology Colloquium,* University of New Hampshire, April.

B. Price (1973), 'Prehispanic irrigation agriculture in nuclear America', in: M. Fried (ed.), *Explorations in Anthropology* (New York: Crowell).

F. Roerig (1969), *The Medieval Town* (Berkeley: University of California Press).

S. Rokkan (1974), 'Dimensions of state formation and nation-building: a possible paradigm for research on variations within Europe', in: C. Tilly (ed.), *The Formation of National States in Western Europe* (Princeton: Princeton University Press).

S. Rokkan (1974) 'Entries, Voices, Exits: Toward a Possible Generalization of the Hirschman Model', *Social Science Information*, 13: 39-53.

E. E. Ruyle (1974), 'On the origins of social classes and the state church', Paper read at the *Annual Meeting of the American Anthropological Association*, Mexico City.

M. Sahlins (1968), *Tribesmen* (Englewood Cliffs (N.J.): Prentice-Hall).

E. F. Schumacher (1973), *Small is Beautiful* (New York: Harper & Row).

E. Service (1966), *The Hunters* (Englewood Cliffs (N.J.): Prentice-Hall).

A. Southall (1965), 'A critique of the typology of states and political systems', in: M. Banton (ed.), *Political Systems and the Distribution of Power* (London: Tavistock).

J. Stauder (1972), 'Anarchy and ecology: political society among the Majangir', *Southwestern Journal of Anthropology*, 28 (Summer): 153-68.

A. Strauss, Schatzman, L., Ehrlich, D., Bucher, R. and Sabshin, M. (1963), 'The hospital and its negotiated order', in: E. Friedson (ed.), *The Hospital in Modern Society* (New York: Free Press).

J. R. Strayer (1971), *Medieval Statecraft and the Perspectives of History* (Princeton: Princeton University Press).

R. Trethewey (1974), 'The establishment of serfdom in Eastern Europe and Russia', *The American Economist*, 13: 36-41.

V. Turner (1967), *Schism and Continuity in an African Society* (Manchester: Manchester University Press).

J. Van Velsen (1964), *The Politics of Kinship* (Manchester: Manchester University Press).

I. Wallerstein (1974), *The Modern World System* (New York: Academic Press).

L. White (1969), *The Expansion of Technology, 500-1500* (London: Collins Press).

NOTES ON CONTRIBUTORS

Hayward Alker Jr. is Professor of Political Science at Massachusetts Institute of Technology. He is the author of *Mathematics and Politics* and the co-editor of *Mathematical Approaches to Politics.*

Bo Anderson is Professor of Sociology at Michigan State University. He is co-editor of *Sociological Theories in Progress,* Volumes I and II, and he specializes in the areas of sociological theory and comparative analysis.

Tom Baumgartner is receiving his Ph.D. in Economics from the University of New Hampshire. He is currently Visiting Professor at the University of Quebec, Montreal. He has co-authored a number of papers with Walter Buckley and Tom R. Burns.

Walter Buckley is Professor of Sociology at the University of New Hampshire. He is the author of *Sociology and Modern Systems Theory* and the editor of *Systems Theory for Behavioral Scientists.*

Tom R. Burns is Associate Professor at the University of New Hampshire and Visiting Professor at the University of Oslo. He is the author of articles on social theory, international conflict, political sociology, economy and society, and planning. He has been a Visiting Professor at the universities of Uppsala and Stockholm.

Manuel L. Carlos holds graduate degrees from Stanford University and the University of California at Santa Barbara. He is currently Associate Professor of Anthropology and Director of the Institute for Applied Behavioral Science at the University of California at Santa Barbara. He has written on political, fictive kinship and family networks, specializes in political anthropology and Latin American societies, and is the author of *Politics and Development in Rural Mexico.*

Ronald Cohen holds a Ph.D. in Anthropology from the University of Wisconsin. He has taught at McGill University and the University of Toronto and is presently Professor of Anthropology and Political Science at Northwestern University. He has carried out field work in Nigeria and in the Mackenzie Valley, Northwest Territories, Canada. He has published on problems of anthropological theory and method, on political anthropology (he has edited *Comparative Political Systems*), and on the Kanuri of Nigeria.

Russell Hardin holds a Ph.D. from Massachusetts Institute of Technology and is Associate Professor of Government and Politics at the University of Maryland. He has been a Junior Fellow of the Columbia University Research Institute on Communist Affairs, and during 1975-76 he is a National Fellow of the Stanford University Hoover Institution.

Tom Koenig is a candidate for a Ph.D. at the University of California at Santa Barbara and is currently Visiting Assistant Professor at Brown University. His research insterests centre in stratification and political economy.

Hans-Peter Meier has studied sociology, psychology and economy at the University of Zurich, where he received his doctorate in 1974. He taught at the University of Zurich between 1970 and 1974, and during 1974-75 held a grant for specialization in political sociology in Poland. He is presently at the Institute of Sociology at the University of Zurich.

Jack H. **Nagel** is Assistant Professor of Political Science and Public Policy at the University of Pennsylvania. He holds his Ph.D. in Administrative Sciences from Yale, is the author of *The Descriptive Analysis of Power* (Yale, 1975), and has contributed articles to *World Politics* and to *Behavioral Science*.

Frank Parkin is a Fellow of Magdalen College, Oxford. He is the author of *Middle Class Radicalism* (1968) and *Class Inequality and Political Order* (1971), and he is the editor of *The Social Analysis of Class Structure* (1974).

Howard H. **Pattee** is Professor at the School of Advanced Technology, State University of New York at Binghamton. He is the author of over 50 papers and the editor of *Hierarchy Theory: The Challenge of Complex Systems* (New York: George Braziller, 1973). His primary interests are in the interaction of linguistic systems with dynamical systems, the evolution of complexity, and the theory of measurement and control. He holds a Ph.D. in Physics from Stanford University.

Peter Schuster is a graduate student in Sociology at the University of New Hampshire.

John A. **Sonquist** is Professor of Sociology at the University of California at Santa Barbara. He received his degree from the University of Chicago and has written extensively in the area of computer-based research methodology.

290